POLITICS OF THE PERSON
as the POLITICS OF BEING

POLITICS OF THE PERSON
as the POLITICS OF BEING

DAVID WALSH

University of Notre Dame Press
Notre Dame, Indiana

Copyright © 2016 by the University of Notre Dame
Notre Dame, Indiana 46556
www.undpress.nd.edu
All Rights Reserved

Manufactured in the United States of America

Library of Congress Cataloging-in-Publication Data

Walsh, David, 1950–
Politics of the person as the politics of being / David Walsh.
    pages   cm
Includes bibliographical references and index.
ISBN 978-0-268-04432-9 (pbk. : alk. paper)—
ISBN 0-268-04432-5 (pbk. : alk. paper)
1. Philosophical anthropology.   2. Transcendence (Philosophy)   I. Title.
BD450.W2375   2015
126—dc23

2015034487

To Mary,

Ronan,

and Michael

CONTENTS

Readers of the present study are entitled to some indication of the relationship in which it stands to my previous works. This is always a matter of curiosity but it is more than that. The development of human understanding follows a tangle of threads whose connections, in retrospect, may not be so obvious. In the case of this book the most evident external continuity is with *The Growth of the Liberal Soul*, a work in which I tried to explore the centrality of the person within the liberal regime of rights. There is also a clear connection with *After Ideology*, which premised the recovery of order on the conversions undergone by a group of exemplary individuals. Personal epiphanies have been central. But it was in *The Modern Philosophical Revolution* that I began to see that experience provides, not only the content of social and historical reality, but the form in which it is realized as well. Human life is inescapably personal. It is borne by that great stream of persons who, from the dawn of history up to its eventual conclusion, in every instance participate by never simply being within it. To be a person is always to transcend where one is. We know one another as persons because we are open to the mutuality that is the openness of persons.

Modern philosophy has arrived at this centrality of the person by way of an indirect route. Descartes was not so much interested in the I as in the thinking that it did, but inevitably the mystery of the I would loom larger. What, after all, is thinking but the activity of which only the I is capable?

Yet the I that performed all that prodigious thinking could never quite be captured in thought. Or, if it could be apprehended, it was no longer the I that did the apprehending. The I escaped every location assigned it. Kant would undertake the transition from an uncritical application of our understanding to full acknowledgment of its limits. We could no longer use our minds to justify the categories in which they sought to grasp the world. From the realization that we cannot ground our self-knowledge, the way was opened to reflection on the entire historical course as the only adequate unfolding of who we are. Eventually the insight would be framed in Heidegger's meditation on being as the horizon within which we think and exist. The idea of the person, the one who is within being and yet outside of it, beats so palpably in this arc that one wonders why it has not been recognized.

It may be that the language of persons has been so familiar that the astonishing reality of persons has not always penetrated. One indication of that lack of awareness is the breezy confidence of the various scientific disciplines that profess to comprehend the reality of persons. No insuperable barriers exist to the analysis of persons in psychology, sociology, neurology, or biology. Eventually we will be able to map the brain so that we understand consciousness more thoroughly than any mere thinking could achieve. Human beings are material and are best grasped in terms of the material processes that constitute them. The notion that human beings are persons, and therefore accessible only in person, cannot pierce the massive amnesia that grips us. Even those who speak for the person, who sail under the banner of "personalists," have not been able to make much headway within this sea of reductionism. The idea that everything in existence must be understood as reaching up to the reality of the person, rather than the other way around, simply cannot prevail. It must be confessed that the personalists themselves have too readily surrendered the struggle. They have been content to call attention to one more entity, the person, within a field of entities, rather than confront the radical consequences of their position. That is, that the person transcends all objectifications, all of those things that merely are. The person is the whole, the one without whom the world cannot go on, as we know in regard to the persons we know. Each is larger than the whole. To say with Kierkegaard that "the individual exceeds the universal" we must be prepared to say more than can be said in the language of universals. In straining toward its fullest realization, politics of the person must become the politics of being.

———————

That radiance of the person who ever transcends what is said has been abundantly displayed by the many persons who have made this work possible. I am conscious of the long chain of teachers and guides on whom my own modest labors depend, and wish to acknowledge them even when I cannot name them. Some special friends have been a more continual source of encouragement and inspiration. Among them I would like to thank Brendan Purcell, Joe McCarroll, Cyril O'Regan, John McNerney, Barry Cooper, Tilo Schabert, Steve McGuire, Chip Hughes, as well as the many participants at the meetings of the Eric Voegelin Society over the years, especially the inestimable founder of that group, Ellis Sandoz. My colleagues and students at The Catholic University of America have often been of assistance in more ways than they knew, and I am grateful for the sabbatical leave during which this project was begun. The process of bringing the work to publication could not have been handled more ably than it has been by the staff of the University of Notre Dame Press, including my acquisition editors, Charles Van Hof and Stephen Little, as well as copy editor Maria E. denBoer, project editor Rebecca DeBoer, and design manager Wendy McMillen. Finally, my wife, Gail, has been an unfailing support of my scholarship during a time that was marked by many trials and joys, but none more momentous than the births of our most recent grandchildren, to whom this book is dedicated.

Introduction

In invoking "politics of the person" we begin at the point of maximum danger. The person is in jeopardy. Exposed to shifting assessments of who is to count as a person, each is placed in perpetual jeopardy. Political power is the power of life and death. It can unleash all of the neglect, destruction, and malice to which frail flesh may be subject. Politics is the realm from which deadly force erupts because it is the point at which decisions are made or unmade. Left to themselves swords would rest as peacefully as plowshares. Mind, especially as collectively activated in politics, is the deadliest thing of all. When the political mind has changed, the character of its threat may be profoundly altered. We no longer have the same fear of the nuclear warheads of the Russian Federation, for it does not possess the mentality of the Soviet Union. At the same time we look to the political as the guarantor of life, fending off the lethality that would render it "nasty, brutish, and short." This is why the political normally assumes the far more benign aspect from which it draws its support. The monopoly of force attained by the state is usually exercised on our behalf. We do not need to arm ourselves as if we are perpetually engaged in a war of all against all. Instead, we can view the political as the guardian under whose protection the bonds of mutual trust may flourish. But we know of its Janus character. The political is capable of great good or great evil. For this reason we have sought to contain it within the boundaries that mark the rights of persons. We are determined to make the state strong enough to suppress the threats, internal and external, that might reach us, yet not so strong that its own supremacy could be turned against the persons it is pledged to protect. The miracle of politics is the attainment of that impossible balance.

Like every balance it is perpetually in danger of collapse. It is never achieved but must be constantly re-achieved. The person is at stake in every moment, for there is nothing in the past that ensures that rights hitherto protected will continue to be guaranteed. None are immune to the process of erosion by which their humanity is imperceptibly devalued. Only the assertion of the rights of persons can halt that silent disappearance, for in the defense of what it means to be a person we behold the full stature of what is at stake. It is for this reason that the great historical struggles for liberty are so frequently recalled. We look to these pivotal episodes as the moments in which our humanity is most fully realized. Liberty, we are told, is a tree whose roots must be refreshed with the blood of tyrants. Why tyrants must thus recur is a topic that is less often broached, or why liberty must depend on their regular execration. Who, after all, are the tyrants but the power in whose misuse we have become complicit? And who are those in whose name we must undertake such an anarchic act of resistance? The political community seems to exist nowhere more than in the effort to bring it into existence, an effort that never reaches its end but seems to demand its perpetual repetition. In the rights of the person we glimpse something of this ceaseless political dynamic in which we live. The state can only *be* through the voluntary transfer of power from the individuals within it and they, in turn, can only be induced to make such an offering through the knowledge that it will be expended on their behalf.[1] How the contract gets enacted may be elusive but once it does the momentum evinces impressive durability. The most powerful states are those most dedicated to the preservation of the rights of their citizens. When every one is weighed as if he or she was the whole, then it creates a whole that is well nigh invincible. Something of that mutual exchange is constitutive of every functioning polity, but its transparence is only evident in the language of individual rights. There must be a state for rights to be guaranteed but there must be a guarantee of rights for there to be a state.

It is through this struggle to preserve the rights of persons that we discover that it is the person who is at stake. Nothing more or less than what the person *is* is at issue in the effort to determine the kind of political association in which we are going to live. How are we going to treat the lowliest member of the social whole? That is the measure by which we are to judge ourselves and, most importantly, the political community in its most visible sense. In saying how we regard the most vulnerable we announce the character of the whole. We are implicated in the defense of the person. Our politics is inescapably politics of the person. Responsibility for the person is thrust upon us before we have sorted through the rationale that is to guide us. Not only are we individually called by the imperative of conscience before we have a moral philosophy but, politically, we are also impelled by the same priority to defend the person without whom the polity would not be. The language of rights by which that precedence has been expressed is a language of abbreviations that has emerged before we have grasped what is being abbreviated. Practice takes precedence over theory because life is there before reflection on it takes place. In responding thus to the imperative that draws us, in recognizing politics as politics of the person, we can never fully grasp that by which we are grasped. We are rather led by intuitions that can be deepened but never fully articulated. Their truth can be enlarged but never surpassed. It is for this reason that theory never fully provides the grounds for politics, for politics is already a realm of truth before theory arrives on the scene. The political must confront its inescapable responsibilities. It is the latter that illumine what politics is about. In living up to what is demanded of it, the political discloses that by which it is constituted. It shows that it answers to that which is more than the political, that which comes before it as that which it must serve. The political is led forth by what is before it exists. That is its intimation. Politics of the person is the politics of being.

Viewed as such a voyage of discovery it is not too surprising to find that it is marked by many ups and downs along the way. Even when the language of rights has clarified the centrality of the person within politics, there remains the possibility of distortion as one of its unintended results. Nowhere is this more evident than in the use to which the heightened awareness of the person is put in the discourse of rights itself. Defense of the rights of persons leads to the easy assumption we know what persons are, or at least to a working definition as the capacity to assert an interest in rights. When persons are the putative possessors of rights attention shifts to the lines by which we define who is a person. It may be a curious consequence of the centrality of the person that it now becomes easier to exclude the marginal cases in which the status of personhood is less than clear. But it should not strike us as so unexpected. An advance in one area of self-understanding always suggests a mastery we might readily extrapolate beyond the limits available to us. As always, however, it is the rise of moral hesitations that is the leading indicator of the errors into which we are about to fall. It is in the moral life that we are closest to life as such. A troubling intuition alerts us to the misconception that refuses to see any difference between a newborn infant and a baby kitten, on the grounds that they each lack an established self-identity. Infanticide and felinicide are equally permissible. What is disturbing is not the lack of sensitivity exhibited, but its justification by the heightened attention to the person that was presumed to avoid it. The greater respect owed to persons has turned the definition of the person into the most contested question. It is perhaps no wonder that many have despaired of rendering the notion of personal rights in coherent form. When a focus on the person supports depersonalization we are given pause.

Yet a sweeping dismissal of the turn toward the person would also be a mistake. What is decisive is that this truncated view of the person as defined by conscious self-identity has not been allowed to stand unopposed. Indeed, it has provoked vigorous and unremitting resistance. The integrity of the person must be defended even against the claim of persons to be entitled to regard themselves in any way they wish. Human rights must not be invoked to override human dignity. We are not simply minds possessing ownership of bodies to be disposed of as we choose; nor are our bodies devoid of value without a proprietor entitled to register such a claim. The self, that innermost core of the person, cannot be so easily separated from all that enables him or her to be what he or she is. Self-expression occurs only through the medium of that which is not the self.[2] Our bodies are our own but not in the way we own anything else. The unity is far more intimate than the language of self-determination would seem to suggest, for in injuring my body you injure me. This is why it is possible for me to injure myself while it is not possible for me to rob myself. The intimacy of the person with his or her bodily presence is not the only continuum that extends the reach of the self. A wider zone of continuity makes us part of the community of persons without whom we could scarcely be. The focus on individual rights may have suggested an atomistic existence, but the web of interdependence making our lives possible constantly refutes that impression. Just as we are body-persons we are also persons-in-community. Indeed, we are scarcely capable of becoming persons, acquiring the awareness of our distinct selves, except in relation to the field of others. I am a person because I am recognized as such by others. It is through the nurturing support of others that I become the kind of self whose independence makes it possible for me to return the same indefatigable care for others. There is, in other words, no such thing as the self pure and simple, without the hyphenated relation to the body and the world of others. The imperative of a more "personalist" account is one of the fruits of the heightened centrality of the person within liberal rights. The turn toward the person has generated a personalist response as one of the most prominent alternatives to the regnant individualism of our discourse.[3]

As such, personalism has enlarged the truncated account of the person that revolves around the autonomous self. Yet it has not really succeeded in responding to the core challenge of the inversion made possible by autonomy itself. What is there to prevent me from using my autonomy to destroy myself? Can it even be destructive or degrading if it is freely chosen? How can we even presume to set our judgment against that of another equally entitled to exercise his or her judgment? The personalists are guided by a profound intuition that there is something appalling about the self-destruction of self, but how is it to be expressed when autonomy has become the highest value? Some notion of human dignity is indispensable if we are to hold the line against self-degradation and the degradation of others, but noting the desideratum is not the same as satisfying it. Kant is in many ways the fount of this preoccupation, and we may regard personalist philosophy as arising from dissatisfaction with the Kantian attempt to ground human dignity in reason.[4] The problem is that personalism has done little more than keep the issue alive, a not inconsiderable achievement, but far less than the revision in the dominant discourse at which it aims. The language of human dignity, with its emphasis on integrity and sociality, will be opaque so long as the source of its inspiration remains inaccessible. It must be within the exercise of autonomy that the enhancement of self and others is discovered. Too often personalists have been content to limit their theoretical reach, falling back on traditional formulations of nature, rationality, and the *imago Dei*.[5] However laudable the deepening of reverence and respect at which they aim, they cannot hope to reach it without articulating the source of the convictions by which they are drawn. Human dignity must be located through the perspective of autonomy if it is to function authoritatively within that realm.

Dignity must be found as the source of autonomy rather than as a possible goal of it. The difficulty is that autonomy is usually so preoccupied with its immediate setting that reflection on the condition of its possibility is somewhat remote. We are propelled by the urges and urgencies of life before we even begin to question it. Yet none of this occurs unconsciously. Behind our decisions lies an awareness of what can never be suppressed, that which will not allow us to freely degrade ourselves. It refuses to countenance the descent into self-deception and self-delusion. The greatest offense, Kant thought, is lying to oneself.[6] But why? What is it that restrains our autonomous freedom before we have even begun to exercise it? Conscience, natural law, right by nature, duty are all possible answers that ultimately beg the question of how we know them. The tradition of moral reflection has always erred in not conceding the difficulty entailed in the starting point it invokes. How can we know what we do not know and yet must know if we are to make a beginning? The conviction that human dignity must at all costs be preserved when the abyss of subjective freedom jeopardizes it is itself testament to an undertow that is all the more powerful for its imperceptibility. It is at this point that the opaqueness of the traditional formulations obstructs us. We cannot penetrate to the source of a movement we sense but cannot discern. The call for a deeper philosophy of the person remains no more than that, a call without an answering response.[7] Overlooked is the extent to which this challenge has preoccupied the history of philosophy in the modern era. It reaches a turning point in the work of Kant when the nature of the challenge comes into view. We cannot answer the question of what makes it possible for us to know or for us to respond to the pull of obligation because we cannot step outside of the perspective of those enactments. The condition of the possibility of knowledge cannot be grounded in knowledge because to do so would presuppose it. No grounding of moral judgment can escape the inexorable imperative of grounding it morally, for the good can be justified only in terms of itself. Even for Kant, however, the perspective of the transcendental, the perspective outside of which we cannot go, assumed a mysterious aspect. To call it a priori hardly cleared matters up since we really need to know the meaning of that priority. Obviously this is not the place to seek such a clarification since the whole book is an attempt to provide just that. It is sufficient to note that the character of the difficulty has at least become explicit and that dismissal of Kant as a formalist merely overlooks his crucial significance in grasping the nature of the challenge.

That was not an error committed by his immediate successors among the German Idealists. They understood that Kant had initiated a new philosophical phase in grasping the ungraspability of what makes it possible for us to know and to act. We know it and yet we do not comprehend it because we are so fully immersed within it. But where Kant was even hesitant to name that about which he spoke, they were more daring in identifying it as the distinct reality of spirit, *Geist*. This had the advantage of making more real what had proved elusive within the Kantian formulations. Antinomies, the ultimate limiting points of his thought, could now be resolved in a certain sense. All that was needed was to note that Kant himself, by grasping the antinomies, had somehow managed to go beyond them. The reality of *Geist* defied univocal and fixed determination for it was apprehended in the movement whereby it included even itself. Philosophy in the Hegelian variant would assume a newly dynamic form that would lead it back to the vitality of life from which it had always arisen, only now with the capacity to include itself in that fluid medium. As the speculation became progressively more elaborate, however, it was evident that the pall of a new fixity had settled over the account. The system threatened to abolish the question from which it had arisen. It too would have to be overturned in the name of an existence that could never be contained within its parameters. That determination has framed the outlook of philosophy up to the present. The existential turn, initiated by Kant and inadequately realized by Hegel, Fichte, and Schelling, forms the permanent condition out of which reflection unfolds. As with the great pioneers Kierkegaard and Nietzsche, philosophy thus becomes radically fragmentary, incomplete, and inarticulate. Correlative to the paradoxical style of thought that knows it can never think itself, there is increasing attention to the inability of language to say what it seeks to say. Falling short has become the mode of saying. Nowhere is this more on display than in the bewildering pyrotechnics of Heidegger and his successors.[8]

Yet in a strange way they are closer than ever to the horizon of the person. We might characterize all of Heidegger's lifelong preoccupation with the question of being as an attempt to identify what it means to be a person without ever using the word "person." He had already turned away from the language of persons, even as invoked by Scheler and Jaspers, as too close to the subject for whom reality must be composed of objects. The whole that contains both of them would be missed, even though it is that capacity to contain them by not being either a subject or an object that defines what it means to be a person. It is perhaps the most striking feature of Heidegger's vast meditation on being as the possibility of apprehending being, that is, of being as self-revelation, that he nowhere seems to notice that this is what it means to be a person. Being is personal through and through because it is that which discloses by never fully disclosing; it is disclosure that ever remains beyond disclosure as its own movement. The tragedy of Heidegger is that, despite it all, being looms as an apocalyptic event that overshadows its recipients. This explains why for Heidegger persons could remain invisible to him, even to the point of countenancing their mass annihilation. Their cry could not be heard because he had not grasped it as continuous with the self-sacrifice of being, even though it was the very same movement of transcendence by which he had glimpsed being. Ontology is prior to ethics for, as he insisted in what is almost a throwback to his scholastic formation, every ethics entails an ontology.[9] Absent is any consideration of the Levinasian corrective that every ontology presupposes an ethics, that we already bear a responsibility before being as the condition for raising the question of being. All of this comes into focus when persons have become the center of philosophical vision. Then we see with Levinas and Derrida that the person, the face of the other, is before all else, including the self.

It is a great mistake to conclude, as a number of personalist commentators have, that this formulation is the imposition of an impossible demand for perfection in human relationships. That impression occurs only if we assume that Levinas is, for example, offering a description of interpersonal dynamics rather than of what is the condition of their possibility. We can relate to one another as persons only because mutuality is the very meaning of what it is to be a person. I am responsible for the other before I even know him or her because that is what makes it possible for me to practice the limited responsibility of which I am capable when we meet. The priority of the other may be the divine command, especially as it is given to us by Jesus, but it is so only because we are already marked by its possibility. God can command only what can be, even if our natural limits usually obstruct the way. We are at least capable of embarking on the way. Eschatology is not some vague destination at which we will arrive in the future. It is the ineliminable horizon of possibility in every moment. Persons, we will see, are not beings within being.[10] No matter how frequently we think of persons as beings, strictly speaking they are incapable of such a status. Otherwise they would be incapable of glimpsing being. To apprehend that within which they are they must somehow never simply be within it. Their genesis is from before being. All of this is amply confirmed by our ordinary knowledge of persons, each of whom we know as unique irreplaceable wholes that exceed in meaning and value all that is in the universe. With each birth being begins anew. This is something that is known to every parent, and it is verified in every encounter with the infinity of the other. The problem is that our language, even in the hands of those attuned to the centrality of the person, has been incapable of voicing that pleromatic epiphany. It is the turn toward inwardness in modern philosophy that has opened up the paradox of the person as what can be contained without ever being contained in what we say about him or her.

The problem of the pre-modern philosophical account is that it never found language consonant with its own apprehension of the person.[11] As a consequence, it always ran the danger of losing what it had grasped. Inwardness is a permanent feature of human existence; it *is* human existence, but its articulation is neither final nor definitive. What has been discovered can also be lost, even if it remains available for recollection. We might even think of the whole history of philosophy as one long effort to regain what had been glimpsed in its very opening. The discovery of being, as well as the revelation of the I AM, is simultaneously the discovery of the interiority within which such events are possible. The beyond and the within are correlative. But they are quickly covered over by the more reliably solid language of beings and nature, as well as the historical destiny that such traces of the ineffable must endure as they wander through space and time. The opaqueness of symbols set adrift from their originating experiences becomes the overarching problem. We do not know what being is when it can only be encountered in the mode of beings, nor do we know what persons are when they too must be assimilated to the finite. The dislocation seems pervasive when we can think about everything except what it is that makes thought possible. There is perhaps no more poignant reflection of the confusion than the preoccupation with what it means to live in a secular age.[12] God is absent, not because he has absconded, but because we can no longer conceive of how he might make himself known. The way of the transcendent seems irrevocably blocked when the inward has shrunk to the subjective. Even while yielding to the abundance of experience we have become incapable of perceiving its reality. God continues to be heard in a secular age; the difficulty is that he can no longer be recognized. The great atheists of the nineteenth century were in revolt against God, which meant that, in their own way, they affirmed him more deeply. Today we have only the unease of the question of God that can no longer be voiced. It drives our new atheists to reject the God that science can never find. Utterly overlooked is the realization that God is nowhere, that he does not exist, because he is that from which everything has come into existence.[13]

To think of God as the first cause is to already draw him into the chain of existence and therefore into the logic of what stands in need of a cause itself. St. Thomas's famous five ways are deeply informed by the awareness of this problematic. Each of them concludes with the formula *quod Deus dicitur*, which makes it clear that we have not proved the existence of God. How could we prove a God whom we already know about in advance of our demonstration? The arguments are really ways by which we arrive at that which we know, the God who is called God and who is vastly more than has been glimpsed. The God who overflows all ways is the ground of possibility of the ways. What is neglected in St. Thomas's meditation is the question of how we know the God whom we recognize as the end of each way. He does show, however, that we ask about how we arrive at the God whom we already know. The question of God comes from God himself. We would be incapable of asking it if we did not already know who it is for whom we search. Our only problem is to account for this revelation itself. The standard response is that God, the transcendent, has chosen to reveal himself to us. But that too begs the question. How can God reveal himself to us unless we already know who he is? How can we hear the voice of God if we cannot recognize it? To know God is thus to know that which is already known and which could neither be sought nor found if that were not the case. But this means that we have no need for a proof of the existence of God because we already know him as that which is beyond existence. We do not even experience God for it is our knowledge of him that makes such experiences possible. We know that which is *not* before we know that which *is* because we are ourselves persons who are not what we are. The inwardness by which we glimpse the transcendence of God, *quod Deus dicitur*, is not the subjective perspective within us. It is the shattering of all subjectivity within transcendence itself. Inwardness is not a private realm but the point from which all that is merely private can be beheld. We do not know God but are rather known by him within the inwardness that is God. Transcendence is not only the way to God but also the very being of God who is known as inwardness. He cannot be other than personal.

The unfamiliarity of such reflections is almost enough to demonstrate the constraints that longstanding conventions have imposed on the spiritual irruptions at the beginning of philosophy and revelation. Each, as Eric Voegelin has suggested, has been content to preserve the results of its illumination, without being excessively concerned about the event of illumination itself.[14] The effect has been the widely lamented opaqueness of what is thus preserved, a still life without the vitality from which it has arisen. To remedy the situation something more than complaint is needed. Voegelin understood this and sought, through the return to experiences of transcendence, to find again the wellsprings of thought. In this he made it clear that there were no such things as ideas of order unless there were first the particular experiences of order that were undergone. That is an indispensable realization. Yet it remains to be carried further, for the invocation of experiences is still tied to the subjectivity of persons who undergo them. Strongly suggested, in Voegelin's account, is that the experiences are not simply subjective. They are experiences of truth, of that which transcends the self. But how can that be said if it is not said in the mode of subjective experience? One can talk about the echo of truth recognized by other selves, but that too is merely to talk about experiences. What has not yet occurred is a discourse out of such events themselves. Even to describe them as experiences is already to have set up a distance by which we stand apart from them. If they are, on the other hand, what makes experience possible, then we can scarcely experience them. We simply glimpse that within which we stand. Of course, this too is an experience, but not of the kind that is simply my subjective grasp. Instead, it is the point at which the subjective stands within the reality of which it is a part. Voegelin struggled mightily to suggest this in distinguishing between the intentionality of consciousness toward objects and the luminosity of consciousness's own participation in reality. Yet he did not quite follow the logic of his own distinction to recognize consciousness as an event of being itself. He saw that consciousness grasps being but not that consciousness is the grasp of being. We experience the transcendent because we are already constituted by it. We know that God is more than he reveals because we are persons who are always more than we say. It is out of the non-saying that all saying arises. This does not have to be established by experience or confirmed by others for it is prior to all demonstration. The order of being is that which we live within. As such we glimpse it without really experiencing it. There is no way of avoiding the recognition that it is only persons who can have such an apprehension of what passes all apprehension. In conceding this we are also acknowledging that what they apprehend is that being is personal.

It is not just that the person is a being. The person is the apex at which the being of being is disclosed. St. Thomas's metaphysics is based on the understanding that every being seeks to disclose itself, to communicate what it is.[15] But he does not ask about how he knows this and, as a consequence, it never becomes clear that being is personal. The person provides the model of being without really showing why. To do that would require the enlargement of perspective to include what it means to be a person. Then it would be seen that the person is not an event within being but the event of being. As that which comes from what is not, the person exemplifies the emergence of being. We can ask about the source of being because we are ourselves engaged in the advent of being. We know that it comes from that which is not. That which can set itself aside, so that being might be, is what it means to be a person. Within inwardness the whole of being is contained in the mode of what is beyond being. To say that the movement of self-unfolding in all things is teleological, as St. Thomas suggests, is itself a perspective that depends on the assignment of purpose of which persons alone are capable. In doing that, however, they are already contemplating it from outside. Freely they assign purpose because they are not subsumed within a regime of purpose. When we ask about what it is that can assign purpose, we know that it cannot be explained in terms of purpose. The only explanation of being remains what is outside of it. Only the person occupies that role. But this means that explanation falls short for we cannot penetrate to what it means to be a person. We apprehend being from within the highest perspective available to us, that is, from the vantage point of the person. The culminating moment is the self-disclosure of the One whose self-disclosure has been dimly intuited all along. We encounter the God whom we have always known.

To be a person is to know what it means to be a person. It is to live within that openness that is there before all communication. Signifying is the capacity to relate to others what can be said but it cannot say what cannot be said, signifying itself. We can point everything out but we cannot point out pointing. It cannot be taught, for all teaching begins with it. We are there before there is a there. Consciousness is very often taken as the starting point for all discussion about the person, and has notoriously been invoked as the sine qua non of being a person. This in turn has led to the question of whence consciousness has arisen. The expectation is that consciousness must derive from some more solid reality outside of it. What is less frequently noticed is that such an explanation would provide us with no insight at all since it would only reduce consciousness to what it is not.[16] We might know what consciousness uses, even what makes it possible, but not what it means to be conscious. Just as we cannot understand money in terms of the physical analysis of paper, so we cannot understand consciousness in terms of anything but itself. The real question is how we understand what it is to be conscious. Given that we are conscious of such an endless stream of things, how is it possible to become conscious of the stream itself? Of course, we say that self-consciousness is the indispensable accompaniment of being conscious of something. But is this not one more of the many things we "say" when we know we cannot, especially since being really conscious of something is usually said to consist in forgetting our selves? To say that the self is merely unconscious or forgotten in that moment is simply to beg the question of how it can then be retrieved. We are hesitant to conclude that consciousness is a form of un-self-consciousness, even though that is exactly what we know. Loath to dislodge the supremacy of consciousness, we know that the knowledge on which the possibility of consciousness turns would also come tumbling down. Like Descartes we would rather build reality from the isolated I than concede that even such an effort is underwritten by what is before the I.

We could not even be conscious without the relationship to what is other that makes it possible. I become conscious of what makes itself known to me, including what disclosure as such means. The world is knowable before I know it. The relationship prevails before the instant when it is actualized in my knowledge. Nothing is so utterly alien that we are incapable of comprehending it. All can be assimilated to what is known because we are borne by an abiding trust in the order underpinning all things. To say that this is faith, that faith makes knowledge possible, still connotes too much of the subjective. We are unused to marking faith with the seal of certainty. Yet what could be more certain than what makes all certainty possible? We may not be certain of what we know but we are certain of certainty. Even to ask the question is to stand within certainty. It is to say, before I know there is certainty. That is what makes it possible for me to know. Descartes's mistake was to think he could ground certainty in something more than itself; it was to confuse faith with knowledge. We cannot know what makes knowing possible. But how then do we characterize what we know of that relationship that makes knowledge possible? It is a relationship we cannot know because we live within it. No one needs to instruct us and no one can receive instruction in it, for all instruction takes place within its boundary. The transcendence of the person can be glimpsed by consciousness because it is prior to consciousness. Metaphysics is not what we establish but what establishes us. This is why it is a great error to identify the person with consciousness or even with the notion of self-identity. Neither would be possible unless the person was more than either of them. Outside of all that marks the person is the person himself or herself.[17] That is what is disclosed in the reverence that is owed to the person from before birth to the moment of death.

We know what it is to be a person before any encounter has taken place. Nothing in what is disclosed can disclose what lies beyond all disclosure, and we know this only because we are persons who encounter other persons. All that matters lies outside of what can be discerned. The person is before being. This is why the question of being, of the ground of that which is, is not just a question incidental to the person. It is the question of the person, for the person occupies precisely that question. The only remaining question is how we know this since as persons we are not strictly speaking in being. We are ever coming into being, but this is a possibility that requires that we are definitively incapable of containment within being. This is the aspect that brings into focus the highest dignity of the person as limitless transparence. The person lives in the luminosity of the person. The beyond being is glimpsed in its transcendence. Language is defeated in its capacity to say only what is, yet that defeat does not have to be final. The very fact that we have adverted to it already initiates a reversal. Through the paradox of non-saying the more-than-sayable can be said. Indeed, it turns out that all language carries that overflowing within it. Containing the uncontainable is what gives the whole vitality and unstoppability to what we say. The problem is that without the constancy of warning signs against it we are prone to lapse into amnesia. We forget the person as the condition of possibility of all saying and doing. Being massively intrudes into the space that previously had been occupied or, rather, non-occupied, by what makes it possible for it to be discerned as being. Otherwise than being, to borrow Levinas's ascription of the project, requires more than the responsibility evoked by the face of the other.[18] It demands an understanding of what it means to be a person who is and is not present within a face.

Being must be discovered, not as the alternative, but as the possibility of the person. It is within the horizon of the person that the whole movement of existence can be contained. There is no other model available. Immanence and transcendence are fragmentary aspects of what the person alone makes whole. There is no ontology of the person because the person is the encompassing ontology. The only reason that our philosophical discourse has not descended into sheer chaos is that we have integrated in person what we could not integrate in thought. In this sense what will be attempted in the present work is nothing new. It is what we have known all along yet never found the way to admit. Persons stand outside of being. Is that not the presupposition of the Parmenidean pronouncement of the Is? Could Parmenides have declared being if he was not apart from it? Even to suggest, as he does, that thinking and being are one, has remained an enigmatic pointer to this realization.[19] We know thinking is possible because it is not subsumed within the being it thinks about. Yet there is the point at which thinking and being are one since thinking is itself in being. But how is this Parmenidean thought itself possible? That is what has proved so elusive for millennia. Only the realization that Parmenides is himself a person furnishes the answer, for then the thought of being is separable and inseparable from thinking it. The person is the pivot of thinking and being, and that thought is inseparable from the being of the person.[20] We cannot step outside of the horizon of the person for it is the person that provides the horizon for everything else.

Our purpose here is to sketch that re-centering of reality within the person. Instead of seeing the person within reality, now we must attempt to find reality within the person. This is not to suggest that we embrace a radically subjective perspective, for subjectivity is only a possibility for persons who are not reducible to it. They can be subjective only because that is not what they are. Persons can behold their own subjectivity, demonstrating that they are objective about themselves. The categories simply do not apply. We know this unquestionably in the persons we know and love. They are neither locked within their inwardness nor exhausted in all they have said or done. Outweighing both the subjective and objective dimensions they are each the unique pivot of the whole of reality. This is how we relate to them. While occupying their particular finite terrain, they become to us the whole world. All human relationships turn on this unsurpassably personalist metaphysics. The person exceeds all other reality. The problem is that our language, with all of its presumptive metaphysical capacity, has utterly failed to capture this. We know what we cannot say for all of our saying consigns the person as a part of reality. It is only within the political realm that an opening begins to resist the dominance of the quantifiable. There we have been compelled to admit that persons are not entities in the same way as everything else. They cannot be commodified, instrumentalized, or reified, for they are inexhaustible sources of meaning and value to whom we owe limitless reverence and respect. None is replaceable and none can be discarded. Whatever benefits might accrue to the whole society, they are not worth gaining if it means the sacrifice of its humblest member. In this sense each is a whole outweighing the whole. The language of dignity and rights, with all its attendant implications of indivisibility and inexhaustibility, is the point at which the transcendence of the person comes into view. Yet even that most deeply affirmed conviction has not found the philosophical means for its articulation. We simply know that we do not wish to belong to any society that would live at the expense of its most vulnerable members.[21] To say why this is profoundly wrong we are thrown back on the vaguest formulas about fairness or reciprocity that only beg the question of the source of their imperative.

What we do not possess is an account of the person as transcending the political community as such. This is not the notion that the person is destined for union with God in eternity but the far more concrete exemplification of the way in which the person includes the association of which he or she is a member. Politics that guards the infinite dignity and worth of the person is correlative to the person who guards the political with an infinite care and dedication. The existence of any polity is secured only by members who are prepared to sacrifice themselves for it. To conceptualize this as a contract is to fall wide of the mark, for what can be given to those who have given all? They have made unmistakably clear that the polity exists, not for the sake of benefits or even for survival, but for the sake of the community of those who have fully transcended themselves. Its only adequate form is one that acknowledges its character as a community of persons, each of whom is a whole for whom the whole must be continually ready to set itself aside. A community of persons is reciprocal, not just in the ordinary sense of mutual courtesy, but also in the sense of that perfect reciprocity of which alone persons are capable. All of this becomes evident in the political realm where action takes place before its meaning has become clear. In this sense the evolution of the language of rights is only a way station on the journey toward the transparence of the person as the founder of the whole that, in turn, embraces the person as greater than itself. For the moment, however, that transparence is elusive. All that will be attempted here is a sketch of how it might be conceived. To do anything more would be to request a far-reaching shift in the prevailing manner of thought and discourse, a request that is likely to go unheard. Perhaps what is offered is less a beginning on that larger task than the issuance of a challenge to begin it.

At stake is the person through whom the political community is possible and for whom the political community must devote itself. Demarcation of the boundary of rights is not enough when we do not know what it is they are intended to preserve. To respond that rights are attached to persons presupposes we know what persons are. It is that easy familiarity that must first be questioned, for anyone who accepts it has not contemplated the nature of the challenge entailed in the task of understanding persons while functioning as persons ourselves. The confusion of persons and things has entangled our reflection ever since the term *homoousios* was introduced to distinguish the *hypostases* of the Trinity (Council of Nicea, 325). Since the two terms mean almost the same thing it was evident that doctrinal affirmation had outweighed philosophic precision, by favoring the language of substance over the language of persons in relation to one another.[22] The later introduction of the notion of subjectivity as what characterizes persons served only to bifurcate reality into two different kinds of things, subjects and objects. As a result we treat subjects as if they were a different category of object. It is for this reason that thought itself has proved to be one of the most incomprehensible of all thoughts. Thinking, we assume, must be intelligible in terms of its neurological accompaniments, even though no neurologist reads his own brain scan as the source of his analysis. Science, it seems, is capable of explaining everything except science itself. What can be more invisible than the observer himself or herself? This is also why autonomy cannot simply be selected as the defining purpose of the person, for autonomy cannot include what makes its exercise possible. Not only must there be something choiceworthy for choosing to be possible, but its emergence cannot be determined in advance of the choice. Autonomy discloses the moral horizon of the person, just as science discloses the intellectual horizon. The openness to others and to reality is a possibility only for persons who are not things at all. They do not even exist within history for history is a possibility for them only because they are always apart from it. Persons may leave their mark but they are not reducible to what they have left. Only art, religion, and philosophy, as Hegel suggested, are the exceptions to this rule.[23] In those instances we deliberately intend to put more of ourselves into what we say than the saying will bear. Art is that enterprise in its most preeminent way. The trail of theological symbols differs as the attempt to convey what is deepest of all and what cannot be conveyed, our participation in the divinity that reveals itself as beyond revelation. How that is possible is the question on which philosophy turns, for it is only philosophy that declares what all the other modes of personal existence know. That is, that the person is transcendence, not only as an aspiration, but also as his or her very reality. Nothing is higher. That is what this book strives to acknowledge. Our task is to do what we can to glimpse what cannot be known because it can only be glimpsed. How else can transcendence be known but as what has already departed? Nothing is left of what was there. That is why only a person can know what it is to be a person.

CHAPTER ONE

A Personalist Account of Persons

At first glance the title of this chapter is bewildering. What can a "personalist account of persons" mean? Is it simply recognition of the respect we owe one another as persons? That we should never subordinate persons to their social roles or functions? That the very language we use must embody the primacy of reverence owed toward persons as such? Or does the title intend all of these meanings and more? We are deliberately installing speed bumps for our inquiry into the politics of the person by reminding ourselves of the linguistic challenge involved. This is different from our ordinary way of proceeding. When we want to discuss something we usually just go right ahead, without asking permission of ourselves. Are we entitled to talk about persons without further ado? Without taking any special measures to ensure we get it right? As if turnips and persons were more or less interchangeable entities? Even our ordinary language seems to bristle with warnings about so casual a mode of discourse. We know, for example, that we must not talk about persons behind their backs. Nor should we talk about them when they are present. Intuitively we are put on alert that this is sacred ground. A proper distance is required. We cannot adopt an attitude of familiar indifference where persons are concerned. Only a sufficiently reverent "Thou" is suited to the delicate touch of encounter with an other "I."

The challenge has been to find the appropriate intellectual means of incorporating that realization. In this chapter we attempt to gain some sense of the scope of what is entailed. This is why we begin with the question as to whether science can in any sense talk about persons. Merely because we have human and social sciences does not mean that their objective method can apprehend this most elusive dimension of the reality within which science itself lives.[1] It is precisely the realization of the inadequacy of science to the task that prompted, second, the rise of a specifically personalist turn within philosophy. Yet despite the promise of this development there remains, third, something inconclusive in personalist philosophy that is attributable to the insufficiently radical character of its project. Personalist philosophy still clings to the language of objects and has yet to carry its logic into a revolution within philosophical language itself. It is for this reason that the elevation of the person, especially in selecting autonomy as the principal criterion of the person, has yielded consequences diametrically opposed to the inviolable dignity of persons. A focus on autonomy has had the distorting effect, fourth, of suggesting that we now possess an absolute means of drawing the line between human beings who are persons and human beings who are not. We witness the outcome in the dehumanization that follows from the assertion that we possess the means of defining a person. Perhaps this is not so surprising when one considers what is implied in such a claim, namely that we as persons can now stand in imperious judgment over what it means to be a person. We no longer find ourselves humbled before the mystery of persons for whom we are responsible, and therefore fail to see the extent to which it is other persons who ultimately define us. The easy assumption that persons can be regarded in the same way as all other entities in existence has misled us. The way back is, fifth, to acknowledge the irreducibly different character of the relationship in which, in regard to persons, responsibility is prior to definition. It is through our responsibility for the other that we can glimpse what it means to be a person. When it comes to persons, a coda will suggest, even the law must be ever ready to become more than law.

Can Science Talk about Persons?

Initially it would seem that persons, and the reverence owed them, is incompatible with the objectification science requires. Surgeons who must carve up the human body as a piece of meat, who indeed can fail if excessive squeamishness deters them from their task, must ritualistically separate their dissection from the politeness with which they greet their patients. Can philosophers do any less in presenting a model of the way in which discourse about human beings might take place? Indeed, the language of persons and personalism has been developed precisely to suggest such an approach. Human beings are not simply beings in the way in which things in general, tables, chairs, mountains, and rivers, are. As persons they may have an external dimension but they are not contained within it. Rather, they contain themselves, in inwardness, and are properly known only through the inward movement by which we know one another. Just as mastery of a name or address does not give us access to the person, neither does possession of even the most comprehensive catalogue of details tell us who the other is. At the core the person is a mystery, St. Augustine reminds us, "an abyss so deep as to be hidden from him in whom it is."[2] But how then is it possible to "know" one another at all? Surely it is only because we ourselves are persons, inwardly capable of bearing the inwardness of the other in the silence of our hearts. It is for this reason that we really only know the people we love, for love is what bridges the gap when "two solitudes guard and bound and greet each other."[3] Through love the inwardness of the other is held fast because it is held within. It is only because we ourselves live inwardly that we can know the inward reality of others, what constitutes the very being of a person.[4]

Conversely, this is a knowledge we must obliterate from our minds if we are to efficiently inflict damage on others. The knowledge that they are persons too must be ruthlessly suppressed. All killing requires the objectification of the other. This is the dehumanization of the enemy so familiar in the experience of warfare, with its attendant cost in dehumanization of the perpetrators as well. Now the question is whether that pattern of reification also extends to students of human nature. Are social scientists in the role of aggressors compelling submission from their defenseless material? Or must they somehow preserve the attitude of friendship by which the humanity of the other is preserved and disclosed? And if it is the latter, how are they going to ensure that their language, of objectification, does not betray the generosity of their initial impulse? Surprisingly this is a question that has received relatively little attention. Despite all of the discussion of methods in the human and social sciences, perhaps even because of methodological self-consciousness, the difficulty of making the transition from a world of subjects to a world of objects has not been sufficiently considered. Eager to grasp refinements we are defeated by the obvious.[5]

Of course, we know the difference between persons and things, between a Thou who calls forth a response and a datum whose structure must be analyzed. But what if that very distinction represents the limiting horizon of our own thought? What if the difference between persons and things is neither an axiom of our science nor a component of our inwardness? What if we cannot comprehend the distinction at all but find that the distinction is what provides the possibility of all of our comprehension? That far from understanding the difference between persons and things we find that our own existence is contained within it? We begin to see that if we did understand the distinction we would no longer be living within it but would have gone beyond it. If the mystery of the intersection between the subjective and the objective were to be penetrated, then it could no longer hold the whole vitality of our existence. In this sense everything depends on our never fully comprehending the distinction we have so easily taken for granted. We do not stand outside of the difference between persons and things and therefore cannot assume we know what it is all about. Rather, we must continually remind ourselves of our inability to penetrate it and thereby preserve a proper respect for the mystery within which the enterprise of science itself unfolds. It is good for students of physical nature to be reminded of the strangeness of their status as thinking parts of the material universe, but it is indispensable for students of human nature to bear in mind that they too are the very same as the object of their study. Then there is little danger they will forget that science is only a possibility for persons, that is, for those who can never be an object of study.

The Rise of a Personalist Approach

It was the need to articulate this ineliminable horizon of the person that gave rise to a countermovement against the monopoly of the scientific model. Science could not completely overlook the scientist. The problem was to find a formulation that would enable us to navigate the two worlds of the subject and the object simultaneously. A promising beginning was the burst of clarity provided by Martin Buber's *Ich und Du* (1923). Of course, the problem of defending other modes of truth, especially the revelatory and philosophic, against the encroachments of science has been a preoccupation since the seventeenth century. "The eternal silence of those infinite spaces frightens me," Pascal had declared.[6] As a project it was unlikely to be fulfilled through a single author or work, not even one encountered as piercingly true. A civilizational crisis can only be resolved, if it ever is, through the formation of the civilizational resistance that is required. However, a single work can play an essential role. It can capture our attention. This was why *Ich und Du* had such a momentous impact. Within a brief 120 pages it reassured dazed modern humanity that its intuitions had not been wrong. Science could not pronounce the truth about our existence; nor could it provide any meaningful instruction on how we should live. Taken in themselves such observations are commonplace, widely echoed in public and private musings of the day. What Buber managed to do was to explain why they hold. Within the pages of his brief treatise he spelled out with unmatched clarity why an objective explanation fails to account for what matters most. We do not live in the external physical universe, a world of objects, but in the interior life that constitutes a universe of persons. Science, its investigation and manipulation of objective nature, remains but it is far from constituting the only, and certainly not the most important, dimension of existence. For this reason we do not have to bemoan the loss of meaning generated by the expansion of scientific reason. That has never been the horizon of our lives. Human beings have ever and always found their meaning within the relationship to others that is disclosed entirely from within. I and Thou always takes precedence over I and It.

Scientific method, Buber showed, is defective as science. It overlooks the most indispensable knowledge of reality through interpersonal encounter. Of course, everyone already knew this. No scientist ever mistook his wife for a hat or addressed his children as robots. Yet we lacked a way of clearly explaining the difference to ourselves. This was what Buber's little masterpiece provided, a handy confirmation of what everyone, including scientists, has always known. There is a world of difference between the

world of Thous and the world of Its. Knowledge of persons is vastly different from knowledge of things. Even when things are denoted by He, She,
or They, the encounter is never in the form of a personal address. We know
persons only as persons who by their very being address us and toward
whom we move in responsibility.[7] There is no knowledge of the Thou outside of the entry into relationship, just as there is no I that is prior to the relationship. Personal knowledge is not available except through the response
by which we become responsible to and for the other person. Objectivity,
by which the I can be held aloof from relationship, is unavailable. We cannot respond to the other with less than all of our being for to do so would
be to fail to acknowledge what persons require of us. That is why there is no
unexposed corner of the self outside of the relationship. Personal knowledge not only expands our epistemological horizon; it also stretches our
existential openness to its breaking point. To the extent that the primary
word of I-Thou can only be heard when we listen with our whole being, the
philosophical challenge of establishing it as an authoritative mode of truth
comes fully into view. Yet the event of relation, of responsibility toward the
other, is no esoteric experience. It is the stuff of our ordinary human existence. To have at least named it, in distinction from the more easily demarcated domination of objects, was no small achievement.

The question was could it be philosophically elaborated? It is one thing
to formulate the issue in principle, while it is quite another to suggest the
full range of its consequences, not the least of which is the development of
a language appropriate to their unfolding. To the extent that our language
has been formed most readily in reference to I-It, including I-He/She/They,
relationships, quite an adjustment is required to encompass the more primordial I-Thou relationship, one whose intimacy has all along shielded it
from the full necessity of philosophical explication. Buber himself continued to push against these boundaries and made sufficient progress to establish that his central distinction contained considerable possibilities, but
he never succeeded in making a decisive impact on the broader philosophical debate. It was left to others, such as Emmanuel Levinas, to more radically develop the implications of his insight.[8] In part this may have been
because of Buber's own involvement with a broadly theological horizon,
one in which he felt called upon to interpret the world religions more
philosophically. It was not a calling that took philosophy itself as its pri-

mary focus. Without taking cognizance of the revolution required of philosophy, he was unlikely to significantly advance it. But identification of such intellectual limits is not the main interest. A more abiding concern is with the features of Buber's thought that not only mitigated against its fuller elaboration in his hands but also stood in the way of successors who took up the same task. What are the obstacles that lie in the way of a philosophy of personal knowledge?

The Insufficiency of Personalist Philosophy

Buber was not the only one to grasp the significance of re-founding philosophy with more deliberate attention to these two fundamental modes of knowledge. Many had glimpsed the possibility of regaining metaphysical openness by beginning with the metaphysical openness of the person. Max Scheler had already shown how the bonds of a reductionist and materialist worldview could be burst asunder through the self-disclosure of experience.[9] Emotions, the interior life of human beings, were not mere epiphenomena but a privileged access to the structure of existence as such. Henri Bergson undertook a similar reorientation of thought toward the vital inner processes through which being itself unfolds as we participate in it.[10] The existentialists, especially Jaspers and the early Heidegger, turned phenomenological analysis to the disclosive power of moods, especially those that reveal our deepest orientation within being.[11] Immanence, the contraction of humanity to a wholly mundane perspective, seemed on the verge of exploding. Metaphysics, that knowledge of contact with higher regions beyond mere finite existence, was about to recover from the long confinement into which the regnant materialism had pressed it. A particular focus on the centrality of the person flourished in France with the growing currency of the term "personalism." Emmanuel Mounier had written a manifesto of *Personalism*, Gabriel Marcel had tilted his existential reflections in a similar direction, and a convergence was also under way from the Neo-Thomist perspective of Jacques Maritain.[12] It is a movement that continued to flourish after the war, particularly among theistic circles who were convinced that if God was to be found anywhere in a godless world it must be within the inextinguishable openness of the human person. Thus, it was not surprising that, when Karol Wojtyla and the school of Christian humanism in Lublin sought to mediate between Thomism and phenomenology, the results would appear in the form of a study of *The Acting Person*.[13] Yet the ambition of a fundamental reorientation of contemporary thought seems not to have been realized. The component parts, phenomenology and Thomist philosophy, have gone their separate ways, and the project of a personalist philosophy has yet to engage the intellectual mainstream. Indeed, the very contours of what has been designated as "personalism" are likely to remain in doubt.

What is it that accounts for the inconclusiveness of such a promising start? In large measure it seems to arise from mistaking the wish for its fulfillment. It is not enough merely to propose a project that wins wide admiration, for nothing is achieved without following through to the fullest possible realization. Advocates of a personalist philosophy never got much beyond advocacy because that is largely where the efforts remained. Further application would have entailed a deeper engagement with the consequences of the shift toward the perspective of the acting person. In particular, it would have required more sustained reflection on the philosophical transformation that was sought.[14] How would philosophy itself be changed in the process? Would it be possible to leap from a largely objectivist perspective on the person to one more deeply attuned to interiority without revolutionizing our very pattern of thought? Could a philosophical revolution be attained without a comparable revolution in its language? The challenges were, in other words, more daunting than the proposed change of direction seemed to envisage. To make the inner life of the person central while continuing in every other respect with a language patterned on subject-object mastery was indeed to have changed very little. A bugle call had been sounded, but little else. To actually wheel an intellectual regiment more arduous attention to the details would be required. It was, for example, no accident that the most powerful philosophical mind associated with existential openness, Martin Heidegger, shifted his own attention decisively away from philosophical anthropology. He saw that fidelity to the project would entail more than naming it.[15]

One could not simply graft recognition of the incommunicable uniqueness of the person onto a general account of human nature. It is one thing to acknowledge that one cannot know a person until one knows him or her personally and another to explain how this relates to the universal category of personhood they all share. If each is a whole in himself or herself, then what is the whole that includes them? Without confronting the core problem that persons can only be known in themselves, never as an instance of something more universal, we can never become clear on why it is that the person must always take precedence over what she or he represents. Heidegger understood that nature could only become a question for a being who could not simply be bound by it, that is, for a being whose very existence is a question. Yet even he did not recognize the source of his insight within his own existence as a person. Too much influenced by the convention of persons as hypostases or substances, he sought to avoid anything that might reify the movement of his thought and, in the process, overlooked the source of that movement itself within the person. Being can only be put in question by persons because they alone are not what they are. The reason why persons cannot be included within the horizon of thought is that thinking is only possible by persons. To think is to exist within the openness that occurs only within each and every person. How can that which thinks be included within what is thought about?

It has been the inattention of personalism to this question that has led to the confusion of personal and essential modes of analysis.[16] As a consequence, personalism has been left with a duality of approaches whose uneasy tension it has been able to neither resolve nor comprehend. We know that over and above everything that a human being says there is the inarticulable addition that can be grasped only by personal encounter. Why this must be so we cannot say until we have understood that the personal dimension is not some optional extra but the very core from which all saying arises. No matter how deeply we may intuit this, it cannot be appropriated until we have seen why it must be so. It is not just that persons always say more than they say, but that all saying arises from an overflowing of its beginning. We cannot separate the personal coloration from its content without draining the latter of all that makes it significant because what is said is always more than what is said. Even the most technical conversations cannot be reduced to their metrics. This is why computers cannot talk or, rather, their talk only makes sense to human beings. In all discourse we listen for the voice of the other that is nowhere contained in the sounds for it can only be heard by listening for what cannot be sounded. We alone can overhear what cannot be heard because we too are not confined to the expressed. Communication and meaning are not only a possibility for persons, they are also *only* a possibility for persons. Nature as such, we must finally concede, can be grasped only by persons for whom it is possible to go beyond nature. The challenge for a personalist philosophy is to incorporate its own insight into its elaboration.

The uniqueness of every single person must not just be acknowledged. It must be understood in its inescapability. Shocked by the suggestion, so nonchalantly advanced by Peter Singer, that human beings should be regarded as replaceable, and appalled by the prospect of homogenization within cloning, we nevertheless must be able to explain why this must not be so.[17] The singular inexhaustibility of each particular person may be deeply embedded within us but that does not necessarily mean we know why. Everything within our relationships to others may be premised on such a recognition, even though the language of generalities seems destined to subvert the possibility of stating it. A personalist philosophy must be willing to concede the scale of the challenge it confronts. How can there be a philosophy of the unique? How can we name it, when even proper names defeat the project of singular identification? We must refuse to be satisfied with the admission that persons are unique in the same way as every blade of grass is an instance distinctly different from every other. The uniqueness of persons far exceeds that numerical identity. In fact, knowing everything about human nature as it has manifested itself over all of recorded history tells us nothing about the one person that stands before us. Nothing, that is, that is of any value in really knowing him or her. To know persons they must be known in all their unique singularity because who they are is wholly contained within them. A person cannot be explained by anything outside for each explains himself or herself or, at least each begins to explain what even he or she cannot exhaustively unfold. Each is unique because each is a whole within himself or herself. To acknowledge this but then revert to the language of substance, as even St. Thomas does in his careful formulation that the name "person is not given to signify the individual on the part of nature, but the subsistent reality in that nature," is to already forget the source of the insight.[18]

It overlooks the extent to which we would not even know what it is to be self-subsistent if we were not ourselves persons. That oversight also goes a long way toward explaining why the notion of substance and self-subsistence became such a philosophical thicket. Locke could not locate any definite meaning for substance and Spinoza could find it only in God, while Kant turned it into the nebulous thing-in-itself. Yet the fault was not entirely theirs. Some portion must be assigned to the ambiguous condition in which the idea of substance had been transmitted by the classical and medieval traditions. As the mysterious "we-know-not-what" that subtends the existence of things, the idea of substance could never claim to be more than the suppositum we must of necessity posit to make sense of phenomena. It was inevitable that under closer scrutiny it would tend to melt away as unidentifiable. Largely overlooked within this hoary dispute is how we might have arrived at such a conception. Self-subsistence is not something we have to attribute to entities we cannot see but the inexorable movement within which our own existence unfolds. We can conceive of that which exists through itself, that which contains and sustains itself, because this is how we ourselves are. This does not mean that we create ourselves but that we take an irrevocable role in our own creation. Self-determination, the distinguishing mark of what it means to be a person, is not a principle but the reality of what subsists through itself. Kant was mistaken in naming freedom a postulate for it is the absolute core of our existence. We know it by virtue of living within it. To be free means to be a substance responsible for its own existence, and to be a substance means to exercise such uncontainable freedom. In this sense, the category of substance does not admit of univocal application, for it is more like a spectrum that reaches from inanimate things, through everything living, all the way up to God. But it is only at the level of persons that the meaning of self-subsistence becomes transparent to itself, for it is persons alone that bear responsibility for who they are.

To gain that insight, however, more is required than simply maintaining Buber's twofold distinction between I-Thou and I-It. The reflection must go on to consider whether the formulation itself could be included within the alternatives. Is the distinction of the two primordial words spoken from within them? If not, then is the distinction itself primordial? If it is, then is it more primordial than primordiality? If the distinction is included within one of the primordial words, then how can it be spoken of both of them? How is it possible for the speaking to stand outside of that in which it itself is contained? The issue, while it may appear to turn on the logic of sentences about sentences, is of far deeper moment. At stake is the question of whether the distinction between I-Thou and I-It relations can be maintained if we are unsure of its own status. The suspicion is that if we have been able to stand outside of the two alternatives in existence we have nevertheless assimilated the whole distinction to the I-It model. After all, this is the prevailing mode of thought in which the thinker is capable of beholding an object of thought. But then we have made the I-It primordial and nullified the primordiality of the I-Thou. The very distinction we have sought to maintain collapses since there is now only the primordiality of the I-It that may, from time to time, choose to enter into an I-Thou relation, only now always from the vantage point of the primordiality of the I-It. If we are to retain the primordiality of the I-Thou, the position to which Buber and the personalists are most deeply committed, then we must find a way for the I-It to arise subsequently to it. In other words, we must abandon the distinction as itself primordial. The only difficulty then is that we must develop a new linguistic medium that is capable of reversing the ordinary evolution from a language of externality to one of interiority. Somehow it must be conveyed that the interior language is not at all derivative from an objective frame of reference but is, rather, prior to all possibility of naming objects present before us. Before there is the word of I-It there must be the word of I-Thou.

The philosophical and communicative task is formidable. It is no wonder that twentieth-century personalists managed to overlook it. But it has not entirely escaped attention. The preceding analysis is not wholly original for it derives in considerable measure from the advances within both continental and Anglophone philosophical development. Of course, the irony of a more personalistically attuned philosophical language arising within circles less ostensibly committed to a personalist orientation should not surprise us. If the intuition of personalism was indeed valid, then it follows that the enlargement and deepening of the philosophical conversation should lead to its confirmation, even if the original personalists were not fully up to the task of sustaining their own meditation. What matters is that the primacy of the personal has been asserted more forcefully through the recognition that its formulation cannot betray its content. To retreat one step into the domain of the impersonal, even by way of linguistic concessions to convention, is already to lose the footing that had been sought. The primordial can only be established through the authority of its primordiality, never by compromises with the secondary. There is no way of defending the priority of the person other than with the full investment of our own persons. Buber and the personalists may have said that we can only hear the word of Thou with the fullness of the I in responsibility, but more is required to give the imperative the kind of evocativeness that leaps from the pages of *Ich und Du*. A way must be found of making the philosophic commitment the exercise in self-sacrifice for which it calls. Only the unconditioned gift of self can adequately bear witness to the inexhaustible priority of the person before us. Generalizations about the value and dignity of the person never quite shake the confident tone of superiority in which they are spoken.[19]

The task asks more than we had anticipated. But this must not be taken as a demand for perfection, that we must always measure up to the immeasurable responsibility required of us. A utopian demand can too readily be rebuffed as impossible. Or worse, we might even feel compelled to impose the impossible as in the revolutionary schemes of brotherhood that sought to achieve through force what could only be reached through love. No, the demand here is more radical because it is more deeply and inwardly present to us. It is nothing less than the demand of the moment in which we live. Philosophy must become capable of articulating the horizon of the person within which its own reflection is conducted. Thinking must itself arise out of the debt owed toward the other before it even came on the scene. Otherwise thought permits itself a respite from responsibility to which it never truly returns. Philosophy is then in the ludicrous position, echoed frequently in contemporary debates, of wondering if it can talk its way back to goodness. "A man who goes undauntedly through life on the category that he is not a criminal but not faultless, either, is of course," Kierkegaard observes, "comic."[20] By beginning with moral self-assurance he has robbed the entire movement of existence of all seriousness. There is no gap between the I and what it owes toward the other. Not even the thought of the other can indemnify it. Existence is inseparable from speaking of it so long as the speaking wishes to retain the truth of existence. A similar imperative of transparence, we might say, has overtaken Christianity in the modern era. For what are the castigations of Nietzsche but a sustained complaint of the failure of Christianity to remain true to itself? But again this must not be taken merely as a prideful assertion of superiority over a desultory theological tradition. Such elements may well be present without exhausting the deepest meaning of his antagonism. The incomparable service he provides is not just the reminder that Christians should bear more faithful witness, but the insight that their witness should never arise out of anything but the awareness of its own defectiveness.[21] The only adequate formulation of Christianity is one that partakes of the very imperative of being on the way from which its content springs. A personalism that arises from any lesser urgency has already failed to say what it is.

Autonomy as a Distorting Absolute

The issue of how we should talk about persons is nowhere more critical than in the many public debates that revolve around the definition of a person. It is at this point that the inconclusiveness of the personalist turn of modern thought is ill prepared for the most aggressively elemental questions posed of it. Rights, we concede, apply to persons, but who is a person? When does he or she begin? What are the criteria of personhood? At what point is the person no longer present? The questions have a familiar ring for they are at the center of the controversies concerning life and death that confound an easy resolution. Mastery of the conditions of our existence suggests an extension of control to include our existence itself. Can we intervene in the processes from which human life begins through a variety of reproductive technologies in concert with genetic manipulation? If we are thus permitted to take a hand in the design of ourselves, then what is to prevent us from taking a role in determining the conditions of our own demise? What can any longer inhibit us from extending control over all of the constituents of human life from beginning to end? Consent would normally be the principal stumbling block but here we are dealing with issues that must be resolved prior to or subsequent to its exercise. Neither the unborn nor the comatose are in a position to issue or withhold their consent. They must have others who speak for them. But that is a responsibility that can only be assumed when we have assured ourselves either that the person is not yet present or is not in a position to make his or her own decision. In different yet related ways we find that we cannot avoid taking a stand on the meaning and limits of personhood. When does personhood begin and at what point do its prerogatives cease? If the capacity to exercise consent defines the boundaries of the person, then what residual respect is owed to the conditions of possibility for self-determining beings? What do we owe to those who are on the way to becoming fully actualized persons and what to those whose possibility of actualization has virtually ceased?

No better example of the danger can be found than the failure of person-centered arguments in the field of bioethics. Indeed, we might suggest that it has been the focus on the person that has been at the root of the elimination of protections for the integrity of the person. By concentrating on the features of personhood the result has been a devaluation of the pre-personal elements that are their indispensable foundation. Personhood has begun to assume a kind of ghostly reality easily detached from its mere physical basis. Biology has become peripheral to consciousness. Despite the widespread awareness of our physiological processes, now studied and understood more thoroughly than at any previous time in history, we are closer than ever to the understanding of ourselves as disembodied spirits, largely indifferent to the fate of our disposable outer shell. It is a strange disconnect.[22] We have never been more concerned with the condition of our bodies, yet we have never been more unable to make them integral to our selves. Bodies lack the dignity of minds whose autonomy must be jealously guarded. We have no compunction about taking a wholly instrumental perspective on our bodies, whose parts can be routinely replaced, exchanged, or upgraded with a view to optimum functionality. Even the prospect that our organs might be traded or utilized according to the dictates of a market does not strike us as so appalling that it cannot be contemplated.[23] A market mechanism of supplying the demand for organs is simply one of the available options because we have so thoroughly accepted the notion of ownership of our bodies. The person is the core, the master of the house, while the physiological residence is a replaceable possession. Why shouldn't we be entitled to dispose of our parts as we wish? Who else might own them? These are the readily accepted grooves along which our thought rolls, not just because we live with the powerful influence of commercial society, but much more because we have become accustomed to think of ourselves as persons first and bodies second. It is no wonder that bioethics is primarily focused on preserving our personal autonomy, and only secondarily on broader considerations of integrity as a whole.

To the extent that we define ourselves as persons, we have already set aside the pre-personal components as outside of ourselves.[24] Everything apart from the activity of self-reflecting consciousness has become objectified. The self holds all of the non-self at that distance from which it can sit in dominion over it. Whatever value our organic basis holds is one that the self has imputed to it and can therefore freely alter in accordance with its absolute prerogative. Far from constituting a republic, the parts of a human being are under the grip of a dictatorship that is entitled to dispose of them at will, and certainly without consulting their needs or interests. Rights attach to persons; none extend to the organism on which persons depend. Absent is any notion of the common good of the whole by which all constitutional rule is sustained. Given the absolute dominion at the center of this physiological realm, the consequences for the members are completely foreseeable. No one can guarantee a limit to the indignity to which the body and its parts may not be exposed. Even the much-vaunted concern with the indignity of suffering does not extend to the corporeal vessel through which suffering enters. Mortal remains are increasingly dispatched with efficiency. We have no difficulty contemplating the endless multiplication of our body parts through cell manipulation, genetic patenting, and reproductive cloning. A longstanding example of such casual disregard is the practice of sperm donation by which a single individual may give life to thousands of children utterly unknown to him. Of course, none of this forgetfulness removes the consequences that inevitably return to complicate our self-sufficient lives. Children of sperm donors do seek out their biological fathers. But the point is that complications are only discovered after the fact. There is nothing in our exclusively person-centered morality that rings alarm bells in advance. Having installed the person as the undisputed master of his or her own mortal frame, we have nothing that reminds us of the intimate web by which we are connected to all other living beings.

Nowhere is the situation more depressing than in the disregard for our offspring. The much-agitated issue of abortion persists because it is couched in terms that are irresolvable. Rights of persons, the mother or the fetus, are posed on either side and with an absoluteness that cannot be compromised. This is in the nature of rights claims. It is not simply that rights are abstractions and inherently unlimited, although that may be a part of the problem. The real difficulty lies in the character of personal prerogatives. A person is a whole, a world unto himself or herself, defined by self-determination untrammeled by outside interference. One cannot exercise partial self-determination, for any mitigation is tantamount to the surrender of control to some other source. No, there is something unassailable in the modern clarification of what is owed to persons as such. Unless one is fully responsible for oneself one can hardly be counted as claiming one's humanity. Even obedience to the law of God requires the free exercise of decision if it is to have any value, for conformity without inward agreement is of little worth. It is because autonomy cannot exist in part that it generates such difficulties, whenever we are nearer than the proverbial distance porcupines must maintain between one another. The whole concept of autonomy requires, therefore, enlargement in the direction of embodied autonomy if we are to appropriately deal with those relationships in which we are closer to others than we are to our own selves. Perhaps an embodied autonomy is not really autonomy at all, especially if the mother's bodily connection with the child has already robbed her of the freedom of choice. What does autonomy mean when we are already obliged before we begin?

It is this deeper meaning that is often overlooked when we use the language of personal autonomy. The situation of the mother and child may bring it into focus but the dynamic of responsibility toward others is inherent in the very meaning of responsibility. We may think initially in terms of freedom of choice for we are intensely conscious of the degree to which the weight of decision falls on us. No one else can accept the call to responsibility on our behalf. The initiative is wholly ours. But is it? Where has the impetus for the decision come from? Does it not begin outside of us? Of course, we are free to decide whether to respond or not, but this is only the most superficial dimension of the freedom we possess. As we enter into the enactment of our resolution we become more conscious of the extent to which we have been robbed of the initiative. We realize that we were never really free in an absolute sense. Obligation always means the recognition that we are obliged, without a choice of alternatives. The other has already presented me with an imperative before the possibility of imperatives has even arisen for me. In any moment of genuinely moral resolution we see that the image of autonomy as a realm of impregnable personal freedom has been a mirage or, at best, a partial perspective on the dynamic of existence in which we find ourselves. We are still free to disregard the call of duty, in that sense we are free, but we are not free *simply* to disregard it for that is the very meaning of duty. Our freedom, at the very point at which we become most aware of it, has already been spoken for. The static conception of autonomy prompts us to think we possess it, in the same manner as we possess our good looks or our lunch, but the truth is that autonomy possesses us, in the way that the ocean carries a wave. Autonomy is the movement of obligation through which it is exercised.

The problem is that the language of autonomy robs autonomy of its most serious connotations, suggesting an unlimited caprice rather than an acknowledged obligation toward others. Those others can lay claim to our responsibility only to the extent that we have opted to make ourselves responsible for them. Responsibility is always conditioned, never thrust upon us in all its unconditioned primacy. Our moral language, the words by which we live, seems to have curiously betrayed us. A strange disorientation pervades contemporary society as we blame the very highpoint, the differentiation of autonomy, for the decline of responsibility universally lamented. Autonomy, utterly disconnected from any other imperatives, has led us into a narcissistic wasteland where the possibility of truly moral action has evaporated. Semblances of the heroic struggle may still be indulged but they rise no higher than the exertions of contestants in trivial competitions. "Reality TV" is of course so-called precisely because of its unreality. Life itself is not a game from which one might withdraw or be withdrawn, nor is it a struggle to which one can commit oneself only in part. Yet everything about the discourse of autonomy suggests that we retain the capacity to opt in or out as the inclination takes us. Too late we discover that this vaunted independence, by which we may choose to give ourselves only in part, is an independence unworthy of the name. A responsibility become wholly discretionary has made it impossible to lead genuinely human lives. Love, tragedy, and joy have become possibilities foreclosed to us, for they are not available to the faint-hearted. Only those willing to risk all can gain all, the only self-determination worth achieving. Interpreted strictly in its own terms, self-determination never moves beyond the self. Autonomy holds out a promise as spurious as any of the self-absorbed celebrities that pervade our mass media.

The Definition of Person as Depersonalization

The deformation we inflict on our true selves is not by any means the cruelest effect of our cultural obsession with the self. Amnesia in regard to the moral enlargement required of us is only a prelude to the callousness we direct toward others. Lives that have become superficial are already inclined to view the suffering of others with superficiality. Indifference to our own destiny is of a piece with indifference toward the fate of others. But what is most disturbing is not only that the language of respect for persons provides no obstacle to this devaluation of persons, but that it is also actually complicit in their destruction.[25] The loss of self at the hands of a language of self-determination is a prelude to the willingness to destroy other selves. How has this come about? The answer returns us again to the insufficiently developed account of the person, the discussion of persons as if we stood outside of the universe about which we discourse. Ironically, it is the heightened sensitivity to the autonomy of persons that has left us so insensitive to the violations we perpetrate. Less inhibited by traditional moral strictures we move ahead, confident that the resources of a personalist perspective are sufficient to guide us. At the point where we least expected it, our conviction of moral superiority, disaster has struck. The problem is so close to us, so inescapably tied into our dominant modes of thought, that our world has scarcely been able to account for the crisis afflicting it. Indefinable anxiety about the moral environment in which we find ourselves is a long way from piercing the source of foreboding. How can we admit that it has been our very principles, about which we were most certain, that have betrayed us? How can we even think about the crisis if we no longer have reliable categories of thought? Such painful reflections are offered by way of a preparation for rethinking our moral discourse, which must begin with the recognition that even its most forceful critics have scarcely scratched the surface. The accusation that an exclusive focus on autonomy yields only a superficial self-absorption is itself only a superficial critique.

The deeper problem is that the discovery of autonomy, our conception of the person, suggests that we have understood ourselves. Now we, as persons, can stand outside of ourselves. A new self-assurance has taken hold where, by right, a deepening of mystery should have been acknowledged. One begins to appreciate why Heidegger turned away from ethics as a realm of peculiar thoughtlessness. Precisely where modern man had discovered the self, the innermost imperative of autonomy, forgetfulness has overtaken him. Now he is in possession of a definition. What could be further from the truth? How can we as persons know what it means to be a person? We can live within and deepen its mystery, but to comprehend it would be to somehow overleap the condition through which we think about ourselves. Nowhere are the consequences more appalling than when the definition is wielded as a weapon. Self-assurance brings with it the unhesitating confidence of drawing lines. Where tradition had left demarcations between the personal and the pre-personal murky, now we approach the task with full mastery of the requisite distinctions. The point at which the person is present and the point at which he or she ceases to be could be identified with precision. No longer would the appeal be made to the standards of an indefinable metaphysics. Now we possess the more concrete and realistic criteria that the language of personal autonomy has provided. Interminable, irresolvable disputes could be dispatched by resorting to the requirements of personal autonomy that inform every discussion. The only problem is that such optimistic expectations have been sorely disappointed. We have not avoided the disputes and it is instructive to consider why.

Could it be that the initial confidence was misplaced? Much has revolved around the conviction that we are in possession of a definition of the person from which unassailable public criteria could be derived. This is certainly the way in which jurists have approached the issue. All of the cases dealing with the permissibility of abortion and, by extension, euthanasia, have conceded that if the fetus or the comatose is a person, then he or she is entitled to the full protection of the law. The law is after all centered on the protection of the rights of persons. This is the one clear point acknowledged by all sides. But having been conceded it is, at least in legal circles, promptly forgotten. The reason is obvious. The law cannot comment on what its operation must presuppose; no legal system can provide its own foundations. Judges cannot be expected simultaneously to apply the law and to step outside of it in order to judge its presuppositions. Already the peculiar nature of these cases is disclosed. Even the admission by judges, that they are uncertain as to when a person, with all of the rights and prerogatives pertaining to such, is present, already opens up a lacuna in the decision that vitiates full legal authority. A fissure has appeared that cannot easily be closed. Could these be the kind of cases in which judges have no alternative but to ask about the presence or absence of persons, precisely what is ordinarily presupposed? If judges must now ask whether these are indeed parties to whom the law applies, then on the basis of what legal warrant will they make that determination? How can the law guide them in assessing what the law itself presupposes? The logical and legal abyss that looms is sufficient discouragement to perceptive jurists who wisely decide to ignore the whole issue. That practical response cannot finally, however, dispel the nagging awareness that "life cases" are not really cases in the ordinary sense of the term. Perhaps they do not properly fall under their jurisdiction.

By default the issue is transferred to the court of public opinion where the question of personhood is debated by the most professionally adept segment, philosophers. There the dividing line is between those who argue on the basis of the autonomy-grounded notion of personhood and those who insist on broadening the terms to some foundation in nature. The latter group generally argues on behalf of what is called a pro-life position, or a more vigorous protection of the rights of the unborn and the terminally ill. They concede that while all of the characteristics of personhood, including the exercise of autonomy, may not be present, the unborn and the comatose should nevertheless be treated as persons. Membership in the human species is sufficient to warrant such respect, while anything less is tantamount to a deprivation of human dignity. To draw the line on the basis of any criteria other than possession of human nature is to select some arbitrary basis that ultimately undermines respect for humanity as such. Now whether this is an argument from nature is somewhat doubtful since it seems to rest ultimately, not on a conception of nature, but on what we owe to others simply by virtue of their membership in the human species. The position is derived, not from a factual judgment about what constitutes a human being, but from the moral conviction that respect for rights requires us to refrain from judging the adequacy or inadequacy of one another's participation in our common human nature. While not proximately an appeal to what we owe to one another as persons, it is nevertheless an appeal that is derived from such a conviction.[26] In other words, it is a variant of a personalist argument that insists on the inseparability of respect for the organic integrity of the person from respect for the person as such. The real strength of this "naturalist" position is the consistency of reverence for the full human being irrespective of position along the spectrum of life. Respect, like the human being to whom it is owed, is indivisible. The weakness of this position is that it has no ready counter to the opponent who argues that we are indeed quite capable of making such divisions. To the extent that the force of the pro-life argument derives from the respect owed to persons, including their full organic integrity, then it remains vulnerable to the ultra personalists who argue that the organic prerequisites can indeed be treated differently. If respect for persons, albeit of different varieties, is the common ground, then the advantage shifts to those who assert such respect in its purest form. It is after all persons that must be respected, not their material parts.[27]

The shift of advantage to those who insist on a definition of the person as the guiding thread explains why this position dominates elite public opinion. It is the position most easily articulated. This explains why some version of the pro-choice position is the one from which debate usually begins, for the presence or absence of personhood is a powerful factor in the moral permissibility of abortion. It is only after the initial concession, of a scale of moral valuation from the fertilized ovum, to zygote, to embryo, to fetus, to newborn, has been made that reservations begin to mount as the consequences are contemplated. Reluctance builds, not just at each incremental step, but also even at the very process of incrementalization. Should we indeed be engaged in the calibration of the value of human life at all? Is there not something profoundly disturbing in a practice by which we sit in judgment over the merits and defects of fellow-species beings? We are, in other words, dangerously close to the reluctance that animates the pro-life side of the debate. The confrontation might even stabilize around some pragmatic compromise on which all sides could converge. But questions of principle cannot be compromised or, at least, they cannot be compromised in principle. Only a clarification of principle can produce a resolution. The assertion of a right to terminate human life, whether in its pre-conscious or post-conscious phase, cannot finally avoid taking a stand on the legitimacy of drawing a line around the emergence or disappearance of personhood. The definability of the person, especially in the constitutive role of autonomy, must be confronted in the full force of the challenge it represents. If we live within a moral order rooted in respect for the rights of persons as such, what is there to prevent us from limiting the application of rights to those whose personhood clearly makes them claimants to rights?

Both sides concede that inviolable respect is owed to persons as such. They differ only in the extent to which they think the person can be separated from the non-personal constituents. How can we demonstrate respect for the person, the pro-life side asks, so long as we disregard the biological substratum that makes the person possible? How can we pay adequate respect to persons, the pro-choice side asks, if we do not sufficiently distinguish the value of the person as such? Persons are inseparable from the whole by which they exist, or they are precisely what give value to the whole. Opposing sides appear to have reached a stalemate, although they are variants of the same position. Knowing what our moral obligation is, respect for persons as such, has generated the impression that we know what persons are. The dynamic of obligation has frozen into a conceptual moment. This is why, despite appearances, the positions are no sooner fixed than they begin to dissolve. The naturalist, pro-life position turns out to be a variant of personalist obligations, while the purely personalist position, of pro-choice, is incapable of maintaining itself against the incrementalist pressures of nature. Each side is in danger of conceding the strength of the other. Naturalism slides into personalism, while personalism gravitates toward naturalism. Inexorability seems to be at work behind positions that all sides assumed could be maintained in their fixity. Why? What is it that frustrates our best intentions to dominate the moral landscape with hard-and-fast demarcations? Could it be that we are ourselves part of that landscape, called upon to play our role irrespective of conceptual mastery? Could it be that we as persons can never fully understand what it means to be a person? That the whole enterprise of definitional clarity has been a massive misdirection? Such suspicions occasionally disturb the assurance of the protagonists, especially as they contemplate the inconclusiveness of the debates. But the murkiness is really only pierced when one side or the other is prepared to follow the logic of its position to its conclusions. In this regard we owe a debt of gratitude to the most extreme exponents of the pro-choice side.

However unwelcome the contributions of writers like Michael Tooley and Peter Singer may be to their fellow positionists, they have performed an inestimable service in clarifying the implication of the ultra personalist foundation of rights.[28] Quite simply they have acknowledged what few were prepared to admit: that there is no essential difference between abortion and infanticide. The reason why the controversy over partial birth abortions has caused such discomfort is because the debate made the same connection factually clear. Late-term abortions are only possible if the fetus is actually killed before full delivery from the uterus. Yet it is one thing to acknowledge such painful medical details and another to declare they are morally permissible. Tooley and Singer have even gone further. They have conceded that the same moral arguments justify infanticide for the first couple of months. The implication is advanced without the slightest hint of irony, unlike Swift's modest proposal to alleviate poverty by making babies available for consumption. Tooley and Singer have not set out to shock us into a repudiation of abortion. On the contrary, their suggestions are advanced with the intention of demonstrating its permissibility. How, we might ask, was it possible for them to overcome the revulsion that most observers cannot suppress at the prospect of treating the tiniest infants as expendable? The question is important because Tooley and Singer are not bad men. They speak out of the best humanitarian sentiments. In many ways they have reached their position by giving excessive weight to the very principle by which our public morality is grounded. Respect for persons, if it is the bedrock on which we erect an order of rights, implies that we know what persons are. To take the task of definition less seriously is to erode the very respect for persons we seek to enthrone. Tooley and Singer enjoy their notoriety largely because they have carried our principles further than we care to apply them. Could it be that the principles contain the seeds of their own subversion? Does respect for persons eventually bring us perilously close to the project of definition by which they are disrespected?

Let us look at the argument. Respect for persons implies that we can specify what persons are. Tooley and Singer propose a list of criteria derived from our commonsense perception of what is necessary to identify someone as a person. The individual must be conscious, capable of deliberate engagement with the world around her or him, and therefore of knowing the self and the non-self in their fundamental distinction. Such individuals would therefore be open to relating to others, just as they would simultaneously acquire a relationship with themselves. Acquisition of a stable sense of identity, a concept of self, is the essential turning point for it is then that the person as person has been actualized. Relationships with others can be mutual. But, most importantly, it is only at the point of conscious self-identity that a person can wish for his or her own continued existence as a singular identity. Legally this is the most crucial step since the assertion of a right to life is dependent on the awareness that one is a wholly separate and identifiable being. Without personal identity there can be no assertion of personal rights. To the extent that this is the fruit of a process of development, we may confidently assert that the entitlement to rights cannot be exercised until the process has reached its conclusion. Adult animals, Singer insists, possess a rudimentary notion of self and therefore entitlement to a corresponding rights respect. But the fetus and the newborn only gradually gain such a notion over a period of months and are therefore not a legitimate locus of rights claims. They cannot expect a certain mode of treatment because they do not yet possess the self-identity from which any expectation can be generated. The logic of infanticide is inexorable once we concede that only persons are the legitimate bearers of rights. Newborn humans are no different from newborn kittens. Lacking even the minimal capacity of self-awareness, they can be disposed of in the same way.[29] No injury is done to beings that cannot even know that deprivation of life is an injury to them.

No doubt this *reductio in extremis* is one of the strongest arguments on the pro-life side, calling attention to the inconsistency of a cut-off criterion at any stage of fetal development. But our purpose here is not to applaud the strengths and weaknesses of the opposing sides. We pause only to note the irony. The strongest argument against abortion is provided by those who favor it. A deep illogic is at work within arguments that follow their logic only to find it overturned. Why does respect for persons cut both ways? Including right through the center of the human beings involved? Is the violence inflicted on bodies, albeit tiny ones, somehow already present in the language through which we think about them? Could it be that the heightening of reverence for the autonomy of the person has not gone far enough, to include a reverential heightening of the language in which the aspiration is itself expressed? In other words, it appears that the personalist approach to the life issues has fallen short in a way that parallels the deficiencies of personalist philosophy as a whole. The mistake has been to assume we could talk about persons in a non-personalist way. Confident that we always know what we are talking about, we could not allow the personalist revolution to challenge the formulations in which it was expressed. Definition of the person was allowed to intrude, rather than submit to the realization that the person remains indefinable. Or this insight might even be conceded in general, but never allowed to penetrate our actual speaking. We remain the owners of language, no matter what the content may acknowledge, for speaking establishes our superiority to the said. We might even have been able to get away with this invincibility, except when it came to discoursing about persons. Then we could not quite shake the awareness that we too are persons and incapable of sitting in dispositive judgment on other persons. We can only regard others as persons to the extent that we enter into conversation with them. The other must always be a Thou if he or she is to escape becoming an It.

Responsibility Is Prior to Definition

When we talk about persons as beings whose autonomy must always be held sacred, we mean that they can only be known as persons through their free self-disclosure. The philosophical naiveté of the attempt to define the person is evident once the project is contrasted with the inner access to the other that is the only basis for our knowledge of others. But the putative definition fails also on its own terms. The very meaning of autonomy, as that which follows its own law, is irreducibly self-determining. What is the value of such a definition, if it is not to proclaim that no definition is possible? A person is, strictly speaking, indefinable. Otherwise he or she could not be a fount of limitless self-enactment and self-disclosure. No matter what a person says or does, he or she is not what is said or done. Whatever the expression, the person has already escaped it. This is the very meaning of what it is to be a person. One is always that which escapes the modes of tangible presence, otherwise one could not carry out the diurnal process of self-unfolding. A person remains a mystery, unfathomable even to himself or herself. Whatever persons are, whatever definition is advanced, even the most exhaustive enumeration, they are not that. A gap has intervened that is not a sheer absence but a mark of the infinity from which each one springs. The possibility of endless love and limitless conversation between human beings arises from this evanescence of what, if it were to be present, if it were to be identified or defined, would suffocate life within the black hole of finitude. Inexhaustibility, unfathomability, unattainability are the marks of the person, but they are always marks in the mode of what escapes all identification. There are indeed no marks, only traces of what cannot be traced because the person has already moved beyond the place occupied in tracing. It is this uncapturability that Kant and his successors sought to designate with the term "autonomy," not its reduction to a faculty psychology to distinguish those who can speak for themselves from those over whom we may work our will.

Even in their least expressive state human beings never recede to the point of indifference in our relationship toward them. It is not necessary for them to be capable of addressing us for the word of address to reach us. "Thou" is said even by one who can no longer say anything at all. This is why we care for them out of the certainty that they never reach the point of expendability. There is no moment at which their value is exhausted, not because of a reserve capacity they possess, but because they have already bestowed the inestimable value of obligation upon us. Before any weighing of contributions and attainments, before any talk or thought of any kind, there is the primordiality of obligation. We are bound in relation to the other before we even know the other is present. We cannot place conditions on a relationship that is unconditioned, for we cannot ordain in advance what the limits of obligation might be. It is the other in his or her need who imposes the limits on us. Nothing of course necessitates our response. We remain free to turn aside, but we are not free to ground our freedom in anything but the unmerited and unanticipated gift of the other. Emmanuel Levinas has emphasized that the other is closer to me than I am to myself, in the sense that the relationship to the other is prior to my relationship to myself. My freedom, the exercise of my autonomy, has no other source than the movement of obligation that the other has already placed upon me even before I have come on the scene. Freedom is the opening toward the other. Response-ability may still fail but failure cannot abolish the possibility from which it itself arises. Nor can that possibility be hemmed in by conditions in advance, for that would be to narrow the range of possibility to the point of extinguishing it. Unconditioned responsibility is made possible by the inexhaustible obligation the other may place upon me.

We cannot define the other for we are already defined by him or her. That is why the project of defining what constitutes a person suffers an inner collapse. We cannot reach the goal before the other has already addressed us in his or her primordial need. The fetus is, in this sense, not a minimal other, a diminished assertion of personhood, but the maximally evocative other, the purest presence of personhood beyond all characteristics.[30] Who could be more in need? Who could be more completely and totally dependent? Who could be more vulnerable? Such questions aim, not at awakening a sense of guilt, the pangs of conscience, but at the more fundamental relationship through which moral discourse becomes possible at all. Appeals to moral responsibility can always be rejected through the most reasonable refusal of unreasonable burdens. We have no obligation to remain tied to the famous violinist who will surely die if we sever the connection, as in Jarvis Thomson's hypothetical illustration of pregnancy.[31] But can we disconnect ourselves from obligation as such? Can we reach the point where we consider in supreme indifference the nature, limits, and rights of all involved? Is it possible for us to choose the obligations to which we will submit? How will such submission ever be obligatory for us? Responsibility is not something we choose but something that chooses us, otherwise the possibility of responsibility would cease to exist. We may not have responsibility for the violinist who needs a continuous blood transfusion, but we can never step outside of the bonds of responsibility as such. Sooner or later the cry of the other will pierce our shell as the voice we recognize precisely because it was already present within us before it was even uttered. Is this not the essence of the fetus? He or she is the purely other that we know as other because it is an otherness we have always carried within. The child, Levinas has emphasized, is another I, but not the same, as truly other.[32] Knowledge of the other is reached through responsibility. To kill the other is therefore not just a possibility, but also the abolition of the possibility within which we live.

The moral language of personal autonomy has failed to intimate the enormity involved in the termination of life. These are not just options within a field of possibilities but the very boundaries by which the range of possibilities can be demarcated. To abort the child is not just an action open to our indifferent choice, one without reverberations for the actor himself or herself. Rather, over and above the termination of the child is the abortion of the mother. It is to turn aside from the possibility of motherhood. More destructive than the loss of life is the nihilation of possibility as such. Physical death is evil but only in the finite way that the foreclosing of a future is always undesirable. Real spiritual darkness arises from the turning away from the maxim of life. In the former case only one possibility is foreclosed, the latter is the foreclosure of all possibility. We are not free to pick and choose between the obligations to which we will respond, for they are indivisible. We can only be serious about one if we are serious about all. To fail in one is in some sense to fail in all. That is why the breach of the moral order is so momentous. It is not an incidental shortfall.

Somehow, our very existence is implicated in the breakdown. Being as a whole is infected by the outbreak. We play a role in the cosmic drama of good and evil whose ramifications go beyond our individual selves. What do such metaphysical extrapolations suggest if not that we cannot step outside of the moral universe in which our lives are transacted? Our preference for developing definitional parameters in advance cannot be supported. We are always too late to define what has already defined us.

The mother does not define the child, any more than the friend defines the comatose patient for whom he or she is responsible. Each is already defined by her or his love for the other that is prior to anything else. Who she or he is in each instance is defined by the other, the unique one who has uniquely called her or him into relationship. To some extent we acknowledge this in accepting that only the mother can decide or only the next of kin can determine what happens to the other. Responsibility cannot be objectively determined by third parties. But we have not quite faced what this says about the one who decides, namely that he or she does not decide. The other, the unique one, has already decided. Responsibility cannot be shifted to an extraneous third party outside of the relationship. What I can know of the other is therefore only accessible from within the relationship. It is responsibility that illuminates who the other is. The other becomes knowable when we become responsible for him or her. This is the deepest affirmation of the personhood of the other. He or she has addressed us, making us responsible all the more by virtue of pure needfulness. Who could be more helpless than the embryo or the unconscious? Without communicating they nevertheless communicate to the consciously living. Their whole personhood, we may say, has been reduced to simply being there, yet somehow that is enough to be counted as a person. Why? How do we know? Certainly not by any objective criteria, for by all definitional tests of personhood they fall short. The only way is through the responsibility they evoke in the caregiver. Even before we know it their call has already reached us; they have taken us hostage without the possibility of escape. All talk of definitions and criteria in that context sounds like rationalizations for evasion of responsibility. Could there be a more powerful testament to the presence of the other than the elaborate schemes of avoidance by which the burden is resisted? Before the silent unaccusing one, the pure presence of need, there is no escape. My responsibility is the measure of the other, for there is no measure that would limit my responsibility in advance. When the other, whether at the very beginning or at the very end of life, depends wholly on me, then his or her call penetrates to the whole of me. Total dependence calls forth total self-giving as the only adequate response.

Communication with the unconscious other has been purified of all that is extraneous. It has become pure inwardness. The situation is similar in regard to the dead whom we can only know in the same way. Nothing overt passes between us. There are no words, no exchanges, no tangibles by which the relationship might be measured. But the dead are not present to us in the same way. They have no need for they have passed beyond all needs. The other, in the case of the pre-conscious baby or the post-conscious patient, has by contrast been reduced entirely to need. They no longer or not yet have anything to offer, not even by way of gesture to let us know who they are. Only their need, the need of the living, brings them within us. Their presence, to the extent that they are no longer or not yet present to themselves, lies wholly within us. This is of course essentially the same with all others who are known, not primarily through the gestures by which they address us, but through the inwardness by which they are held in themselves beyond all gesture. Even the name by which the other is familiarly known fails to attach a stable identity to the other. Only the inwardness by which the other is known beyond all fixity of names gives us access. That is paradigmatically the case with the fetus who has not yet been named and the comatose who can no longer answer to a name. Far from falling short of the requirements for personhood we might say that they exemplify them perfectly. Their claim rests purely on the inwardness by which they are known, thereby bringing to light what it is that enables us to know persons at all.

The project of defining the person, an unfortunate consequence of our heightened perception of what constitutes a person, fails because a person is precisely what escapes all definition. Abortion and euthanasia cases, far from turning on the definition of the person, are in effect the point at which the definitional project is overturned. Personal relationships through which we assume responsibility for the other cannot be subsumed within universal categories outside of the concreteness of those relationships. We can no more assume impersonal responsibility for the other than we can come to know the other impersonally. Somehow the personal exceeds the universal. This is what Buber sought to convey in insisting on the irreplaceability of the I-Thou relationship. So long as we remain at the level of generalities we have not even begun to know the concrete otherness of the person. No one is exempt from this imperative of concreteness or this concreteness of imperative. The other cannot be known outside of relationship to the other and relationship is impossible outside of the acceptance of responsibility for the other. The person is that which exceeds the universal.[33] This formulation of Kierkegaard is the closest we come to a definition, that is, a definition that operationally cancels itself. The challenge of developing a personalist language of persons cannot be avoided. It certainly cannot be sidestepped by simply distinguishing between a personal and an impersonal formulation, I-Thou and I-It, as a distinction that can be maintained simply by stating it. The divisions bleed over into one another, as the abortion and euthanasia debates illustrate, because we must constantly shift from the language of others to the language of third parties. The personal and the impersonal cannot be so neatly held apart unless we want to risk the kind of confusion in which talk of the dignity of the person opens the prospect of depersonalization. A far-reaching change is required. From the easy confidence in our ability to conceive a resolution, so long as definitional arguments are sufficiently mastered, we must shift to a perspective in which our capacity to talk about others as third persons, with all the unavoidable objectifications, is utterly abandoned. Before we talk about human beings we must first take responsibility for them.

The suggestion seems elementary, even pious. Suffused with the superiority of discussants we are inclined to regard the admonition as perfunctory. Having conceded its desirability we can force our way through the amnesia that overhangs our debates. Perhaps we could not even debate if we allowed ourselves to be interrupted by the cry of those whose distress scarcely makes a sound. But the hollowness of argument would have reached our ears. Even in the absence of a sound from the other there is still the echo of our own voices become irritatingly noticeable. The illusion that we talkers are alone in our discourse has been shattered. Yet even for those who allow the unease to penetrate and disturb their serenity the situation is not easy. How do we talk about third persons in the mode of otherness? We do not have a readily available means of making the transition. Nor can we simply avoid the topic altogether. We have to address the rights of the unborn and the comatose while we are not immediately and directly responsible for them. Policy is not generated out of each person's individual world. The otherness, the personhood, of those coming into and departing from life must be protected while they are not at this moment others to us. Merely pointing out the difficulty, as personalism has done, is not sufficient. A way must be found of taking the language of third persons, with all of its definitional and calculative character, while simultaneously subverting it, in the name of the other who exceeds all categorization.

The Law of Going beyond Law in Responsibility toward the Other

More than merely recognizing the one who speaks for the unborn and the unconscious, the law must find its own way of assuming responsibility for what lies beyond the law. An opening is already provided in the acknowledgment that we are not all equally situated to speak for those who cannot speak for themselves. Special weight is assigned to those who carry the other inwardly through personal bonds, whether of blood or affection, that affirm the irreplaceability of the other. Law has thereby secreted within itself the question mark that overturns its own universality. Contrary to the conception of law as applying impartially to all, irrespective of individual differences, here it is conceded that the relationship of individuals makes all the difference. This is more than the self-recognition of the limits of law. It is tantamount to the admission that the prerogative is usurped by the uniquely positioned individuals. Their responsibility exceeds the responsibility of the law. Why? Because they have been entrusted. By whom? By the other who cannot speak for himself or herself. In other words, it is the authority of the I-Thou, of the other who addresses me before I have even been able to decide whether I am ready to be addressed, that surpasses the external authority of the law. The vulnerability of law is unexpected but only if we assume that law is invulnerable to the unexpected. To the extent that law is rooted in the unanticipated call of the other, indeed of all others, it shares the vulnerability of the person that is the very possibility of relating to others. If we are the sort of beings who can become responsible for others, then there is no stepping outside of the perspective of responsibility. Openness to others is the very root of law itself, for it is from that source that the demand that all third parties be treated as others arises. The modification advocated here is, therefore, not that law be radically overturned, but that it recollect its own emanation from the imperative imposed by the other. Recognition that those personally responsible are entitled to speak on behalf of others is not merely a desirable modification; it is indispensable to the very principle of the law itself. How then would such an acknowledgment unravel the tangle of the life debates? In particular, how would such an approach conform to the universal responsibility of law that must step in when personal responsibility fails?

The answer is that law's intervention must be informed by awareness of its own incapacity. It cannot put itself in the place of the mother or the next-of-kin, yet it must, if it is to be in touch with the reality it engages. Why should the law value the other less than the one to whom responsibility for the other is addressed? Even though the law is not thus addressed, is not made personally responsible, it is nevertheless in the same position if it values each as much as a mother or a friend does. In other words, the law is in the position of the mother or friend but more secure against the possibility of failure. This is its guarantee, a protection against the vicissitudes of personal relationships. As the overarching mother or friend the law must bend itself toward the perspective not naturally available to it. Indifferent to the particular, the law must be prepared to acknowledge the pull of the particular other as the inestimable. Only in this way can respect for persons be accorded as that which can never be fully enough respected. Without entering into relationship with the other the law must acknowledge that disclosure of the other is only reached by such relationship. If the law steps in, as it is intended to do, in place of the relative or friend, then it can no longer be neutral in regard to the other. Law too loses its freedom. It has no choice but to see the other as a person who calls on it because the other is nothing but the need of the call itself. Whatever definitions of personhood law brought in advance to the situation, the urgency of the call of the other has shoved them aside. To raise them anew would be to murmur tones of dissembling that only thinly veil a desire to avoid the exertion that responsibility brings. The law too, once it has become responsible, has no choice but to regard the other as a person, no matter what vague generalities about consciousness and self-concept may be floating around in the background. The one who is responsible, whether it is single or multiple, is in no doubt that the other is fully a person in all that matters. The address of the other has penetrated all the way through. How can there be any doubt about an other who, even in silence, has been able to lay an imperative upon us from which there is no escape?

Law makes use of fictional persons but it might also itself be viewed as a kind of artificial person. Failure to live up to the responsibility uniquely placed upon it will have the same devastating effect. The viability of law, its capacity to represent persons in the care it exercises towards them, is deeply affected. If law turns its back on the most defenseless and most vulnerable, how will it any longer be able to claim the authority of their protector? Why should anyone care about the condition of law if it turns out to be least useful when it is needed most? Who needs the law more than the most marginally existent members of the human species? If it is not made for them, then whom does it serve? These are difficult questions for a legal system to confront when it has immunized itself through professions of neutrality and anonymity. Yet things stand very differently if we follow out the logic that law is rooted in respect for persons. That requires law to place itself on the side of persons, leaning against an indifference that might be deaf to their call for life. The pressure is such that law too cannot afford to do anything less than lend all of its weight to their defense. In case of doubt about their status it must always lean toward giving them the benefit of the doubt. The task should not prove too difficult, given that the law is not entitled to doubt the other whose responsibility has been placed upon it. Just like the mother, the relative, the friend, law too shares in the uniqueness of the one called, even when that call is generically extended to all who stand in need of its defense. Studied indifference is no longer an option.

CHAPTER TWO

Persons as beyond Good and Evil

The title of the present chapter deliberately invokes Nietzsche's *Beyond Good and Evil*. Like much else of the great iconoclast this is a work that challenged our very idea of morality because it exposed the instability hidden within it. Conventional language seemed to reassure us that we knew what we were talking about when we applied judgments of good and evil to persons. We were in possession of categories that permitted us to pronounce on the worthy and the unworthy because these were the criteria to which individuals subscribed in giving an account of themselves. What could be more natural than to speak in terms of good and evil as if we knew exactly what we meant by them? What distinction could be more fundamental? If we were not able to maintain it, was there any line of demarcation that could be retained? All threatened to dissolve into an abyss of relativism from which no lines of meaning could any longer emerge. The crisis of nihilism would, as Nietzsche predicted, overwhelm us. Little noticed in the cataclysm he foresaw was that it had been reached by carrying the logic of moral aspiration beyond its self-enclosed limits. Nietzsche's critique of conventional morality was at root a moral critique. But he was not a moralist in the ordinary sense of those wits who note the extent to which human beings fail to live up to their self-image. Nietzsche's trajectory was the far more radical one of pointing out the inconsistency in any idea of morality that remains satisfied with a finite actualization of its principle. To the extent that a finite morality is the only one we have ever known the critique has wrought havoc on our moral universe.

Characteristically it has been Nietzsche, the messenger, who has most often been blamed. Little incentive existed to examine the mode of his arrival at such devastating conclusions. The situation is understandable when one realizes that a more accurate rendering of Nietzsche's path would require a large-scale revision of prevailing patterns of thought. It would have required the major concession that our thought really indicates patterns of non-thought. We would have had to admit that we really possess no understanding, or very little, of what we mean when we bandy about terms like "good" and "evil," "moral" and "immoral," "persons" and "principles," "freedom" and "necessity," and so on. Such linguistic indices are more in the way of markers along our journey than accounts of the terrain as a whole. We cannot exhaustively enumerate the content of our moral language precisely because it is our language. It is not an object we can hold at a distance to view its undistorted essence. Instead, it is the language we live within, the means by which the dynamic of our lives is unfolded. We cannot keep ourselves apart from that which is so internal to us that it is this side of our own skin. Yet the language we use, of an objective morality, has failed to take account of our inextricability within it. There is no moral language apart from the persons who bear it as the inescapable undertow of their existence. Even that, however, is a formulation that suggests a distance that in reality is simply not there. It is almost as if we sought to discourse about the nature of morality without noticing that the discourse itself should partake of the same moral imperative. Can we talk amorally about morality? Can we speakers fail to intimate that we too are subject to the same inexorable demands? Can we allow even the respite of discourse itself, the moment of leisure snatched from the urgency of obligation, to rob talk of obligation of all seriousness? Nietzsche had an unfailing ear for the humbug that crept into the most well-meaning exhortations to goodness. And he never failed to expose it.

In that perhaps he himself took the easier path. The task of exposing the hypocrisy of others is a source of satisfaction and, as such, fraught with the risk of an even deeper mode of hypocrisy. What can be worse than the moralist whose superiority has been vindicated? Where do we go from there? Certainly these concerns also occurred to Nietzsche, and they troubled him. He had no way of dispelling the unease, or of knowing if it was an unease that ought to be dispelled. Even Nietzsche, it appears, had not fully understood the nature of the demand he had placed on European morality. Certainly it was not just exposure of the mendacity of moral shortcomings. Nor was it simply despair at the prospect of any moral code finding sufficiently devoted practitioners. Elements of each of these perspectives were undoubtedly present but they were too commonplace to capture the originality of what Nietzsche evoked. That novelty was nothing less than a reinvention of moral language. In place of the static conception of fixed quantities and permanent attributes, Nietzsche sought a language as fluid and dynamic as the unending moral struggle itself. A moral language that remained tied to the very demand of which it spoke would be one in which the moral life was not simply examined but actually lived out. The inseparability of persons from the moral struggle in which they are engaged is at the source of Nietzsche's insistence on the primacy of the perspective of life.

Some indication of the difficulty of rendering our language transparent for the vitality of the moral life is provided by the failure of most readers to grasp this as Nietzsche's project. Despite being one of the most widely read philosophers his thought remains peculiarly opaque. We may be able to follow his call for self-overcoming, but to see this as a requirement that extends even into the formulation of the call itself is more than we are prepared to concede. Yet the whole moral tradition from its Greek and Christian beginnings has been rooted in the recognition of life as an unending struggle. We have simply not made that acknowledgment integral to moral discourse.[1] The present chapter attempts a beginning in this task. Nietzsche, we will discover, is not so bewildering, once we see that the instability of his thought is of a piece with the instability of existence itself. The strangeness dissolves once we remind ourselves that the arrival at a moral language is the inward movement of morality itself. A first step is the acknowledgment of the origin of this realization within the whole moral tradition, a path of self-overturning that did not have to await Nietzsche's reflections. Second, we will examine Kant's evocation of this dynamic as a mysterious unfathomability that has not been well served through its identification with the notion of autonomy. This will, third, provide us with a way of enlarging the conception of moral language as one that is borne by the persons who continually exceed its boundaries. Persons charged with moral responsibility are strictly speaking beyond the categories of good and evil with which they must contend. Persons, we finally see, are more than the categories applied to them. Kant was surely on the right track when he formulated autonomy, not as self-expression, but as universal legislation, a process through which we become responsible for the sum total of good and evil in the universe. Beyond the moral categories there is the more fundamental decision for or against being enacted by every one of us.

The Sermon on the Mount as Deconstruction

Acceptance of moral responsibility is a risky affair. Moral commitments are not easily stabilized in advance for, having responded to the need of an other, one never knows what else one may be called upon to surrender. We are still free to disregard the obligation that takes our freedom captive. Giving alms is not the same as being robbed, although the material losses may be roughly similar. Robbery might even be preferable since it is over and done with, while generosity is an emptying of self without consideration of the cost. Only the need of the other imposes a limit on what may be asked of us. Certainly an appeal to our own resources, capacities, and needs is never enough to permit relief. What kind of moral code could impose such an impossible and insupportable burden on us? Surely there is a madness within the morality of the Sermon on the Mount that counsels a perfection unattainable by mere human beings. "Be ye perfect as your heavenly Father is perfect" (Matthew 5:48). The Church has always conceded that the requirement of living within the tension of transcendent perfection is imprescriptible. Christ had not come to abolish the law but to bring it to a perfection that lay definitively beyond all law. At the same time he opened the possibility of its eschatological fulfillment through the perfect sacrifice of himself on behalf of fallen creation. That resolution of the conflict between an impossible demand and its impossible fulfillment through the perfect love of Christ answered the basic theological issue. But it left the status of its moral force uncertain. Were Christians called to lead a life of perfection in this world, or could they tolerate the compromises that the necessity of survival imposed on them?

A wide range of responses to the question was explored over Christian history. The early Church sought to live out the vision of a perfect community of believers, but then the pressure of institutional differences mandated a more differentiated responsibility. No one, Augustine explained, was absolved of the obligation of inner obedience to the divine call of perfection, but in undertaking action they must first consult the obligations of their station in life.[2] Judges were not free to simply follow the counsel of forgiveness toward wrongdoers, for they were specifically charged with the defense of justice for the common good. The weak and defenseless must not be sacrificed for the sake of satisfying the inner imperative of public officials. The compromise between transcendent truth and pragmatic limits has remained the classic formulation of Christian political thought up to the present. Nowhere was it more eloquently enshrined than in the just war doctrine that also saw its first comprehensive formulation with Augustine's carefully balanced reflections. What could be more of an affront to the Christian commitment to love of one's neighbor as oneself than the readiness to violently terminate his life? How could Christians be soldiers? They could, Augustine explained, if death were not the worst evil to befall human society. Worse than death is injustice, especially its proliferation to the point that even more death and destruction are perpetrated. War is justly prosecuted if it is undertaken, not for the evil it entails, but for the sake of the good that cannot be secured in any other way. The Christian soldier must, therefore, fight always with the attitude of the peacemaker. His external duty and his inner disposition cannot be separated. But not everyone over the Christian centuries has been content with this uneasy tension to which Augustine, far from resolving, had delivered them more profoundly.

Some decided to give themselves wholeheartedly to the pursuit of perfection and took the requisite step of severing their responsibility for life in the world. Hermits, desert fathers, and the early monastic communities flourished to become the rich variety of religious orders within the Catholic Church. Even there, however, perfection was not reached but pursued with a focus that made the failure to reach it even more palpable. It was from these sources that the call for monastic reform became an ever-widening pressure within the Church, to include the hierarchy, clergy, and the ordinary faithful. One way of reading the fracture of the Reformation that splintered the Christian Church in the sixteenth century is precisely as a failure to keep this periodic call for perfection within institutional bounds. Loosed upon the modern world the demand for perfection would work unpredictable effects, including the secularized spirit of widespread social control. A radical and unsatisfiable demand could metamorphose through the tyranny of virtue into the revolutionary ideologies of perfection that devastated the twentieth century. The madness, by which the best becomes the enemy of the good, was unleashed with a fury that set aside any finite achievements. From that catastrophe we look back longingly at the unstable stabilization that Augustine effected between the twin mandates of our existence, for survival and self-transcendence.[3] Even more wistfully we look toward the Greeks to whom the thought of definitively escaping the tension between perfection and imperfection simply had not occurred.[4] For the philosophers and the poets it was just not an option that the conditions of existence might be fundamentally altered or that we might be called upon to play any role in such a process. The turn away from religion in our secular age is in large measure provoked by just such a reaction against its excesses, although even that response is moderated by the return of religion nonetheless in societies that seemed to have been done with it.

The pull of transcendence, it turned out, was more deeply embedded in the movement of existence than commonly suspected. Religion with its excessive impossible demands could not be so easily put aside, even by societies dominated by the comfortable placidity of the reasonable. Yet admission of the irrepressibility of transcendence did little to provide a framework for comprehending it. The best that a secular thinker like Habermas can attain is the acknowledgment that we live in a "post-secular" age, a formulation that concedes the incapacity of a secular horizon to understand the unassimilated guest in its midst.[5] It is a peculiar situation in which the previous tone of self-confidence, secure in its dismissal of religion as obsolete, is now noticeably diminished. Even the voices of popular atheism, periodically resurgent, no longer have the capacity to shock once enjoyed. Now they are seen as quaint curiosity pieces from an era of battles, between religion and science, long gone by.[6] Meanwhile religion endures with a shocking originality we are still incapable of surpassing. It is an offense to ears soothed in immanence. Settlement in the routine is decisively and permanently disrupted. Such is the logic of the Sermon on the Mount, a logic that exceeds all logic and an economy that overflows all economy. The structure of Christ's dicta has a repetitive force that drives deep into our hearts. "You have heard it said . . . but I say unto you . . ." To the one who asks for a coat we must give our cloak, the one who desires us to go a mile must be accompanied two miles, and to the one who slaps us on one cheek we must present the other too. Nothing is too much for the giving that is required of those who are prepared to yield all without counting the cost. Let not your right hand know what your left hand is doing. When we ask the reason for submitting ourselves to this endless outpouring of self, we are given no answer but the imperative of giving itself. The injunction, of becoming perfect as the Father is, is itself just one more formulation of the imperative. Why should we want to become perfect like the Father, especially at the cost of the ceaseless pouring of existence without return? That is the question that cannot be answered for it is the question that underpins the whole discourse. We are called upon to give without asking why and, in that, is brought to light the extent to which all giving is made possible by such self-forgetting. Finitude is definitively ruptured.

Christ's most famous sermon is thus an instance, perhaps the decisive instance, of the instability of all moral codes. It is a crucial demonstration of the impossibility of a morality that seeks to remain within its own self-contained parameters. The irrepressible drive to transcend its own limitations cannot be forever repressed. A finite or secular morality is impossible in principle. This observation will have a more substantial basis after we have considered the modern attempt to establish such a morality in the principle of autonomy. For now it is sufficient to note that the most well-known moral exhortation is structured by a dynamic of going beyond itself. Morality cannot be fulfilled merely by fulfilling it. It is a paradoxical conclusion that, like all paradoxes, is difficult to take on face value. Only on closer inspection do its contours reveal themselves as confirmation of what we have known all along. The Sermon on the Mount is not a unique formulation of the instability of morality. It is simply the most celebrated of what is the case with all attempts to set limits to the moral imperative. Their very formulation calls into question the intended rationality. If obligation is to contain inbuilt indemnifications, why should the stopping point be placed just there? One coat rather than two? Why not even earlier, or perhaps later? Why should any amount be sufficient? The secret of the sermon is that Christ speaks, not out of his own authority, but out of the authority of the moral impulse itself. It is a Nietzschean "transvaluation of all values" without the incautious implication of departing from all "values." Christ, we may say, remains closer to Nietzsche's intention of showing how all moral principles drive inexorably beyond themselves because they are incapable of finding a resting point short of the perfect gift of self. The moral trajectory is structured by the horizon of the infinite.

What this realization means, how we are to understand it, and what its status is are all questions that in the simplicity of the sermon remain in abeyance. They have, as we suggested, prompted millennial struggles within Christianity, many of them fought over how the sermon is to be interpreted. How is an eschatological text to be applied? The difficulties recede only when we begin to see that such a text shatters the very notion of a text. Ordinarily the reader sits in judgment over what is read. He or she remains free to determine a response, usually in the leisure of a detached distance. But what about a text that announces an urgency we cannot ignore? One that warns we have already taken too long in the task? A text that reverses the ordinary relationship, by reading the reader rather than the other way around? The words of the Gospel are sui generis, but only because they are the supreme instantiation of the authority from which all morality is derived. No preconditions, calculations, or bargains are announced in advance. We are simply plunged into the imperative to which we must respond, not because of the favorable or unfavorable consequences that may follow, but simply because we have already heard it, before the words of the imperative reached us. The "voice of conscience" is too tame an expression to capture the jolt of awareness it entails. As an authoritative command the imperative remains distinctly beyond the self. Yet it is a voice that is closer to the self than the self of self-awareness. We cannot turn aside from its call or, rather, we can turn aside but only at the cost of the very self that makes it possible to be a self. It is our own voice and at the same time utterly beyond our expectation. No tests of authenticity are required for us to know that this is the voice of God for it bursts upon us with all of its unanticipated fullness. Physical miracles could provide no greater verification than the miracle of unconditioned love unmistakably affirmed before us.

The light that radiates from the sermon is not limited to its application within the Christian context, for it casts a reflected light on all other moral and legislative enactments. No longer can they rest secure in the stability of their expression, a stability that perennially tempts the response of merely fulfilling the letter. The radical literary impact of the sermon is to upend all possibility of encapsulation in a code. Certainly the classic philosophers understood this condition well as they focused on the centrality of virtue. Law was never sufficient to ensure lawfulness since it could never adequately encompass the multiplicity of requirements that flow into the good life and the good society. Following directions without understanding the science of rule hardly constituted a human order at all.[7] Only the free response to transcendent goodness, undertaken in the full awareness of the direction and validity pursued, could be counted as the properly human mode of fulfillment. But that could not be reduced to a set of rules, even as comprehensively elaborated in Plato's *Nomoi*. Aristotle opted for the evocation of a concrete human type as the only norm and measure of right action. This is the mature man, or *spoudaios*. When he thought then about the character of his own discourse, the *Ethics*, Aristotle had to engage in his own little noticed self-subversion. Ethics, he declared, is not a science whose truth is found even in the general principles announced in his book. Such attempts at a definition of virtue, as a rule of reason, aiming at a mean, and so on, are no more than indications of where virtue lies. To really encounter it, it must be found in life, for ethics is a science whose truth is found in concrete action rather than in the universal principles that merely abbreviate it. Most men, he warned, prefer to talk about good action rather than engage in it (*Nicomachean Ethics* 1105b14). How are we to take such retractions if not as a deliberate overturning of what the whole work of the *Ethics* appears to be doing? This is of course not to render the text superfluous, no more than the sermon removes the value of its own reading. But it is to call attention to their peculiar instability as texts, an instability that is deeply embedded within them.

In one sense their theme is instability, for that is the existential dynamic they aim at communicating. Obedience to law requires going beyond law. That is presented, not as a means of making the fulfillment of law more desirable or even of exhorting the generosity of over-fulfillment. It is rather in the very nature of law that it calls forth a more than legal response. To merely satisfy the letter of the law is to fail, perhaps even to break, the spirit of the law. No law that aims at being taken seriously can afford to ignore the distinction for it is not only respect for the law that is at stake. The very operation of the law depends on a whole range of considerations that cannot be included in the law. Contracts, for example, must be entered into in good faith but there is no way of stipulating all of the elements needed to satisfy good faith in advance. Laws too rest on a broader background of tacit support for the entire political and constitutional order that sustains their functioning. A virtually limitless set of conditions could be adumbrated without approaching the possibility of explication within the code itself. Their absence from the rule is not a fatal defect but an inevitability of the nature of rules. The latter cannot include the injunction that is most indispensable of all. That is, that the rule ought to be obeyed. In its absence the rule may be taken as an invitation to avoid what is enjoined, by meeting only its minimum requirement. Work-to-rule is a well-known means of bringing any enterprise to its knees. Legalism drains all respect for the rule of law. Even the rules of politeness entail more than the formality required. Law is, despite all the appearances of self-containment, not a realm apart from the whole of existence. It is rather a moment within the dynamic that contains the whole life of a human being and cannot be properly understood without that gift of self as the infinite possibility of the person. The Sermon on the Mount dispels the illusion that virtue can be gained on the cheap.

With a relentless exposure of our vulnerability, Christ drives home the impossibility of satisfying the law through any response short of the complete surrender of self. The economy of reciprocity is ruptured beyond repair as he points out the impossibility of limiting the circle of recipients. If one gives only what is expected and only to expectants, then what kind of giving is this? One has merely given in order that one might receive in return, but then the very meaning of the gift is undermined. To give, the gift must be outside of the economy of exchange, as an outburst of the unexpected, the uncalculated, and the unreciprocable. The rule of giving can only be fulfilled by going beyond the rule. "But if you do good to those who do good to you, what credit is that to you? For even sinners do the same" (Luke 6:33). The injunction to give cannot be fulfilled if the giver is to receive credit for the transaction. It is for this reason that the gift must exceed the requirement, must be directed toward the least deserving, and must annihilate its connection with the giver. The supererogatory abundance Jesus advocates goes beyond the madness of the famous potlatch ceremonies of gift-competition, even to the point of destruction, so beloved of anthropologists.[8] On such celebrated occasions the gift-givers are at least mutually present and their excessiveness at least serves a rational goal of prestige. With Jesus the pure gift has removed even the possibility of return. It opens the possibility of reconceiving the whole mode of communication between persons. But for now we need only note that the requirement of going beyond the rule is already embedded within it. Could it be that rules, our whole conception of morality, function in just such a way? Rather than stabilizing an order, are rules a perennial invitation to go beyond them? And if imperatives are to be conceived dynamically, how are we to regard the persons who bear them as their inner mode of existence?

Surely such persons are beyond good and evil since their final assignation has yet to be determined. So long as they remain alive the identification of the city to which they belong, the City of God or the Earthly City, remains unknown. Inescapably drawn in these two eschatological directions, so memorably formulated by St. Augustine, we do not know which will be our end. Our existence is held within this eschatological tension that definitively precludes finality. So long as we remain alive we cannot be sure, despite the resolve we may summon, that we will sustain the commitment to goodness to the end; nor are we entitled to despair, even in the face of the most resolute choice of evil, of discovering an unexpunged corner of goodness within. It is the impossibility of turning ourselves totally in one direction or another that seals the unknowability of the self. Just as we cannot sit in judgment over others, we cannot even sit in judgment on ourselves. Persons are the kind of beings about whom judgment cannot be rendered, for to be a person means precisely to be engaged in a process about which the outcome is unknown. Conversely, it is the unknowability of the end that guards the possibility of the process. Nothing so obstructs the Christian life, Augustine also discovered, than knowledge of our predestination.[9] Why work for what is already a foreordained outcome even without our work? Knowledge of the goal toward which we are moving cannot be allowed to eclipse the struggle by which the goal is attained. The moral dynamic by which personal existence is disclosed and enacted takes precedence over every formulation of it. As such, the moral life is neither good nor evil, but beyond them.

Human beings are not reducible to what they do. Actions may indeed be characterized as good or evil but not the persons from whom they have arisen. What they are to be has not yet been decided for that is what occupies their whole existence. The problem is that as we sit in judgment over the quality of actions on a continuous basis, the tendency to elide that outcome into a judgment of the actor is often irresistible. This is why the counsel, "Judge not lest ye be judged," is so often invoked in the Gospels. We are not in a position to sit in judgment of persons as such, not because of the impossibility of adequate knowledge but, more importantly, because who the person is has not yet been finally determined by himself or herself. Even characters in novels are hardly believable unless they are able to retain some element of the unexpected in their development. To be a person is always to escape encapsulation in the character given to him or her. If stabilization were possible, then a point could be reached at which the moral law could be fully satisfied. But then who the person is would be fully disclosed. Is there such a moment in life, an action in which I can place the whole of myself without remainder or reserve? One is inclined to think that there must be, for that is precisely what is aimed at in our best action. But to the extent that our whole life is one long effort to live up to such a commitment we have not fully disclosed who we are. We have only announced our intention. Only perfect action is a perfect disclosure of the person. The paradigmatic case of Christ's passion, death, and resurrection is simultaneously the limiting possibility and the impossible limit. For all other persons a more mundane language of disclosure is required to intimate the irresolvable tension within which their existence unfolds.

A moral language of attainment and non-attainment must be found to suggest the imperceptible dynamic of the person. Moving always toward the ever-fuller donation of self, the whole of a person's existence is found to be insufficient to the task. Seeking to give more, we are always more than we give. Even in our best-intentioned efforts, the shortfall trails into inextinguishable darkness. Just as we have never fully been able to serve the cause of goodness, so we have never finally severed the connection with evil. Yet so long as we remain alive we have neither gained nor lost definitively. The difficulty therefore is to talk about what cannot be talked about because it only exists in the movement. If there is neither good nor evil but only the movement toward or away from them, how are we to discuss them in the language of fixed quantities? Even Christianity with its focus on doing rather than saying has not yet been able to find a language that makes the saying transparent for the doing. Nietzsche's critique of both Christianity and philosophy hits its target. That is, not just that Christians have not lived up to their own moral imperatives, but the deeper objection that their very language invites such a side-stepping response. By making morality a matter of attainments they had lost the unattainability that is its source. This, as we have suggested, flies in the face of both the Sermon on the Mount and the classic insistence that virtue can properly only exist as a way of life. We do not have to follow Nietzsche's anathematization of the whole tradition for us to recognize that he had hit a weak spot within it. Philosophy and Christianity had not always managed to say what they sought to say. Life must be privileged over its conceptualization. That is what successive generations sought to affirm even if the linguistic means was not always adequate to the task. A turning point would be reached only when autonomy had emerged as the defining notion of the person.

Autonomy as Unfathomable

Autonomy had the advantage of placing the understanding of the person within a dynamic context. No longer tied to fixed parameters in nature or a moral code, the centrality of emphasis had shifted to the person himself or herself. Initiative lay within the person whose most crucial dimension consisted of the freedom of self-determination. It was this aspect that particularly captivated Kant, who regarded it as the centerpiece of the dignity of human beings. Rational beings in general occupied an exalted position in reality because nothing could move them to action but their own free grasp of the necessity of duty. They could be bound only by their own free assent for nothing could oblige them but that to which they had already permitted themselves to be obliged. Conversely, no obligation worthy of the name could arise from any source other than the free and rational consent of persons determining themselves in serene detachment. Incentives and coercion are to play no role for they demean the very meaning of moral obligation. What is the value of an action that is compelled? Or even one that is entered into out of interest? Such tawdry considerations, fear or favor, merely devalue the proposed action. By contrast, what renders a moral action of supreme worth is that the agent chooses it entirely on a rational basis, that is, in accordance with his or her conception of what obligation requires in the instant. This is why Kant could announce in the imperious opening of the *Groundwork* that the only unqualified good in the universe is a good will. Compared to the inestimable worth of autonomously chosen action all other goods are merely instrumental. It is from this realization that he derived the categorical imperative. Always act in such a way that one can will that one's action should become universal law.

Obedience to law is inseparable from its enactment. We do not find the moral law ready-made, either in the command of God or in the inclinations of nature, for every such instance begs the further question as to whether obedience is required of us in this particular instance. Nothing merely factual relieves us of the burden of moral judgment. Whatever is proposed as good must be such, not simply because it is, but because it ought to be. We are charged with rendering a judgment that cannot be transferred to another. Responsibility for affirming goodness is inexorably ours. There is no stepping outside of the moral horizon within which our whole existence is transacted, for nothing stands higher than the imperative of deciding in relation to the highest. If nature or the voice of an other occupies that deciding position, then we are not ultimately free, nor do we live within a moral horizon. It is because not even God or nature can take away our responsibility for following them that we remain free in relation to them. But this is what the law of God and the law of nature always meant.[10] It was never the mere acknowledgment of an irresistible necessity, otherwise God would have no need to utter his commands and nature would merely prompt without our reflection upon it. Kant understood that he was bringing about a clarification in the conception of divine law and natural law that illumined our point of access to them.[11] Whatever God or nature declared as our good remained for us to take up as the authoritative good for us. Ours is the primordial freedom of that which creates itself, if not in every sense, at least in the most decisive choice of direction. To be thus charged with bringing the good into existence does not mean we are free to invent it in light of our own imagination, for it is a good that is prior to our engagement with it. To be free means we are more deeply bound than we thought, for we share in the responsibility of the Creator.

This is why neither natural law nor divine law relieves us of responsibility for their interpretation. It remained to us to determine what was required within the specific applications. Every set of axioms contains their own conflicts. How were we to decide when preservation of the self might override preservation of the other? When the care of the body might be subordinated to the care of the mind? When life could be purchased at the risk of death? No neatly ordered hierarchy could preclude the struggle with concrete alternatives, and proponents of divine law and natural law never pretended that intuition of the source of law resolved the issues once and for all. It was always somewhat disingenuous to suggest that natural law and divine law failed merely because they did not finally preempt moral evaluation. On the contrary, natural law and divine law have always been concerned with the arguments to be adduced in their application. Laws do not furnish a decision, only persons do that. What natural law and divine law have done is issue an appeal to the person to weigh that decision in light of existence as a whole. She or he is charged with upholding, not a specific provision, but the integrity of law as such. In the end it is not the particular norms that are dispositive but their evaluation within the whole, a perspective that requires us to stand outside of them in the primordial light of the good as such. The law of nature or the law of God reveals itself to us only when we are prepared to submit ourselves to the principle from which it derives. It is because we are free that neither commands nor inclinations can determine us. What they mean is what we are charged with determining. We are responsible for the enactment of the morally good.

The imperative is categorical, applying irrespective of all circumstances, because autonomy is indistinguishable from it. Autonomy is the categorical imperative in action. What else can self-determination mean but the enactment of one's own law? The enactment of one's own law must of necessity be a universal law for only that is rationally grounded. A law that is chosen for some consideration other than its rightness is not properly speaking a law. It is merely a hypothetical action, chosen as a means to some particular end. To rise to the level of a moral choice it must be untainted by other factors, including the particularities of the agent engaged in making the choice. As rational creatures, persons attain their highest self-realization when they are no longer particular selves but wholly rational agents. Universal selves enact law for all similarly situated universal selves. Only by responding to the pure incentive of reason do they attain the freedom of those who can be moved by no other consideration. The general structure of Kant's formulation is well known. Its familiarity has often caused us to overlook the novelty with which it initially struck its author, for this is an indispensable aspect of Kant's own effort to come to grips with his discovery. Along with the starry sky above, the moral law within was one of the things that filled him with wonder and awe. This famous remark is not a mere throwaway comment but an indication of the deep mystery Kant sensed in the principle of autonomy at the center of the person.[12] It is almost as if Kant himself realized that there was something unfathomable about the whole notion. His moral writings are replete with references to the dignity and reverence elicited by autonomy as the highest calling of human beings. This dimension of Kant's own response, generally neglected in a commentary literature that focuses on his arguments, is important because it directs us to the indefinable within the definition of autonomy.

Definitions in general, we have suggested, encourage a false sense of mastery of the matter. This is particularly fatal when definition aims at encompassing the definer himself or herself. Kant did not quite grasp the imponderables in this conception but he had a profound intuition of their imponderability. Nothing puzzled him more than the question of how it was possible for the individual to be so utterly detached from his or her own interests that a decision could be reached within the supreme indifference of reason alone. The difficulty centered, not so much on the process by which the individual arrived at such an exalted region, but, once there, how he or she resolved on a course of action. What was the moving force of it all? Would there even be momentum once the motivating sources had been left so far behind?[13] Perhaps we would simply recede into ataraxia, the state of supreme self-sufficiency well known to the Stoics Kant had read so well. He knew of course that human beings never or very rarely reach such a condition. Their experience is more commonly dominated by the awareness of the struggle of ascent toward it. The arduousness of the task will rarely yield moments in which the leisure of such pure reflection becomes available. Agents will more normally be propelled forward by the quest for the good of which they are in search. They are unlikely to be tempted toward quietude when they have still not reached the goal of their striving. But the mystery of the limiting case remains. We may not be in danger of confronting it but its prospect structures the whole account. What indeed is the point of the struggle if it ends in a condition in which the struggle itself is eventually suspended? A similar consideration affects Kant's theological adumbrations. God's denomination as "holy," meaning that he is above the temptation to turn aside from the good, pure duty, renders him both less relevant and less interesting for human existence. Divine remoteness is not just a function of our incapacity to hear the voice of God. It arises much more from the sense of the unlikelihood of his having anything to say to human beings. Holiness would render its pursuit obsolete.[14]

Perhaps it is the remoteness of the attainment of holiness that renders it so inexplicable. At any rate the awestruck response to which Kant confesses exactly captures the mood of mystery. He cannot understand how a person can be moved to act purely out of rational motives because that is the limit of his own horizon. To the extent that we human beings live within that imperative we cannot fully explain it to ourselves. We simply find we are capable of it, no more. To call it God-like or holy as Kant does on occasion is not to dissolve the mystery. We only deepen it by dwelling upon it. In the absence of any possibility of stepping outside the highest viewpoint available to us, action chosen simply out of duty, we can never fully apprehend what it is about. Only the perspective from within the exercise of autonomy is available to us. No explanation is possible. This is in stark contrast to our knowledge of the external world, the realm of causality in which the inexorable laws of necessity hold sway. There the connection between cause and effect accounts fully for the phenomena, as Kant detailed in his *Critique of Pure Reason*. Categories of understanding exhaustively permit us to organize our knowledge within the world of objects. It is only when we seek to apply them to ourselves that theoretical reason fails us. Despite the superior access we enjoy through our internal perspective on the self, we remain more of a mystery to ourselves than the most remote constituents of the universe. Could it be that our very closeness to the moral horizon within which we live is the source of its insuperability? Kant only touched on this consideration, without elaborating a reflection. His thought remained transfixed by the contrast he had identified between the two utterly different realms to which we belong, without a possibility of grasping the bridge between them.

This is his famous antinomy between freedom and necessity.[15] We simply find ourselves inhabiting these two distinct realms. On the one hand we are part of an order governed by causality in which there is no effect without a cause and no cause without an effect. Even our own actions are covered by this inexorability for, once initiated, each element in the series transmits its force to a successor, and in turn to another, and so on indefinitely. The chain of cause and effect can be traced back to a prior cause in the same way in which every other reality can be analyzed. Human action is no different from any other phenomenon. It can be explained. But the exception lies in its innermost beginning. How is it possible to explain where that initiative came from if it has no other source beyond itself?

For it has no other source beyond itself if it arises utterly without motive or incentive, that is, if it is rational. Nothing outside of the will has resolved it to action in a particular direction. It cannot be explained in relation to anything that came before it. Only its own inner determination to act solely on the basis of right or duty has compelled its movement. But this is tantamount to admitting that it has no cause, that nothing comes before it, that it has always been. These were the extraordinary implications that Kant acknowledged and, far from resolving the mystery he confronted, they only drew him deeper into it. To concede that moral action originates in eternity, not in the causality of time, is hardly to shed light on the issue.[16] Kant, however, was convinced that the concession was unavoidable. How else could we understand a process of decision in which nothing predetermined the outcome but the free exercise of reason? Even an action that occurred spontaneously could be explained in terms of an impulse unknown to the agent. But when the agent has intentionally excluded the possibility of acting out of any other motive but his own conviction, then nothing can explain it but the movement of conviction itself. His reasoning may be defective but it yields to no authority beyond its self-correction. To explain this would be to explain the operation of reason itself, a task that would require the very thing we seek. Autonomy, Kant knew better than his successors, marks not the beginning of an explanation but its limit.

Autonomy cannot be foreclosed, even by its own definition.[17] The truncated account of autonomy that has dominated moral discourse must therefore be overturned. We must admit that autonomy, as the self-determination of moral existence, is in effect a non-definition. For too long we have simply assumed that the autonomy that made possible all of the enactments of the moral life could be comprehended as if it itself were one of those finitizations. The journey seemed to be assimilated to the way stations. The truth is that they are of a very different order from one another. For every particular assignment of value, judgment of good or bad, we can always ask whether that itself is a good estimation. Even a definition of autonomy can be subjected to the same scrutiny. Is it good that we should privilege the self-determination of persons? What this suggests is not that moral judgments are irreducible, demolishing what G. E. Moore called the "naturalistic fallacy," but that they are even more mysterious still. Their irreducibility extends to include even the talk about them as irreducible. Somehow we can never fully understand what is entailed in rendering moral judgments because we are incapable of radically stepping outside of them. In talking about what it is to be a person we cannot cease being persons ourselves. Our only access is from within a process in which we participate. At its most profound level autonomy is not really a concept but who we are. Definitions suggest something that we possess, not what possesses us. It was this latter dimension that Hegel sought to capture by turning Kant's conceptual language into a radically altered form in which the concept itself becomes the moving force of existence. The mystification thereby generated could have been reduced if he had dwelt longer on the source of the problem, in the widespread tendency to overlook the difference between concepts we contain and concepts that contain us.

The issue is of course of millennial scope, reaching all the way back to the Platonic Ideas and their forebears. The status of Ideas that are normative for us is a notorious source of uncertainty. Nowhere was it more famously exposed than in the tension that pervades the *Republic* between the city in history and the city in speech, a tension that remains irresolvable although Plato lacked the means of acknowledging its irresolvability. Kant, by contrast, conceded irresolvability as the mode in which autonomy exists. Autonomy cannot function without postulates it can neither suppress nor surpass, for God, immortality, and freedom are extrapolations from the innermost unfolding of autonomy. Ramifications of mystery exceed our penetration, while simultaneously guarding autonomy from the transparence that would abolish it. As such, acknowledgment of the self-limitation of our definitions is not just a matter of parsimonious commitments. It is an intellectual modesty that is indispensable to our continuing existence as persons. Only the unattainable preserves the expenditure of effort to attain it. This is what Kant intimated, without explicating, in his celebrated invocation of the postulates. He saw that what could not be said directly could, nevertheless, be said by not saying it. In order to find a definition of autonomy that would do more than define, that would call attention to the impossibility of definition, it would have to be a definition that simultaneously undermined itself. He initiated an approach to the definition of persons that recognizes the superiority of misdefinition. In this way Kant becomes not only the great inaugurator of the concept of autonomy but the decisive point at which the notion overturns itself.

Beyond Good and Evil

Once the morality of morality is admitted as the crucial question then the impasse at which autonomy seemed to be immobilized is broken. The question as to whether the isolated individual could generate a full account of morality, from within his or her own resources, is no longer relevant. Morality is not what is generated through the exercise of autonomy but what makes that exercise possible. Even before the individual raises the question of what ought to be done, he or she is already implicated within the unfolding of the good. The self does not invent the values by which it is guided but rather discovers them as prior to the self. Nietzsche was the first to seize on the crisis generated by the very notion of self-chosen values. He understood it as the catastrophic collapse of the Western tradition of morality, for it meant the exposure of bottomless caprice. Usage of the term "value" as a moral reference originates with him and the degree to which it has gained almost universal currency bears out the prescience of his foreboding. Nothing any longer would be of value if its value were rooted only in subjective preference. Without some metaphysical depth beyond the ceaseless variability of the self nothing permanent can endure. A subject without an anchor is driven by the unceasing winds of whim. The exercise of limitless mastery meant the complete loss of self-mastery. This was the great crisis, the advent of nihilism, the "uncanniest of all guests," against which Nietzsche expended his great philosophical energy. Yet it was a contest he never quite brought to the conclusion he sought, that of thinking his way through to the other side of nihilism by which he might inaugurate a new spirit of European morality. By immersing himself so deeply in the problem, Nietzsche overlooked the degree to which he had transcended it. Like so many of his successors in the crisis, he failed to see the extent to which the announcement of nihilism as the crisis is already a step beyond it. Only Heidegger, with his particular affinity for the uncanny, could diagnose the extent to which Nietzsche's nihilism had begun to negate itself.[18]

Other commentators have tended to see Nietzsche as epitomizing the crisis he sought to address. Largely overlooked in this rush to judgment is what it was that made Nietzsche such an unerring diagnostician. How was it that he could pinpoint so exactly the crisis of values that would overwhelm the autonomous self? Was it not that he had already seen farther down the road and had already begun to occupy a position in which autonomy has yielded, at least in part, its vaunted independence? The fault, as we have suggested, was not entirely attributable to the limitations of Nietzsche's readers, for he gave more than a little encouragement to the view that he had fallen victim to the impending disaster. His own increasingly vituperative writings at the end, as well as the shattering collapse of his powers, all worked to confirm this impression. But the impact of his personal crisis should not be allowed to obscure the brilliance with which he held the wider civilizational crisis at bay. The sense of liberation, of a joyful superiority over all dark forebodings, which marks the writings of his creative peak, derived from this certainty that only one who had so thoroughly understood the problem of nihilism could decisively stand beyond it. This was the major trajectory of his thought. It began with the critique of morality that emanates from the rapier dissections of the moralist. Stripping away the illusions of self-satisfaction that perennially envelop the moral life, he could expose the bankruptcy that lay at the heart of the most cherished progressive ideals. Endless talk about the improvement of morals had become a substitute for anything that might require real self-sacrifice. Beneath his deft probing, the mendacity that masqueraded as idealism was allowed no shreds to conceal it. The operation had been carried so far it was easy to conclude that Nietzsche had stripped the principles of morality itself away. But that would be to rob the impact of the very critique itself, and he understood that problem very well. It was for this reason Nietzsche conceded that, despite all he had said about truth merely being a prejudice, he still worshiped at the same altar of truth as Plato had.[19]

The difficulty was to find a way of retaining both the impact of the critique and the foundations from which it drew its force. Part of Nietzsche's genius was that he understood that the problem had no solution, or at least none that could be formulated in such a way that it would convince everyone who came upon it. Besides, any "solution" would itself be immediately exposed to the harrowing force of the same critique, by which it would be accused of not having gone far enough in the direction it advocated. There would always be something imperfect about every moral formulation. No matter how unconditioned the demand it made on us, there would still be some unsurrendered corner of the self. Nietzsche understood that even the categorical imperative harbored an unacknowledged note of cruelty and pride. Yet this did not vitiate the whole possibility of moral existence, for this would also deprive the critique of its force. It was rather that a new way of understanding the moral dynamic as a whole was required. Where good and evil had been conceived as the fixed parameters between which the autonomous self made a choice, now the real meaning of autonomy is that it is the process by which good and evil are revealed. What makes the moral life possible, its autonomy, is that its struggle between good and evil provides no resting points. There is no moment at which the pursuit of good is achieved or evil avoided, for that is to betray the imperative under which it operates. Embrace of a purely finite good or rejection of a purely limited evil is the point at which the corrosive pride of self-satisfaction gains access to the moral life. The insight is profoundly Augustinian, and Nietzsche understood his affinity with all of the great psychologists of history, but the language is one that strains toward a consistency that even Augustine never achieved. To the extent that existence remained an unending struggle between good and evil, then it could only be understood as a process of emergence beyond good and evil.

The crisis of morality thus resolves itself. There can be no diagnosis of crisis except from within the unfolding movement by which it is simultaneously transcended. Such a hopeful self-understanding is a far cry from the despair that tends to overwhelm the preoccupation with modernity. The widely lamented loss of meaning weighs most heavily when it robs the initiative by which it might be regained.[20] But this was not the position of Nietzsche who saw, as clearly as Kierkegaard, that endless discussion of the crisis was merely a means of postponing any response to it. The attitude was, moreover, inherently unstable, for one could not diagnose what one had not already begun to surpass. Deferral of responsibility became in essence an avoidance of what had already been conceded as unavoidable. Diagnosis marks the beginning of therapy. It is a logic that could be overlooked through the proliferation of discourse whose endlessness seems to take up the space and time for action, or at least to produce amnesia sufficient to block awareness of the failure. The strategy of course does not work. Bad faith cannot suppress what it must continuously remember in order to forget. At its core, Nietzsche suggested, it is not even a form of faith for it would prefer to turn its back on existence altogether.

This was the fatal misstep in the Western intellectual tradition. It was not so much the search for a metaphysical beyond that had perverted the path of existence, but the notion that a certainty might be found in advance by which we might dispense with the entire moral struggle. It was the turning aside from life that so appalled Nietzsche for, whatever else we can know, the one thing we cannot cast aside is the faith by which the opening toward being is itself sustained. We cannot substitute certainty for faith, as the trajectory of philosophy from Descartes on had sought to do. The loss of faith in the God of revelation, datable from this period of growing self-confidence in the power of reason alone, is accompanied by the quest for a certainty that will leave faith as such redundant. Its most telling consequence is, as always, in the moral realm where the effort to provide a rational grounding to morality demonstrated the impossibility and the irrelevance of the project. Ever since Grotius suggested that morality might be able to dispense with what it ought not to dispense with, a theological foundation, the philosophical current has moved through a succession of alternatives in the form of natural law, natural rights, a priori reason, contract, utility, and history, without finding a principle with sufficient authority to dispel rival challenges.[21] The subsequent collapse of moral justification into emotivism, relativism, or decisionism seems to confirm the outcome as evidence of the impossibility of a purely rationally grounded moral order. Again the exhaustion of possibilities without issue is taken as proof of the crisis in which we find ourselves. Yet morality as such has not collapsed, or where it has, the collapse has not been irreparable. Restorative forces have asserted themselves in the wake of the most horrific outbursts of inhumanity that periodically overwhelmed modern societies. More often than not the moral resurgence has been expressed in the most rationally abbreviated language of all, human rights.[22] As a consequence, we begin to suspect that the collapse of the project of a rational justification has not only been irrelevant to the moral life, but may even have been contributory to the most ideologically driven excesses.

The quest for foundations strikes a post-foundational age as particularly futile. A readiness to admit that we live in an irreducibly pluralist world, in which "overlapping consensus" is the best for which we can hope, has replaced the foundational project.[23] But what the positive significance of this turn is cannot be grasped until we have understood why the foundational project failed. It was not just that the object sought, a universal rational justification of morality, was not found, but that the goal was fundamentally misconceived. To have located a compelling argument for doing good would have been to rob goodness of its purpose. Autonomy, the self-enactment of universal law, would have been rendered obsolete if the path is already foreordained in advance. No longer would the dimly intuited pull of the good draw us into a greater actualization of it, nor would the inner growth of fidelity to its promptings give rise to the virtue by which the commitment is sustained. The very exercise of autonomy presupposes its engagement in a process of discovering a good that is never fully disclosed to it. When self-determination is reduced to a foregone conclusion the process of arrival at it renders thinking unnecessary. A similar process is at work in the realm of theoretical reason. According to a famous remark of Lessing, the whole interest of science derives from the process of investigation rather than from the conclusion at which it arrives.[24] Paradoxically scientists are driven, not by truth, but by the quest for it. A similar paradox governs the moral life, in which the underlying movement toward the good takes precedence over any particular achievements or failures along the way. The person is more than what he or she has done. It is this unlimited capacity for surprise that is preserved in the prioritization of the moral life over all of its manifestations.

The problem with naming it, as the term "autonomy" has done, is that the vitality of the moral life is arrested. Once again the congealing power of words is evident, although more than the ordinary fixation by what we have objectified is involved here. The very notion of autonomy seems to present a limitless range of possibilities, none of which provide a sufficient impetus for action. Overlooked in the process is that the self that does the contemplating and the self contemplated are the same. As a result the self thinking about the problem of autonomy bears no relationship to the self called upon to exercise responsibility. Autonomy as such looms as an empty expanse that must be filled from we know not where. This is the origin of the demand that a source must be found in nature, reason, or the social whole, anything beyond the punctuated self. The charge of formalism leveled against Kant's categorical imperative, a charge he struggled mightily to refute, stems from the same problem. Posed as an abstract possibility, autonomy almost invites the impression of unrelieved isolation. What can compel the action of one who recognizes no valid motive outside of self-validation? Can there even be an impetus to action when the self has so thoroughly distanced itself from all potential urgings and urgency? The sadness of the self lost within the cosmos of its own making, cut off from all that could furnish a reason even for existing, can become a pervasive mood. Autonomy reveals its cruel obverse in this state of bereftness in which it is condemned to play endlessly with the creation of values without value. This was what gave rise to Hegel's unfair characterization of Kant's moral philosophy as lacking in seriousness, although there was an uncomfortable element of truth to the charge.[25] The categorical imperative lacked nothing except purpose, for it could not provide what it sat in judgment over.

A variety of remedial efforts have sought to remind the autonomous self that it is embedded within practices that already commit it in specific directions. To the extent that the self engages in a task certain moral presuppositions come into play, presuppositions from which it is not free to distance itself. Playing a game, for example, entails more than merely following the rules. It also calls forth a more unspoken and deeper engagement with the rules about rules, the morality of rules, for mastery of a game cannot be acquired by circumventing its rules. Honesty and fairness are prerequisites so universal that no task can be undertaken without them. Neither baseball players nor mathematicians can be considered masters of their craft if they cheat to achieve the results. A more philosophical version of this appeal to the internal dynamics of a practice invokes the parallel within autonomy itself. If choice or self-determination is to take itself seriously, then it must recognize that more is at stake than mere subjective preference. Somehow a moral dimension beyond self-chosen values must inform its unfolding. In this way at least the beginning of an opening of autonomy beyond the closure of the self is intimated, for this appeal reminds us that autonomy has little value unless it opens upon a universe of moral seriousness. Kant was sensitive to this danger that choice might devolve into mere arbitrariness and sought to preserve the full dignity of the person involved in self-determination. But it has never been enough merely to hold out the aspiration of moral seriousness, for that still leaves the self-enclosed individual with a further choice to make. The crucial issue is whether there preexists any direction by which he or she can be guided. Calling on the autonomous self to respond to such invitations is still to leave it on the far side of all that can move it.[26]

What is needed is an understanding of the moral order that would draw it closer to the self than the self is to itself. Rather than conceiving of autonomy as what makes morality possible we must think of morality as what underpins autonomy. It is not therefore for autonomy to sit in judgment over the moral imperative but rather the reverse. Then autonomy would be robbed of the distance by which it holds its moral decisions apart, pondering the desirability of acting on them or not and, in the process, discovering that there is nothing to prevent its endless postponement of action. Instead, autonomy will discover that it has already failed, that it has come on the scene too late, that it stands guilty of dereliction. This is not to insist on some primordial fault of the will, an original sin that hinders its realization of the good. In many respects the self-enclosure of autonomy is already such a condition. Rather, the point is to break the hold of such obstructions. It is to think through what the only sin against autonomy can be, namely the refusal to exercise it. The greater awareness of the role of autonomy has, as we have suggested, heightened the danger by focusing attention so exclusively on the self-determination involved. The effect can be a mesmerizing paralysis that robs autonomy of its momentum. Autonomy can sap the vitality of autonomy. Lassitude and depression must be ruptured by a judgment that is more searingly intimate than the self. Kant's own concern with ensuring that autonomy is used to sustain rather than destroy itself, that self-determination not be used to abandon self-determination, the promotion of virtue by which the obligation to duty might be sustained, answers itself. It is a question that can only be raised by one for whom the question is no longer an issue. We cannot step outside of the boundaries of morality to demonstrate the truth of morality. The inseparability of autonomy and morality is the deepest meaning of each of them.

The Individual Exceeds the Universal

It is through the moral imperative that the arrested development of autonomy is overcome. Nothing can still the unstillable drive toward the good, for the dynamic is the very definition of autonomy. There is no higher authority recognized by the individual than the good that calls it from within. Autonomy does not in that sense require a moral grounding for it is such a moral grounding in action. Submission to the imperative of duty has no other end than its own being. There is no *telos*, or goal, beyond it for, while good action may serve a range of purposes, none stand higher than the "ought" itself. We might even say that it is the point at which being transcends itself. Fidelity to the good, to what duty requires, can compel us to leave all other being behind as we endeavor to remain true to the one unqualified good in the universe. The "metaphysics of morals" is a term to which Kant gave currency but it is not clear that even he plumbed the depths of what it contained. Conventionally it has been taken to mean the a priori of practical reason, although the degree of imprecision as to whether the a priori were a groundwork (*Grundlage*) or a metaphysics should alert us to the uncertainties involved. They seem to go back to Kant's initial assumption that he could separate morals and metaphysics, an assumption that made it difficult for him to later conceive of morals as a species or mode of metaphysics. Yet it is difficult to deny that the imperative that seized the autonomous will came from a reality beyond it or that the direction in which it drew the will inexorably lifted it into a more real reality than the will itself. It is not that the attainment of greater being is the goal of the moral life, but that it is the only viable self-understanding of the dynamic involved. At its peak the categorical imperative, the performance of duty simply for the sake of duty, attests to human existence as a movement beyond being. Refusing to be captured by what is, the autonomous person is one who is capable of living in accordance with what ought to be. Freedom is the mystery from which being is.

The best Kant could do was to hint at these inexpressible depths of the moral life, although those hints are a precious and indispensable access to its inwardness. They begin to reveal the powerful inexorability that drives the moral life. Even the person himself or herself cannot fully penetrate the necessity entailed, for clearly it leaves all thought of natural or causal necessity far behind. Kant's own formulation of it as a necessity of freedom adds little in the way of insight; it merely concedes the limits of our capacity to penetrate the pull of that to which we are called to respond. All that we know is that we must and, in that acknowledgment, confess that more is at stake than our purely individual selves. It is at this point that Kant usually lapsed into talk about the worth and dignity of such beings who could set everything aside, the whole world and its welfare, including their own, for the sake of imperious goodness.[27] Reverence and awe are owed to such beings who outweigh all of creation for they are virtually its source. To say that their actions originate in eternity, as Kant did, is not therefore such an impossible notion.[28] It may have given notorious difficulties to his readers, but for Kant himself this famous characterization was of a piece with the profound inexorability within the categorical imperative itself. Always act in such a way that one can consider one's action as the enactment of universal law was more than an aspiration. It was the very meaning of action and the very meaning of autonomy. There is no law other than the law one has enacted. The purely private self that might set itself outside the law is no more, for it has wholly subordinated itself in obedience to what is universal. Once this is taken as the very meaning of action then the possibility of conflict with the law has disappeared. The self has become universal and, as such, dwells in the eternity in which the universal has been accomplished.

It is because the self within the categorical imperative enacts a moral universe, one so true that the merely empirical one pales into insignificance, that it has no need of a *telos* beyond itself. Purpose has been reached in the beginning.[29] Whether this is to be interpreted as a teleological perspective or not is a matter of interpretation. Kant himself seemed to take issue with Aristotle on just this score and for many commentators this underlining of the difference has confirmed the deontological character of Kant's moral philosophy. On this account Kant goes out of his way to emphasize the irrelevance of any extrinsic motivation to the process of forming a moral resolution. Anything heteronomous, whether it is pleasing God, attaining happiness, or securing the common good, robs action of the purely moral worth of that which is done for its own sake. Autonomy seems to define a world utterly free from purpose or incentives outside of itself. Yet that is not to liberate it from purpose altogether. It is rather to see purpose as consummated in that which is highest, that which cannot reach anything further because it is the summit of all purpose. In thus invoking that which is done for its own sake we hear echoes of the Aristotelian definition of virtue. The affinity should not surprise us. Aristotelian ethics, despite its teleological reputation, also seems to serve an end perpetually accomplished and yet never finally accomplished, otherwise the good life would be no more. Strange as it may seem to suggest, Kant, even in his sharply etched distinctions, may simply have been remaining more faithful to Aristotle. A *telos* that we live within may be both present and absent at the same time. Indeed, how else could it be except as the presence whose absence makes possible the movement toward presence that never abolishes the absence? Yet none of this is a mere idea. It is a mode of being through which being itself becomes luminous to itself. Metaphysics may no longer define a realm available for our contemplation, ideas or forms existing apart from us, but it does point to the order of reality as a whole that can be known from within.

The mystery of the moral universe we inhabit, a mystery that is never fully penetrated, is one that also never fully escapes us. Transparence is a dimension of the moral life. We know that we ought to act purely out of a sense of duty, for this is the very meaning of right action. It is action undertaken irrespective of all other reinforcing or opposing considerations, impervious to every appeal but one, the unsurpassable truth of what is right in itself. Of course, from our subjective perspective this is couched in the terminology of ought, as the requirement to which we ought to conform despite all of the struggle of self-overcoming involved. But in order for it to be an ought imposed on us we must first somehow already exist within it. This was a dimension that Kant's successors, the German Idealists, sought to convey, with admittedly, mixed success. We would scarcely be able to fail in fulfilling our obligations, they insisted, if we did not already live within that fulfillment, at least to the extent of acknowledging its obligatory force over us. Only someone who already lived within a moral universe could acknowledge the duty of living within a moral universe. Obligation, the ought, has already imposed itself on us even before we have confronted it. We find that we already live within obligation by discovering we have failed to live up to it. Our lives become then one unending effort to repair the fault from which every beginning begins.

It is at this point that we begin to realize that more is at stake than the worth or worthlessness of particular actions. Even the consequences implied in the formation of character, the kind of person I am becoming through the actions I have undertaken, are not quite large enough to capture the scale. The moral life is the nexus for our involvement in a drama of good and evil that is greater than ourselves. Kant's formulation of the categorical imperative, by which individual action is taken as the establishment of universal law, suggested something of that larger context. The only problem was that it could also be taken as a grandiose expression of the ego enlarging itself to the whole universe. Kant sought to correct this misimpression in *Religion Within the Boundaries of Mere Reason*, a work that takes as its starting point the acknowledgment that a purely individualistic approach to morality misses the more than human scale of good and evil involved. We are both called to a greater goodness than seems humanly attainable and tempted by a descent into evil more abyssal than we can plumb. But what is decisive is that this drama is not an event in some remote future or past. It is present as the unfathomable depth of the actions by which we uphold the maxim of goodness or, failing, embrace the darkness of evil. Actions in themselves may be relatively slight, while the maxims behind them are fraught with metaphysical significance. In choosing we choose not just for ourselves but also for the whole of reality. The responsibility we assume in enacting universal legislation is truly awful in scope. Within the concision of the *Groundwork* such implications were present without being elaborated. It was only later that Kant came to see that morality itself could not be properly understood unless it was located within this larger than human drama.

Deepening the mystery did of course nothing to relieve it. What it did do was raise awareness of the responsibility of the individual whose autonomy assumes an almost cosmic significance. A person chooses on behalf of the whole order of being, not merely as a private occupation. In this way we begin to see what the individual is. He or she is capable of bearing this primordial responsibility because there is something primordial about him or her. This is what Kant sought to suggest in talking about the dignity of rational beings, a dignity that derives from their being more than simply logical deducers. He meant that there is an unsurpassability about each human being that is ultimately what makes them capable of rationality. They can think and act rationally because of their metaphysical openness as originators of order within being as a whole. Even before they think or act they already stand within that primordial relationship of responsibility within the whole. They bear the whole within because they are its originators by virtue of their capacity to give themselves as a whole. It is a Godlike status, as Kant surmised, for in a certain way the world begins with each person. This is not just in the subjective sense that for each one the world is just what it appears to him or her, but also in the far more objective sense that the existence and order of the world is the unique responsibility of each one of us. We are not God and thus we do not create the world out of nothing, but we bear a God-like responsibility for enacting its order. All that we do is done with a view to the whole that is thereby established through the maxims of our action. Through endowing the universality of the whole each has uniquely given himself or herself as a whole. Each is the singular without which the universal could not be.[30]

The intriguing consequence of this mystery of the genesis of moral action is that it sheds light on the peculiar metaphysical status of the individual. Is there even such a thing as the individual given that he or she must be prior to any of the universal categories by which they might be identified? Kant's origination of action within a moment of primordial freedom is an attempt to address the problem. It is a far cry from the disintegration of the subject that has occurred in the subsequent history of philosophy. The source of the difficulties lies, however, in the admission of an autonomy that could not give an account of its own possibility. All too frequently the superstructure of Kant's thought has been taken as an unproblematic starting point without paying sufficient attention to the infrastructure that, even by his admission, seemed peculiarly unsubstantial. We are left to puzzle over how it is possible for the individual to be the source of universal legislation while standing outside of it. What does it mean to suggest that the universal is enacted through the self-determination of a self? Is it because the individual is the whole of reason, for it is only as such that he or she can be the source of a multiplicity of universal enactments? The self-government of reason is only possible if reason is fully present in such a way that it is not present at all but remains to unfold itself in a panoply of directives. Most of the time Kant took for granted that there were rational beings and that we could be confident we knew what they were. It was only when he turned his attention to the grounds of their possibility that he was forced to admit the non-grounds of their possibility. This was the point at which he introduced the mysterious postulates, especially the central one of freedom exercised in a moment of eternity outside of time. About this unspecifiable source of all autonomous unfolding nothing more can be said, for it can only be glimpsed in its operation and not in its invisibility.[31] The furthest reach of Kant's reflection on the topic was to acknowledge that this limited penetration was a good thing. If we were to see through the whole purpose of our actions from beginning to end, then we would be robbed of the only incentive for rational action. Reason can govern itself only if self-government is indispensable to its self-realization. A mind that knew everything in advance would have no need to stir itself.

Existence is crucially bound up with this self-ignorance of the self. This notion of the between character of human existence, held between the poles of knowledge and ignorance, the human and the divine, has its classical origin in the very self-understanding of philosophy. Yet even in its

Platonic formulation little attention was paid to the self susceptible to this intermediation. Emphasis was placed on the between status of the existence in which it finds itself. Largely overlooked was the implication that a self that could participate in such a tension, especially a self that could grasp such an observation about itself, would also have in part transcended the polarity.[32] Indeed, it is this tension between the self that grasps and does not grasp the tension that is the deepest form of the polarity. What is decisive is that the tension not be fully grasped, as Kant indicated. But this is to heighten the mystery of its condition of possibility. The temerity of Kant's successors in specifying the Absolute or the I as what makes possibility possible ran the risk of specifying the unspecifiable. Given the greater interpretive uncertainty with which their works have been shrouded it is not clear that the risk has paid off. Yet their efforts have yielded an important further dimension in acknowledging that the boundaries cannot be drawn simply around the empirical self. Only a self that is transparent for an unreachable beyond can sustain the full dignity of autonomy at which Kant aimed. Unfortunately the readiness of Fichte and Hegel to name what could not be named has often been taken as just the kind of foreclosure of self-knowledge against which Kant warned. Whether that is a fair or justified reading of these figures is not the most significant issue. What matters is that the subsequent development of philosophy has understood itself as firmly opposed to all such misplaced concreteness. Now naming of the ground of possibility of autonomy must assume the form of a naming that fails to name.

Morality, we have seen, is not confined to its resting points, those moments in which it is closest to encapsulation in a definition or standard, but is most truly itself when it surges endlessly forth to raise the question of the morality of its morality. How can that inexpressibility be expressed except by suggesting its inexpressibility? But this is not to say nothing about the dynamic of the moral life. It is to say everything about it, only in the mode of not-saying that is closest to the not-saying by which it itself perpetually refuses to be confined to the said. Often that invocation of an unsurpassable freedom has been taken to mark the end of metaphysics. But the priority of ethics does not abolish ontology so much as raise its status to a very different mode. In contrast to the image of an ethereal other world that somehow lies just beyond this one we are now more inclined to regard metaphysics as the unattainable horizon of the life we live. It is unattainable because we cannot step outside of ourselves to view the whole in which we exist.[33] All that we can do is notice in passing what makes the enactment of our existence possible, that is, the presence of a moral order with all of its eternal ramifications that can never really be present. The mode of presence is eschatological. This is the thought intended in Kant's famous postulates that could neither be dispensed with nor grounded in knowledge. We have only our own participation in the moral life to reassure us of God, immortality, and freedom. Outside of this perspective their validity has no meaning. What then does this say about the person whose response to the call of duty renders a glimpse of what cannot otherwise be glimpsed? It is surely that an individual exceeds the bounds of the universalities in which such adumbrations can be couched. They can be known only by someone who has already in some sense gone beyond them. We might say that this is what the person is, an endless capacity to transcend what *is* that brings what *is not* into view. The collapse of metaphysics, so widely proclaimed in contemporary philosophy, is directly attributable to the failure to find a way of talking about that within which we exist and which, for that reason, cannot simply exist. Kant's postulates, despite their rather cryptic character, are not by any means the least plausible versions of this insight. They have the unique advantage of signaling what the moral life cannot signal directly.

To embrace the logic of such self-overturning signifiers, however, would require a more deliberate acceptance of the linguistic revolution taking place. In this regard Kierkegaard stands out for the boldness of his grasp of the implications. He was the one who formulated the admission that the individual exceeds the universal with all of its antinomian hazard.[34] When we concede that the individual is beyond good and evil, then morality itself seems to be lost. There is more than an element of this foreboding in his analysis of Abraham's sacrifice of Isaac. Could there be a higher obedience within the inwardness of the person that would surpass the universal fidelity to duty? That would even justify action contrary to duty? Kant did not consider the disturbing implications of the existential dynamic he had imparted to morality in the form of autonomy. For Kierkegaard, however, the point was to dispel the unease by showing how the overturning of morality arises from the thrust of the imperative itself. In this endeavor he found the means of saying what could not be said, through the introduction of the individual who was already living out what could not be said. Duty then always requires going beyond duty in fidelity to what cannot be fully known. As a consequence duty itself is changed from a goal to a way station at which we have the duty of not allowing ourselves to rest. Beyond duty is the voice by which we are personally addressed. We can hear it only because we have already heard it, an event that transforms the imperative into recognition. The person is therefore not simply a process of self-determination but the prior openness that is ready to respond and that guarantees that the process never settles down. Talk of an absolute I before the I tends to confuse the situation. At the very least such formulations overlook the extent to which the response is rooted in the uniquely personal nature of the calling. There is no depth beyond the personal depth from which we have been called and toward which we personally respond. Autonomy overflows into a metaphysics of the person. This is the decisive consequence of the prioritization of the person within the movement of autonomy: autonomy is itself overturned in the direction of the personal horizon within which it unfolds. Rather than looking for the person within an account of metaphysics, now we must think of metaphysics as an account of the person.

CHAPTER THREE

Reality Transcends Itself in Persons

It is often said that the modern world, the world in which we live, is afflicted by disenchantment. Reality is impersonal. No longer do we encounter those mysterious presences that to our forebears seemed to populate a magical cosmos. Instead, we must endure a largely inert universe indifferent to the pleasures and pains it elicits within us. Communication and conversation occur one way as we continually probe a reality that never appears to address us in turn. We are alone with all the frailty of thinking reeds in the vastness of things. Who would know or care if we were to be wiped out entirely? Only the warmth of our common humanity, as well as the bond we share with all living creatures, sustains us in the great mindless ocean in which we find ourselves. The contrast between our exalted status as autonomous beings and nature's obliviousness to our fate only underlines the poignancy of the human condition. Pascal was not alone in crying out against the emptiness of space, for we moderns have irrevocably departed from the closed world into an infinite universe. We are no longer at home in the world in which we live because it is no longer our home. The best we can do is gain access to the secrets of nature by which we might employ its powers for our own preservation. "For the relief of man's estate," Bacon's battle cry, carries not only the connotation of our superiority over nature but also our alienation from the forces we are determined to exploit. Indeed, the twin perspectives are correlative. Only a mind thoroughly set apart from nature could assign itself the task of subduing it so thoroughly. Whatever mute resonances might flow from nature, they can no longer be detected by a humanity severed from its source.

Of course, mastery does not arise without lingering after-effects. As moderns we are haunted by the memory of primordial oneness from which we have separated. We are more and more aware of the impossibility of dominating with a good conscience the reality of which we are a part. It is surely no coincidence that as modern civilization has extended to the limits of the world we have simultaneously been seized by the guilt of overreaching. Global warming, we are ready to concede, is the consequence of human activity. We have upset the delicate balance of the orb whose sheltering protection has made human life possible. Only a species that has so completely stepped outside of nature could assume responsibility for the harm it has inflicted on nature. At no point can we simply entrust ourselves to the great forgiving whole. The path may have been imperceptible by which human beings raised themselves above that which gave them birth, but now its fruits have become inescapable. We are no longer part of the natural order. The damage we inflict on its balance may become, we worry, irreversible. All we can do is initiate a fearful withdrawal from the precious limits we have breached. But again we are on our own. Nothing in nature speaks to us of the harmony that must be restored. It is we human beings who must assume responsibility for a natural order that no longer leads or instructs us. Returning to nature is no longer an option for those who have eaten the fruit of mastery. Consciousness may have been the first unnoticed step but it has carried us inexorably beyond all natural limits. By stepping outside of that which conditions our existence we have radically departed from its guidance.

We are more than lost in the cosmos, for we seem to be even more deeply lost within ourselves. Overconfidence in our ordering of nature falls apart as we perceive its hollowness. Nothing but the sheer will to dominate lay behind its drive. Nature itself had provided no responsive support. The whole project seemed premised on our capacity to forget that we are ourselves a part of nature, for it was necessary to overlook the impossibility of the part coming to dominate the whole. Even when a part had set itself this

Promethean task it could not quite shake the awareness of whence it had come. Mastery over nature is itself a drive of nature, one whose viability depends on its purely natural status. Problems arise only when it is extended to the whole. Limitlessness becomes the enemy of attainment. We can assert our power over nature only to the extent that we do not seek to impose our power on the whole of it, for then we would no longer occupy a place within nature from which our power might be employed. Who are we if we are not a part of nature? What is the basis for our self-assertion if it is not a natural drive of self-assertion? By stretching our hands ever farther, to include the unencompassable grounds of our own exertion, we have snapped the connection that made all possibilities possible. It is only from within nature that we are capable of imposing our will on nature. By making our power coextensive with the whole we have lost the vantage point from which we might operate. The disorientation of the denatured self is virtually complete. Set loose from our mooring within nature, disembodied humanity is condemned to drift as aimlessly as the Flying Dutchman, capable of traveling everywhere but of never reaching port. Endless instrumentality is the obverse of unassuageable guilt. Without any sense of natural limits we no longer know who we are.

The great temptation is reversion to the polar opposite. From the undisputed masters of the natural universe we rush to the alternative self-identification, that we are merely natural beings. That is, that we are simply material. This is especially the case as the growing mastery of nature turns to focus on human nature. Increasingly we think of ourselves as available for intervention and manipulation in the way that all physical entities are accessed through their constituent parts. Are we any more than the biological, chemical, and physical processes that are evidently the basis for our existence? Darwinian evolutionary theory has given credence to the emergence of the higher forms of life from the lower. One might be inclined to suggest that it is the unassailability of this world picture that has provoked a fundamentalist backlash against it. Lost in the furor is any hint of the irony entailed. How is it possible to argue for the truth of a conception that seems to suggest that all conceptions arise from the blindness of biological necessity? Freud encountered similar hesitations but, so far as I know, managed to suppress them. Darwin, by contrast, allowed himself at least a few unguarded moments, as he wondered about the implications of his own theory for its truth. He averred in a letter his "innermost conviction" that "the universe is not the result of chance," but then he wondered why his convictions should carry any higher status than those of any other organism.[1] Is thought epiphenomenal, a mere byproduct of electrochemical impulses? And, most importantly, how could we know it was epiphenomenal if we did not already assert that it is more? In holding what is true have we not transcended all motivating factors? Are we not saying that this is the case irrespective of whatever sustaining processes may be occurring within us at the time?

The problem is we have been so transfixed by our intellectual success that we have overlooked the extent to which the process of knowledge escapes our apprehension. We assume that it must be similar to the natural processes that we know. Everything can be known except the knower. Simply because the electrochemistry of the brain affects consciousness we jump to the conclusion that the latter is reducible to the former. If only we can map the correspondence between the two, then the barriers to human fulfillment, intellectual and emotional, will disappear.[2] The inclination to take control of our lives, through ingesting substances or inflicting violence, is not a new one, but it has received an enormous boost through the prestige of scientific investigations that themselves attest its falsity. Science itself proceeds, not by external manipulations of the brains of scientists, but under the analytic rigor of a discipline that is capable of setting aside both interior and exterior influences on the investigators. So why is it that we cannot include the activity of science within its results? In part it is the self-forgetfulness required in the practice of science. We must set aside the personal component, the concerns, motives, and idiosyncrasies of the individuals involved. But this operational amnesia then becomes a general discounting of the personal as such. Reality is the externality that is under investigation, even though there would be no investigation without persons capable of such self-transcendence. By the time we become uneasy about the blind spot in our worldview, it is too late. The perspective has hardened to such an extent that the accent of reality falls so entirely on the material, with its inbuilt dynamic toward reducing all to the most elemental, that we overlook the extent to which matter can only be apprehended by that which is not material. It comes therefore as something of a shock to suggest that reality is ultimately spiritual since it is only illuminated by that which is not material.[3] Could it be that our ancestors were right in insisting that the material is only a veil through which spirit is addressed by that which alone can address it, namely spirit? Is reality personal?

This chapter takes up the question of our place in nature by attempting to think through what it means for a part to assume responsibility for the whole. Already the question suggests its overturning. Contrary to the conventional image that we should fit within the order of nature, we find ourselves stepping outside of it in responsibility, to contemplate the possibility that nature finds its place within us.[4] A very different worldview is opened up when we begin to see that persons are the point at which nature arrives at its culmination. Yet that is precisely what the adventure of knowledge indicates, once we realize that it is in knowledge that nature comes to know itself. The first move in this reflection is to recognize that knowledge is only made possible by the mutuality of persons who sustain it. Interpersonal openness is both the horizon of knowledge and the goal toward which it drives. A second reflection reminds us that the implementation of knowledge requires a forgetting, a deliberate setting aside, of all that is really personal. This is why we can think of machines becoming intelligent. The raising of such concerns demonstrates, however, that persons are always more than what they say or do. It is because they occupy that unique position that they can contain the whole of reality. This is why, third, reality as a whole is open to the truth about itself when it is so grasped by the persons who are the point of its self-transparence. Reality can be known only because it is knowable. It is through persons that the meeting place of truth is announced. In this way we discover that persons are, fourth, the point at which the epiphany of the supererogatory occurs. Reality transcends itself.

Knowledge as Inseparable from Persons

Whether reality discloses a personal meaning is of course the question to be settled through its investigation. Science has taught us that we are not likely to be well served by assuming that the world is peopled by spiritual beings within and behind the visible manifestations. By taking such a route we run the risk of missing what can be known for what remains unknowable. We are counseled to follow the humbler path of observation and experiment of the empirically given. Ultimate ends and final causes may escape us, but we gain the satisfaction of the verifiable. By taking objective truth as the authoritative model we eventually come to overlook its unsatisfactory aspects. We are aware that the disclosure of factual patterns and conditions entails no normative implication for how we should regard them, but we regard the detachment as a small price to pay for the impartiality of perspective we have gained. It has been by rendering ourselves impervious to any personal appeal from the reality we investigate that we can behold it as it is. The human factor has been relentlessly eliminated so that nothing, not even the experiences or interests of the investigator, is allowed to influence the contemplation of reality. The personal must be set aside in favor of a truth that is impersonal. It is therefore not surprising that the prevailing conception of science can find no room for a personal dimension it has disavowed in principle. Individual scientists may have their particular motives, ranging from the pecuniary to the vainglorious, but a cordon sanitaire separates them from the practice of science itself.

It is this swerve away from the personal that made Michael Polanyi's insistence on "personal knowledge" all the more unusual within contemporary philosophy of science. Along with his parallel notion of "tacit knowing," he seemed almost alone in calling attention to the inability of scientists to give an account of the operational presuppositions within which they move. Polanyi's work went a considerable distance in dislodging the unassailable authority of the scientific method. He demonstrated that, far from standing on an utterly presuppositionless foundation, science comes into operation only on the basis of a range of implicit convictions that could scarcely be rendered thematic. His work sought to show that the scientist already approached reality with a knowledge of its regularity, reliability, and intelligibility before he even knew the specifics of his investigation. Tacit or personal knowledge formed the most comprehensive background within which the examination of particular realms became possible. Like Kant, Polanyi had understood that the methodology of science could not provide a justification for itself without presupposing it. But unlike Kant, Polanyi never quite raised the question as to the status of that insight into the limitation of self-knowledge.[5] Was the observation itself a mode of knowledge? Or did it arise from what made knowledge itself possible? In other words, is the self-limitation of knowledge an epistemological or an ontological event? Of course, Kant too did not fully unfold the adumbrations of this philosophical conundrum that he bequeathed as a question for his successors to ponder. It may even constitute a mystery we are unlikely to exhaust and we will certainly not attempt to plumb its depths here. For now all that matters is that it calls attention to the more profound meaning of the personal horizon of science. Not only is science an activity of persons, but also its very meaning is derived from the openness to reality that is identical with the person. We will discover that it is only persons who are capable of reaching an impersonal point of view.

A far deeper appreciation of this personal dimension becomes apparent when we consider the process by which one becomes a scientist, for the acquisition of intellectual self-detachment is hardly a spontaneous human attitude. It is rather the fruit of a pattern of socialization, what we call scientific training. Again, this is a well-investigated aspect of the science profession. At its best this line of reflection generates a kind of sociology of knowledge, as exemplified in such titles as *The Social Construction of Reality* and *The Structure of Scientific Revolutions*.[6] We recognize that intellectual inquiry is far from an individual enterprise, that it is a pervasively collaborative project at its very core. As such, it is not surprising to discover that the development of science is susceptible to the same social forces, such as competition and conformism, that are synonymous with social existence itself. Yet the status of that insight into a sociology of knowledge, one that intimates its own capacity to escape the sociological limitations of knowledge, slips past the nets of scrutiny. The point, however, is not to block the evasion but to call attention to the inescapably personalist character of the maneuver. Not only is science an irreducibly social activity but so is the analysis of it and both in ways that scarcely merit explication. Indeed, we might say that it is the non-necessity of self-explication that is its innermost horizon. Science is not just social in the extrinsic sense of requiring the cooperation of others. It is also intrinsically social in the sense of the mutuality of presence that is the very mode of scientific existence. What is meaningful or significant within any topic of investigation is what every other would perceive as meaningful or significant as well. We measure not just reality but ourselves in the minds of one another. It is through the other that I am able to gauge what is. Community is not just a social necessity of science but a metaphysical one. In this sense the collaborative enterprise of science is derived from the mutuality of all scientists, past, present, and future. Somehow they are all present from beginning to end. This is the capacity for non-present presence that marks the being of persons.[7]

But the personal horizon is not just what makes science possible, it is also what frames its investigation of the universe. We have become so used to the conventional understanding of the scientist as aiming at impersonal knowledge of things that we overlook the extent to which even scientists cannot avoid aiming at a personal encounter. Thinking, we have suggested, is never an isolated activity for, even when we are alone, we are always thinking in the company of others. Now we must acknowledge, it is not just the process of thought that requires others but that its content is also oriented toward others. It is not just that others provide confirmation for what we judge to be meaningful, but that they constitute the very purpose of the search. Our ancestors encountered mysterious presences within and behind things, not just because they were credulous, but also because at the deepest level they were already in quest of such encounters. Are we then any different? Do we believe that the universe is a dark and empty space in which we are alone, or do we strain with every research dollar spent to discover others like ourselves? Even the possibility of life elsewhere in the universe is enough to excite and intensify our interest. It gives the lie to the notion that we are merely interested in an impartial account of the nature of reality, for we already know that reality is hierarchically organized. The apex is occupied by persons, and it is they that constitute the meaning and purpose of all else. No doubt the merely physical and chemical understanding of reality has a value in itself, but that value is inestimably enhanced when it underpins the understanding of beings with whom we can begin to relate. Already plants begin to stir our interest more deeply since we share the bond of life with them. Our exploration of reality is not, in other words, indifferently distributed but has a specifying intensity that culminates in the encounter with other persons.

The pattern, both in regard to the practice of scientific inquiry and to its warrant of purpose, is well illustrated by space exploration. In the first place our approach is amazingly wedded to manned space flight, a fact that has long been remarked upon given the dangers, costs, and inefficiencies. Nothing in the quality of the data sent back by remote probes to Mars and beyond is in the slightest way deficient in comparison to what might be obtained by a live astronaut. When the enormously expanded size of the space vehicle for manned flight, with its exponentially increased costs as well as the incalculable dangers to human life, are entered into the comparison, there seems to be almost no case left for anthropological transport. In addition there is the sheer impossibility of extending human travel beyond the immediate neighborhood of the solar system. But the mystique is such that we are willing to send men and women into low-orbit space, on the shuttle and the space station, for no other reason than that human beings need to be in space. Why? The question is intriguing because it illustrates the inescapably human dimension of space exploration. Somehow the universe cannot be known unless it is known through a human being. Data may be received but only human beings can know. Part of it is that the full richness of the human experience of landing and departing from another planet cannot be captured by the most sophisticated probes. But the core of the preoccupation is what is to count as knowledge for, even when we send machines, human beings are present through those very projections of themselves. The attraction of manned space exploration will not disappear because when the vehicles carry no human life they still carry our minds forward to the point of contact. Unmanned flight is inwardly manned.

It even heads toward the same goal as manned flight for the target is nothing short of communication with others. The overarching goal of space exploration, one for which we have so far not the remotest shred of evidence, remains the meeting with other intelligent life forms. Merely encountering other life forms will not be enough. We long to meet others like ourselves. So far this may be in the realm of science fiction but that does not diminish its nonfictional influence. It is our very willingness to invent the prospect of extraterrestrial life that is the most powerful evidence of its hold upon us. Our whole outward reach through the universe would be profoundly disappointed if it could be demonstrated that there is no possibility of encountering other rational beings. Curiosity is certainly a factor within this quest but it is not reducible to that merely external interest, one that looks on the other as an object of investigation. We long to go farther to actually meet the other, a possibility that is only available for persons. They, of all the beings in the universe, can become mutually present to one another. No other reality satisfies that longing. Like Robinson Crusoe we carry a whole social world within our thoughts, indeed, we think by means of that imagined discourse with others, but it is only the prospect of encountering an other that raises and focuses all our attention. We are searching for the footprints in the sand that shatter our solitude. The romance of science is thus no different in essential terms from the romance of meeting through which every human life is ruptured by the other.

Objective knowledge turns out not to be what it thought it was, that is, a perspective from which we can contemplate and master the universe in which we find ourselves. Science is rather a way station on the road to the complete unmastering of ourselves that the other alone can accomplish. The line that Buber had sought to maintain between I-It and I-Thou relationships cannot hold, for there are no I-It relationships that do not head toward I-Thou encounters. Even when there are no presences to greet us we imaginatively extrapolate them as if to say that they alone can give meaning to our voyage on the vast cosmic ocean. Humanity may not encounter its Man Friday but its search is already structured by the anticipation by which we bear the other within, before we have even met her or him. That is the real meaning of the extraterrestrial project, for our realistic chances of meeting with other intelligences over the expanse of space and time are slim. Yet somehow disappointment does not matter.[8] What counts is that we are ready for the meeting because we already hold the unknown other inwardly as the overarching horizon of our journey. Robinson Crusoe was alone but he carried the other within him. Everything tangible and useful gained incalculable significance within this light. The finitude of the routine, the island that could be exhaustively enumerated, opened upon an infinitude when related to the other. The boundary of the I-It had been shattered and the disintegration occurred because the I-It never really contained our existence. Even while engaged in an objective exploration of the universe we continually lived in relation to the Thou that would set our mastery of reality at naught. Now the other came first, an event that could not have happened if it had not already been the truth within which we lived from the start. For persons the universe could never be a limitless space and endless duration. It has always been the meeting ground of the other.

Even astrophysics does not live within the astrophysical universe. Proof of this is that despite the infinitesimally low prospects of encountering other intelligent life forms the aspiration endures. It may indeed be held all the more firmly the more the calculation of the chances diminishes.

Enormous encouragement would be drawn from irrefutable discovery of life elsewhere in the universe. The science is, in other words, not driven by an utterly disinterested interest in knowledge of reality as such, but by a passionate quest of persons for our own kind. A structure of intensifying interest shapes the investigation as it ascends from the more elementary to the intermediate and finally to the possibility of advanced forms of life. There is nothing impartial about it. Our approach to reality betrays the highly partial conviction that persons are its culmination. We are carried forward by the assumption that persons must be present elsewhere in the universe for, otherwise, its vastness would seem considerably diminished in purpose. Of course, we are buoyed by the knowledge that if there are persons they too will be moved by an interest in meeting us. The encounter is not entirely random. Each side is already from the start, even before stepping outside of their planetary homes, in search of the other. Imagination, amply reflected in science fiction, carries us to where science and technology still have to reach. The possibility of the latter is that we have already visited it inwardly. When the voyagers are washed up on a foreign shore the question that structures their whole being is, what are the inhabitants like? The thought that the natives may have absolutely no interest in making their acquaintance simply does not occur.

The interpersonal horizon within which science is practiced has pervaded its subject matter. What makes scientific inquiry of interest to us is also what makes it of interest to others. From there we extrapolate to others with whom the exploration of reality may put us in contact. We are prepared to enter into relationship with them. At that point they cease to be objects of scientific inquiry since we cannot simultaneously study them and get acquainted as persons. To really know them we must drop the superior vantage point of investigators who stand outside and approach them as equals, in the way that persons know one another from within. Anthropologists who do field research by living with archaic or primitive people know that the most important part of what they learn can never be included in the treatises they produce. They are humanly affected in ways that radically escape the scientific categories of thought. Yet the imperious stance of science remains scarcely challenged by the outcome. We may be personally affected by such encounters but science itself exists in splendid isolation. The disconnect between science and the persons who bear it makes it impossible to locate scientific inquiry within its indispensable horizon. Instead, we are recurrently surprised by those episodes in which the personal exceeds the scientific. We literally have no way of making sense of them and, as a consequence, we never quite grasp the nonscientific setting of science itself. The result is the characteristically schizoid state in which the practice of science is conducted, a state that because of the pre-eminent authority of science colors the entire way in which we understand ourselves today. The issue, most bluntly expressed, is that science is capable of understanding everything except how science itself is possible. We think that science must be like one of the natural processes it investigates. Completely overlooked is the impossibility of science being anything other than a mode of personal existence, absolutely incapable of setting aside the openness to others that defines what it means to be a person. Scientists, we know, have friends and families that mark the boundary of meaning for their lives. Could it be that science too is meaningful only when it constitutes a bridge between the persons who sustain it? Can we forget that truth becomes such only when it is seen through the mind of the other? In adopting a perspective that utterly departs from ourselves can we at any point recall what we do in doing science?

Science as Forgetting the Personal

On one level the amnesia of the person within science is a deliberate stance. If we want to behold reality objectively, then we must set aside all that derives from the merely personal point of view of the observer. Especially repugnant is the notion that the observer matters, that he or she counts for something in the whole order of things, a center of meaning or value in the universe. Correlatively, we must eliminate the implication that reality has any investment in us as persons, that the universe addresses or is even oriented toward us. Sentiment, subjective inclinations, must be firmly thrust aside as we struggle to gain an impersonal perspective on the way things are irrespective of how we might wish them to be. Truth requires this radical rejection of self, of all that may stand between our minds and the objectively real.[9] The cold unblinking stare of science permits no vestige of the yearning subject who sustains the contemplation. Transcending the self we have left the self behind. It is not surprising, therefore, that what science has so resolutely pushed away, the self, should find so much difficulty in locating a place for itself within science. Or that science would experience the corresponding difficulty of not knowing whence it itself has derived. Einstein's remark about everything being intelligible in the universe except its intelligibility is echoed here.[10] The problem is not just the inability of science to locate itself within any extra-scientific perspective. There is the even greater difficulty of locating humanity when it has been set aside through the canon of scientific method. How can science understand itself? Quarantining all legitimate questions within the parameters of scientific method, the default position of the discourse that neatly separates facts and values, is hardly a workable option. The questions that are repressed and excluded return to disturb us in ways we can no longer acknowledge. This includes the question of the validity of scientific method itself, which cannot be established through scientific method.

Science without scientists, a paradoxical requirement of science, has resulted in the obstruction of the most indispensable component of science. Relegation of the personal foundation of science to irrelevance has in turn contributed to the dismissal of the personal from reality as a whole. At best, the personal reenters as the epiphenomenal, that which while not reducible to phenomenal causality nevertheless mysteriously persists. This is tantamount to the admission of the unreality of the personal as such. What to the self-perception of consciousness has all the marks of a free self-subsistent activity will, eventually and on closer examination, turn out to be the result of a causally determined neurological network. There is no realm of autonomous personhood because to yield to such a suggestion would be to admit that there could be no science of the comprehensive reality of the person. It would be to allow the partiality of the investigating self to influence the outcome of the investigation. This is the ultimate infraction of the scientific rule. Predilections must be resolutely removed, especially when they favor the kinds of entities that have predilections. Science itself has no preferences, not even those that favor science itself. The perspective of science is thus one that has rigorously separated itself from the reality within which it is. Disseverance is what enables it to take its dispassionate view. The strategy is one that works perfectly well so long as science represses the awareness that it too is part of the reality it studies. Only when this renders it incapable of understanding itself do the difficulties mount. Then we discover that the universe disclosed by science is one that allows the mapping of every aspect except the activity of science itself.

Everything can be comprehended except comprehension. The observer alone occupies the blind spot that cannot be included in the field of vision. It is a process that can, given the thoroughly materialistic and reductionistic emphasis that dominates our self-consciousness, extend rather far.

Mind and purpose have no role when everything can be explained by means of efficient causality. Admission that we too are the result of an unintended sequence of events seems a small price to pay for the mastery thereby gained. We behold the world as it is, not as we would wish it to be. Only then is there any possibility of doing what we can to ameliorate the human condition. Besides, what does it matter if my exalted self-conception has been diminished in the process? That is merely what is required for the apprehension of the way things are. Science has already taught us to set ourselves aside in the investigation. Surely it is no great loss if the self disappears entirely within this development. We are the sum total of the constituents that have come together in our formation, just as we are the result of a chain of events bound together by nothing more than the randomness of their convergence. An element more or less, a slight deviation in the timing or coincidence, and everything would have turned out very differently. We might not have been, or we might be no more. Nothing great or glorious adheres to such insubstantial entities, and we certainly cannot alter the situation by wishing it were otherwise. By thrusting partiality aside we have come to see more clearly the reality of which we are made. We have even been able to contemplate the nullity of our existence so long as it discloses the truth about us. So long as we have avoided interposing anything of our selves into the depiction we are satisfied with a knowledge that leaves us without consolation. The austerity of science, Nietzsche remarked, is as stern as any ascetic ideal.[11] And like any ascetic practice the goal is to winnow the practitioner to the point that virtually annihilates the self. But, unlike earlier ascetic disciplines, science holds out no spiritual enlargement once the purgative way has been completed. In this regard scientific asceticism surpasses all others in rigor. It periodically evokes the cri de coeur as to how we can live within the universe it has revealed. Can human beings live without consolation?

The question fairly aches through the consciousness of modern man who is less and less able to find a place for himself within the perspective of science. Not only is the universe overwhelmingly indifferent to his existence, but also he is no longer sure why even he should value it so highly.

Having learned to put aside all purely personal elements, nothing is left but homogeneous matter capable of being organized into ever-higher-functioning entities. Certainly there is no reason to hold on to the notion that the observer has escaped this continuum, that he or she is the one exception, a unique irreplaceable center of meaning and value in the whole. We are on the verge of accepting the disappearance of the person. Perhaps no more poignant expression can be found than in the debates surrounding artificial intelligence.[12] Machines, we are ready to concede, demonstrate the same qualities of intelligence as we perceive within ourselves. It is only a matter of time before they are our equals and, perhaps, even surpass us. With the relentless indefatigability of the mechanical they may be capable of learning without the exhaustion, distraction, and deterioration so characteristic of the humans we know. Machines that learn seem to hold out an unlimited possibility to which we can scarcely aspire. What can humans add beyond some vague notions of creativity and unfathomability that are mere holdovers from the time when we had souls? The debate rages with amazing durability precisely because we have not been able to shake the idea that intelligence is indeed a mechanical process.[13] It is testament to how thoroughly science has forgotten itself that it could confuse thought with its object. All of the interest has focused on what the machines do, the more readily understood element, but what humans do, the more profoundly inaccessible, remains shrouded in mystery. We know what the "artificial" means but not what "intelligence" does. Can machines think if it is merely an imitation of what human thinking is? Could we say that the thinking of the machine means anything if there is not a human being there who understands it? Even if the machine achieves "consciousness" is this anything more than an anthropomorphized imitation of human consciousness?

It is at this point that we begin to see the cost of the regime of self-forgetfulness that science imposes on us. Initially it left us lonely and isolated in an empty universe, vulnerable to the appeal of a cosmic search for other intelligent life forms. But now that science begins to address the boundaries of the human, the disorientation effected by the loss of the uniquely human vantage point becomes more evident. Not only does it lead to the dehumanization by which human beings are to be engineered through biotechnology, but even the meaning of such manipulations ceases to be clearly understood. If human beings are to be regarded more on the model of machines, then what is the nature of the operations we elicit from machines? The erasure of the boundary between inventor and invention is not just a question mark for the reality of the inventor. It also eliminates the possibility of understanding the invention. Artificial intelligence epitomizes the problem, although the dilemma extends to the whole range of biotechnologies. Is there any such thing as intelligence if it can be engineered? Why not simply call it what it is, accelerated computational capacity? The rapid switching on and off of the binary code of modern computers, even when it becomes self-directed, is still no more than a machine that takes a hand in its own construction. Creation of machines that "live" presents a fascinating engineering challenge, replete with echoes of the old dream of overstepping the human condition in creating a homunculus. But it is an aspiration that depends on maintaining the boundary between creator and creation. If we have replicated ourselves in a machine, then the nature of the achievement is itself mechanical reproduction. What makes artificial intelligence exciting is that it is artificial. We have developed machines of such prodigious capacity that they are very like us without actually being the same as us. The marvel of the engineering is how much the machine can approach us; it is not how much we can approach the machine. Artificial intelligence would disappear if we lost the meaning of intelligence. It is the artificial character of the intelligence that is so impressive, but that depends on our retaining the irreducible understanding of intelligence as such. When robots "know" as we do, then there will cease to be anything striking about them. They are amazing inventions only so long as there are persons whose capacity to be amazed attests to the surpassing criterion by which our creations are measured.

Reality Requires Persons

It is persons alone who can stand within and provide access to the whole, albeit without naming it since they are themselves contained by it. Their standing within the whole is radically different from the way all other things are.[14] Persons alone know that they stand within the whole. That does not give them a satisfactory knowledge of being but it does give them a glimpse of what is hidden to all non-knowing participants. Their knowledge consists of knowing more than they can say. The widely lamented decline of metaphysics that marks our contemporary cultural condition is merely one more testament to the failure of saying. Wittgenstein's injunction to remain silent about such matters is itself a refusal to remain silent. Even in the mode of denying the validity of a metaphysical horizon, human beings bear witness to the metaphysical horizon within which they live. Metaphysics still remains a question to them, one that they continue to take seriously enough to renounce. They thereby preserve it even more purely, for they show that metaphysics is essentially the question of metaphysics, of the horizon of the whole within which we are while the whole itself is not in the same way as all that it makes possible. It is at this point that the supreme meaning of the person is revealed. Not only does each one of us bear the question of the whole but we also attest to our affinity with it. We can catch the sense of the non-present character of the whole only because we are ourselves constituted by the same mode of non-presence. Human beings stand in a transparent relationship to the whole because they exist in the mode of the whole, of presence through absence.

But that means that they are the only way by which the absent whole is present within existence. They not only bear witness to transcendent truth but also actualize it to the extent that it can be actualized. Persons are indeed necessary for knowledge of things to emerge but they are more than machines for knowing. They also know what knowledge is, the capacity to absent oneself completely in occupying the perspective of truth. Only that which is not can behold that which is. But that is an event that is not just of significance to the knower. It also says something about the known, that it is knowable, that it can be beheld from the transcendence of truth. The knowability of reality is not just the conviction that animates the knower, for it is also silently affirmed by the known. Of everything that exists there is a truth that can be grasped about it although it itself does not grasp it. The tension that is transparently present in the knower is non-transparently present in the known. Knowledge affirms what the known cannot affirm of itself, namely its standing in relation to the truth. To know something is to say what the thing would say about itself if only it had the opportunity to do so. The traditional notion of the connaturality between knowing and the known, even the hoary correspondence theory, all reflect this insight although they still retain an excessive emphasis on what happens in the knower. A more accurate account would place just as much weight on what happens in the known. The known is what yields up its secret, that which is unknown to it but nevertheless true, while the knower merely puts himself or herself in the position of sympathetically absorbing what it has to "say." The union thereby effected between the two does not entirely occur within the knower, although that is commonly how it is described. If that were all, then knowledge would be indistinguishable from mere subjective opinion. What makes it knowledge is that they are united by truth. It is because persons stand in relation to truth that they can become the point at which the truth of everything can be illuminated.[15]

The universe needs persons to interpret itself back to itself, not just for the sake of the interpreters. Newton talked about science as reading the mind of God in things and, while that remark seems to presuppose too much, it nevertheless points us toward the larger significance of the quest for knowledge.[16] Even if we are not sure of God we do read the mind of nature in things. We do not live in as thoroughly a disenchanted universe as we have been led to believe. It may be that the order of things is largely indifferent to our fate and refuses all purely personal discourse with us. We cannot read our future in the entrails of birds, but reality does invite us into its secrets. We are not wholly shut off from nature.[17] Science proclaims the connection in all its splendor. Nature welcomes us into its inner processes, inviting us to probe ever deeper into its mysteries and, as a consequence, to discover that we are united by a bond far deeper than the utilitarian interest with which we first approached it. Now it is possible for us to understand nature as it is in itself, quite apart from calculations of our relationship to it. Science literally tries to get inside of nature and discovers in the process, not only that it can, but also that nature has an "inside." We may no longer personify natural phenomena, and therefore have diminished some of the magic of that fairytale world, but we have become privy to complexities that nature works within its own silent depths. Hearing nature may no longer be plausible, but only because we are all the more focused on overhearing it. In performing this task persons are uniquely equipped for they alone can grasp the purpose that everywhere else must be mutely obeyed.

Kant was perhaps the first to see this crucial connection as he grappled with the strictly non-teleological presuppositions of modern science. He understood that science looks not for purpose but only for patterns within the phenomena it investigates. It refrains from an anthropocentric injection of final causes and abhors any theological attributions. But he also understood that teleology could not be so completely eliminated. Even when we renounce a teleological account of nature we still retain it as indispensable to our understanding of it. Nature may not be obeying a guiding purpose but we cannot understand it unless we view it as if it were. Whether teleology is a law of nature we cannot be sure, but we are certain that it is a law of thought, or what Kant called a regulative idea of our thinking.[18] We have no choice but to think in terms of teleological patterns, otherwise reality sinks into unintelligibility. To the extent that we continue to understand it we assimilate it to some loose framework of purpose. The issue became particularly acute when science turned its attention to living things. Then it was evident that while all of the parts of an organism could be understood in mechanical terms the entire organization could only be comprehended as one that was more than mechanical. They are more than the sum of their parts, for they live in relation to what they are not yet, a goal or purpose that lies beyond them. Even survival is more than the moment, for it is what drives the moment forward. Living things somehow contain their existence in the form of purpose and can only be understood in such terms. They cannot be viewed from the outside; they require the affinity with inwardness that only living beings possess. It is because we ourselves are living, Kant maintained, that we can understand living things. The irreducibility of biology to its elemental components means that it can only be understood in its own terms. It is because understanding is itself constituted by the transparence of purpose that it can comprehend the unfolding of purpose within its non-transparent forms.

In making this case, however, Kant was congenitally hesitant to embrace its implications. This was what defined his strange role as the instigator of German Idealism who yet refused to follow its logic. He finally could not shake the sense that ideas, including regulative ideas like teleology, were anything more than constructions we impose on reality. Nothing in the order of reality confirmed them, as science resolutely attests. All we can say are what the processes of nature are, not why they are the way they are. We can still read in purpose, but that is precisely what we are doing. Nothing in the empirical analysis of reality authorizes such a conclusion. In this sense Kant's reluctance to pursue a way out of the antinomies he so brilliantly formulated reflects the ongoing quandary of thought all the way up to the present. It accounts for the schizophrenic condition in which science itself must be carried on, one that enlarges science while omitting the scientist. This was what the Idealists saw. Kant's antinomies constituted an impasse only so long as one overlooked the impossibility of formulating them without simultaneously transcending them. But that has been a difficult knot to untangle. The inconclusive state of its clarification is perhaps best reflected by the absence of any scholarly consensus on the meaning and significance of the work of Kant's successors. We remain with Kant, rather than follow Hegel or Schelling into their speculative extrapolations. It is with some trepidation therefore that one suggests the possibility of movement out of the stalemate, a movement that only becomes plausible through a shift from the language of subjects and objects to the more unsurpassable horizon of persons.

It is because persons take their stand in relation to truth that they are capable of knowing reality.[19] Already they have transcended the perspective of the subject, for the person is what is capable of setting itself aside in order to enter into the mode of being of the known. Nothing is foreign to the person, everything is knowable. Not everything is of course known but it can be known only by persons. This is not a process of assimilating all things to itself, but rather of assimilating itself to all things. The old conception of man as a microcosm discloses its relevance. Persons can find themselves in all things because there is something of the trajectory of personhood in all things. Even the inanimate is not simply what it is, for, while it does not unfold its existence in the manner of what is living, it does maintain itself within the condition that makes it what it is. When it can no longer remain within its governing idea, then it undergoes change into something else, following the idea of a different realm of being. Atoms and planets may not know what they are doing but their existence obeys the principles that maintain them in their condition or that govern their transition to a different one. Nothing in existence has such a hold on the idea that constitutes it that it must exist of necessity. The contingency that afflicts everything in existence mirrors the mode of existence of persons who are always going beyond what they are. The idea of each thing is what it aims at because it does not fully possess it, at least not to the point of such complete identification that it is assured against the loss of it. Survival, the goal of all living things, is only a particularly intense case of this. And the unfolding of personal existence, the process of self-determination, is the ultimate expression of contingency, the movement from nothing into being that is the very meaning of freedom. Only that which possesses reason, that which exists through the exercise of its rationality, is capable of such freedom. Everything else is on the way toward self-determination by virtue of determining forces that maintain it in existence. Change happens to what is inanimate, it is reflexively undergone by what is animate, but it is only chosen by what is rational. Persons are thus not just the highest point of that which is, but the veritable disclosure of what everything aims at. Self-determination defines every reality, including that which lacks a self, because everything seeks to remain true to its being. The truth of everything is the idea to which it must remain true. Persons who stand in relation to truth stand transparently toward that within which everything else stands non-transparently.

Teleology is thus not just a regulative idea of our minds but also the regulative idea within which every reality exists.[20] To the extent that entities approach the transparence of minds they make the regulative idea their own, or more accurately, exist within the tension of realizing their idea. The point of complete self-realization is never reached for if it was then there would be no further tension within which existence could unfold. To reach the goal is to close the space of existence. It is only so long as striving is possible that anything can be said to exist. The goal therefore bears a strange relationship to anything living and, by analogy, to anything non-living. It is that which constitutes the whole purpose of existence and yet must not be attained without abolishing the purpose of existence. The status of final causes is eerily metaphysical in the way we have previously encountered the term, that is, as defining the horizon of existence that from within cannot be named or identified with any certainty, although it is the most intimate reality of all. Final causes, Kant understood, are preeminently the province of rational beings although for all other realities they are what illumine the rationality they obey. Yet as defining the horizon of existence they remain necessarily elusive and, for that reason, have largely been eliminated from modern science. When analyzing a reality in terms of the parts and forces that constitute it, one confines the investigation to the quantifiable. It is only when we are compelled to deal with the whole that preserves itself, as with organisms, that teleology must be presupposed even if it is not invoked. Scientists are loath to personify the objects of their investigation and ask what entities would say of themselves if they could speak. Kant's hesitation to see teleology as anything more than our way of thinking was well founded. It is only if everything in existence aims at becoming a person, itself a teleological assumption, that teleology provides the basis for understanding them. Can such an assumption be justified?

It is hardly justified if nature is a jumble of forces that have no conscious intentions governing their effects. In the absence of significant evidence to the contrary we must assume this to be the case. Certainly the individual components of nature are clearly of that elemental character, lacking intelligence or will. It is only later that the latter emerge and only then as the result of interactions bereft of any such directional purpose. Whatever may be the forces behind nature, the investigation of nature must confine itself to the forces themselves in all their stark brutality. We must be prepared to accept the unsatisfactory features of accounts that leave us with the emergence of mind as the fruit of a purely accidental train of causes, unrelated to any overall design. Scientific parsimony requires us to remain strictly within the empirical boundaries of data that evince nothing of the inwardness sustaining life, let alone any hint of higher intelligence. To see intelligence or life inchoately present in materials that patently lack them is surely an egregious anthropomorphism.[21] Science is built on the rejection of all such personifications, in order to arrive at an objective estimate of reality. The fact that particles and molecules might play a more significant role within cellular processes, or that the latter might condition the functioning of a whole organism, becoming the vehicle for a conscious and even intelligent life, is hardly relevant to the investigation of such discrete constituents. Elements must be taken on their own terms, not in relation to the part they play in the whole. The moon is merely a satellite of Earth, not a presence that bestows the magic of romance. Of course, everything does play such multiple roles, but we are compelled to overlook all but the most elemental. Reductionism, by which explanation is sought at successively lower levels of reality, is not just a pattern of scientific method; it is virtually a requirement. How else can we be sure that we have obtained an objective account, one from which every shred of self-insertion has been eradicated? The introduction of higher purposes, of any suggestion of a teleological horizon, strikes us as wholly illegitimate. At best the *telos* is hidden from elements that follow their own autonomic processes without reference to any larger wholes. That means that, even if design does govern reality, it is irrelevant to understanding its operation.

We may still continue to think in terms of teleology, as Kant suggested, but we have no way of knowing whether it is anything more than just the way our minds function. How can we know that nature is governed by a *telos*? The only answer is that our minds too are a part of nature. If we can grasp its teleological structure, then the order is not simply extraneous to nature. Indeed, if this is the only way that nature can be grasped, then this seems to confirm that nature is teleological. All of the constituents that work as parts without knowing what they do are not simply haphazard, for they realize themselves by contributing to a task greater than they can comprehend. They play a role that transcends the level of reality within which they operate because they make possible a higher type of existence than their own. Reductionist accounts are so far off the mark that they virtually deny the reality they seek to explain. Everyone knows that physical and chemical components obey their own immanent laws within living things; what needs to be explained is how they can fulfill a function within a whole that is neither physical nor chemical. Self-generated motion and reproduction are not features of purely inanimate matter. Only the category of life encompasses such features, but that is strictly speaking outside of the capacity of the parts. How then is it possible for the less differentiated to take part within the more differentiated order? How is it that what is purely random at the molecular level becomes ordered at the cellular level? It is evident that we cannot explain the activity of the cell in terms of its molecules, for it is intelligible only in terms of its own dynamic patterns. We are compelled to admit, when we can no longer simply ignore the issue, that the physico-chemical components are not simply discrete entities but are already open to the possibility of integration within successively higher levels of organization.[22] We do not live in a dead physical universe, but in one that carries the potency toward life within it. What this means is that even the most elementary particles stand ready to play their role within a vastly more complex whole that can only be comprehended from the apex they make possible. We live in a cosmos, not a chaos.

The truth is that the parts are not what they appear to be, for they are parts of the wholes they constitute. Their real meaning is the role they play, not what they are in themselves. Instead of thinking we can understand the higher in terms of the lower it is evidently the reverse. Merely physical and chemical processes carry within them a finality that is achieved only in sustaining living, sentient, and rational beings. Far from being the most real things there are, the more elementary levels point toward the emergence of the higher as their own truth. It is life and mind that explains their unfolding even while they remain outside of such transparency. Spirit is capable of containing all the lower levels of being, while they are incapable of reaching the self-transparence of spirit. Unfortunately we lack a word for this complete overturning of the reductionist perspective. We cannot call it the spiritualization of reality without suggesting the negation of the material. Not surprisingly, when we find ourselves linguistically shorthanded, the situation arises because we already live so intimately within the perspective of spirit that we can scarcely distance ourselves sufficiently to name it. Yet the conviction that reality is ultimately governed by ideas is at the very core of the project of seeking explanations. We spiritualize or intellectualize reality every time we seek to comprehend it. There is not the slightest doubt that it can be grasped by mind even though it evinces nothing intellectual in itself. One might say that each element of reality reaches its culmination, not just in fulfilling its role within a larger whole beyond it, but also in being known to do so. Things are not only graspable by mind, they aspire toward it. It is thus in being known that the known comes to know itself, in a certain sense. Mind is not just capable of apprehending reality, it is the moment when reality apprehends itself.

What is apprehended is therefore not just subjective, the concern that preoccupied Kant, but is the truth of reality in its self-unfolding. Reality may not know it, for only mind knows, yet it is what reality would know about itself if it could know. That is what knowing is, the capacity to so put aside the perspective of self, everything that smacks of the subjective, that mind puts itself in place of what it knows. Mind becomes the vehicle for the self-knowledge of things. It is in this sense that reality requires mind, not in order for things to be, but in order for them to go beyond being to being known. It is mind that illumines reality, not reality that irradiates mind. This is because knowledge is the culmination of the process that is under way in all the levels of being from the most elementary to the most differentiated. To the extent that each is governed by the idea that determines it, then it heads toward the kind of self-transparence that is minimally present in the sentience of animals, but only maximally present in the conscious self-realization of rational beings. If we were to reverse the direction, and attempt to understand reality in terms of its most elemental units, then we would overlook the very process of understanding itself. To think of everything, including mind, as merely particles in motion is to ignore the self-unfolding of ideas that thinking is. This is not to deny the material constituents of reality, or to ignore their conditioning role, but it is to insist that they cannot be taken as defining the criterion of what is real. Even the characterization of what is real, including the assignment of reality to the most elemental building blocks of being, is a judgment that can only be made by a mind that is not so confined to materiality. The very actualization of knowledge means that all things must be seen in relation to it, rather than the other way around.

Kant's concern that mind might be supplying more than was present in reality was not justified. Mind is itself a part of reality. What it supplies in the process of knowing is merely what reality itself would supply if only it had the transparence of mind. It is only because we are inclined to think of reality as true and mind as doubtful that we are inclined, with Kant, to concede the priority of reality. The attitude is marked by a certain strangeness, for why should we be inclined to think of mind, that which we inhabit most intimately, as less real than the surrounding reality with which we are in touch far less continuously? It is notable that Kant was less concerned about the mere subjectivity of mind in the realm of moral reason. There the imperative of mind remaining true to itself, not only in independence from the rest of reality but even in defiance of its pressures, seemed to be precisely the source of its authority. It was only in the intellectual realm that mind remained uncertain of itself. There it could not be sure if its grasp of meaning in objects was only what it had brought or had actually found. Where Kant did advance the argument, however, was in insisting that it could not be otherwise. Mind could operate in no other way than in thinking of reality as purposive in the same way as it itself is. From there it is only a small step, although a step we have yet to complete philosophically, to the recognition that reason's grasp of the rationality of things is validated by its own culminating position within the order of things. To see this all that is needed is the realization that this is precisely what knowledge itself is. Reason sees itself in things because it is that which is capable of knowing every thing as it would know itself if it could. It is because reason is open to all things that it is capable of knowing them and, conversely, it is because all things are open to reason that they are capable of being known. It is through reason that everything becomes intelligible, while nothing else renders reason any more intelligible.[23] In itself reason remains a mystery.

This is also why the so-called argument from design cannot prove the existence of God. Design is the circle within which reason operates, as

Kant understood well. We cannot assume the intelligibility of nature and then use this to infer the presence of an intelligent creator. Intelligent design is not just a circular argument but also the very condition for the possibility of argument. Kant famously turned God into a postulate of practical reason, but he also conceded the same in regard to speculative reason. We cannot think of nature except in a teleological framework that ultimately points toward a creator beyond nature. Yet, Kant also insisted, this is not to establish that there is such a divine source.[24] We cannot use reason to ground that which reason presupposes. It is rather that we move within what is presupposed and thereby apprehend its reality even more deeply. Presupposition is what we do in advance of rational inquiry; when we engage reason we affirm that reality is structured by it. The situation is more emphatic in the case of moral action in which we not only postulate a rational order of things, but also effectively bring it about. Reason itself is a mode of the same moral faith that guides all of our practices. In the moral life we do not ask ourselves if we will find confirmation of what we know to be true, that goodness outweighs all rewards it might garner, or that virtue is its own end. We need nothing more, for what could count as more worthy of admiration than the will that is anchored in the good apart from all costs and benefits that may accrue to it? Our whole notion of what the good *is* is thus transcendentally constituted. There is no disclosure of the good that surpasses the movement by which the person is wholly turned toward it. There is no higher epiphany of the good in existence. It is the same with the rational order of the whole, the cosmos, within which we find ourselves. Of course, the regularity that nature discloses confirms this conviction but it is only conclusive because reason itself is the preeminent instance of its teleological unfolding. We are not the designers of the natural world, except within the very narrow limits in which we effect such a scheme on a small scale, but we are the point at which its design can become transparent because we are the ones who live transparently within it. Design that is precariously confirmed in the natural world has its deepest confirmation within the moral responsibility of persons. Teleology is quintessentially the mark of rational beings.

The question then is what are we to make of the teleological configurations tentatively disclosed within the natural world? Is there indeed an intentional design at work behind it all? On the basis of the mere presence of intentionality within us it would be hard to conclude anything further. We might well be the accidental result of a vast accumulation of blind events. This is the classic Darwinian suggestion of natural selection through random variations. Even this, however, sneaks in an unnoticed teleological component. It assumes that nature "aims" at the survival of the fittest, that it has an in-built drive toward the emergence of ever more capable forms of life. But it is surely the baldest self-flattery of the higher forms themselves to assume that everything serves their emergence. A far more plausible assumption is that the whole is as doomed as the parts, that the world process is headed for exhaustion and extinction, species as well as their individual members. Why should we presume that life, especially the higher forms, will escape the most fundamental law of the cosmos that what comes into existence must go out of it? And if that is the case what are we to make of the alleged order or design of nature? That the cosmos ultimately aims at becoming a chaos? That evolution is merely a prelude to devolution? The questions could only be asked by a mind that, by raising them, attests to its own invulnerability to them. It is because mind is not subject to the law of the cosmos, because it already occupies the stance of truth eternal, that it can accept annihilation with equanimity. Whatever there is of purpose, or *telos*, in this world is reached only in the spirit that transcends it. This is the source of that relentless quest for meaning within a universe largely indifferent to such aspirations. Yet this is not to suggest that reason merely reads itself in where evidence refutes it. What defines reason is precisely the capacity to remove its self-interest from the scene and, in doing so, to confirm even more deeply the higher purpose that is carried forward only by that which can comprehend the order of reality. Purpose is the prerogative of mind and exists elsewhere only by attribution. It is mind alone that can stand outside of purpose and thereby provide the possibility of contemplating it.

The connection between mind and the rest of reality is far more intimate than the subject-object dichotomy would suggest. Objects are capable of participating in a teleological order only because there are subjects who can interpret them as doing so. To insist that this is mere projection is to assume that mind is not itself included within the whole of reality. It is to assign the accent of reality to what lacks mind, flying in the face of the capacity for knowledge that evinces its unity with matter. What makes it possible for us to know reality is that both the mental and the material are governed by ideas; the one is determined consciously while the other is determined unconsciously. Kant was correct in insisting that we cannot think apart from ideas, including such overarching ones as purpose, but he was mistaken in concluding that the ideas are only ours, a mere subjective possession. Knowledge is itself a transcending of what is merely held within our minds to affirm a genuine encounter with what is apart from us. Such a meeting can occur only because ideas in some sense "govern" the reality known. A proto-personal striving for the self-determination of reason must be assumed everywhere. Naturally this is not something that can be demonstrated, at least not without begging the question of that in terms of which it is demonstrated. To suggest that the whole of reality evinces a movement toward personal self-transparence is not to reach an understanding of spirit or of matter, one that would select either as ultimately real. They are rather the irreducible poles of the reality within which we find ourselves and by virtue of which we can think. We can no more think outside of them than we can comprehend what it is that makes knowledge possible. The mistake Kant made was in assuming the conditions of the possibility of knowledge all lay on the subjective side, as transcendental ideas through which we order sense intuitions. In fact, the knowability of reality is dependent on the predisposition to be known in such ideational fashion, so that the determining ideas are as much a mode of being as of being known. Knowledge is not just a subjective event. It is the point at which subjectivity is surpassed. Without comprehending it, knowledge attests to the metaphysical horizon within which it is.

It is because knowledge is an event within being, indeed, the privileged event in which being becomes transparent, not comprehensively but in principle, that it can shed light on the process of the whole. The subjective dimension, that I as a particular individual am the possessor of this knowledge, is the least decisive aspect. We might say that knowledge is precisely the assertion of the opposite. This knowledge that I possess has nothing to do with me personally. It is true, public, an event open to all that as such is no longer tied to the one who happens here and now to actualize it. The decisive aspect is its universality, as that point at which knowledge occurs within being as a self-knowledge or self-transparence of being. When we ask therefore about the significance of the moment when mind first emerges within the unfolding of reality we cannot treat it merely as an event indifferently related to all others. It is of more than incidental significance when from the process there emerges a mind capable of grasping the process as a whole. This is because knowledge is not simply a private event within minds but the point at which the self-transparence of reality has occurred. We are perhaps more inclined to jump toward the further implication that reason, once it is emergent, will take a hand in more deliberately shaping the unfolding of reality. But this is the old habit of instrumentalizing reason while overlooking what constitutes it. The mystery of the emergence of reason must also be contemplated for reason, once it has emerged, cannot be subordinated to any instrumentality beyond itself. Strictly speaking as the Greeks, who first made reason self-conscious, discovered, reason is utterly non-instrumental. It can of course be put to work like any tool, but then it degrades itself in the service of goals far beneath its noble liberty. By refusing such servitude reason performs the greatest service of all. It demonstrates that reality is not closed in upon itself, employing everything in order to keep its perpetual machine in motion, but that it explodes into the realm of the supererogatory, freely giving itself without considering the cost or aiming at a return. Once reason has emerged, the goal of mere survival, the only goal accessible at a purely natural level, has been definitively transcended. The logic of an evolutionary process aimed at mere survival has been irrevocably shattered.[25]

The Personal as the Epiphany of the Supererogatory within Reality

What is remarkable is the extent to which the instrumental perspective still exercises a hold on us despite its contrary exemplification by science itself. Within the logic of survival as the highest goal, the emergence of mind is often regarded as a significant although not revolutionary event.[26] Reason merely allows a more efficient application of means to guarantee the survival and flourishing of the species. The notion that the arrival of mind exponentially surpasses biology does not seem to arise. Perhaps only humor can capture the situation in which scientists dutifully calculate the positive and negative effects on survival, while themselves operating within a realm of rationality impervious to all cost-benefit considerations. Their own thinking has left the motivation of survival so far behind that they are scarcely disturbed by the prospect of their own epiphenomenality.[27] So profound is their commitment to the free unfolding of reason that they are even willing to overlook its significance in their dedication to understanding the process of emergence. Truth, they proclaim with every fiber of their being, is their goal, not mere survival. Yet they continue to think only in terms of the logic of survival as the only viable explanatory basis. It is the self-forgetfulness of persons we have already noted, although now brought to a sublimely glorious extreme. The reason for it, however, is not too hard to discern. It is the dominance of a purely objectivist perspective that lacks any room for the spectator. The solution is, not to find room for intelligent design within science, but to find room for the intelligence of science within it. Once it is recognized that science itself is free from the servitude to any purpose beyond it, then it begins to radiate the light of the supererogatory over the whole of reality. Survival, even of the fittest, is only one of the possible goals presented by nature and not by any means the highest. The apprehension of truth, even when it is not instrumentally useful, stands far higher. Having thus loosened the straitjacket of utility within its own thinking, science can then become the means of recognizing the overflow of purpose that seems to occur on every level of reality. Science is, in other words, not alone in transcending utilitarian calculations. In itself it attests to the degree to which rationality always exceeds any confinement within boundaries defined in advance and thereby alerts us to the extent to which the supererogatory pervades the reality it investigates. It is not just that science cannot comprehend itself. There is also a profound respect in which all that it seeks to grasp eludes it.

More is shared between the wonder from which science itself originates and the expansiveness that carries everything in nature beyond itself than we might have suspected. Neither can be fully captured by the logic of instrumentality that is undoubtedly present, for they exhibit a persistent tendency to exceed what a strictly utilitarian calculus would justify. At the deepest level, both thought and nature demonstrate a vitality that exceeds every purpose attributed. We know, for example, that the smile of a baby serves a well-calibrated design of ensuring a regular supply of care and nourishment, just as the blazing color of the flower serves the efficient ecology of pollination. But why does the child smile and the flower bloom even more than is required? No doubt there is a design at work in the sheer profligacy of nature that countenances numerous failures in order to ensure the transmission of life. But that larger perspective only begs the question always in waiting for us behind any scheme of rational purpose. What does the process as a whole serve? Why indeed should life be continuously and uninterruptedly transmitted? What is its consummate value that over-rides and justifies all else? The answer is, of course, nothing. That is, nothing beyond itself. Life is its own reward, just as thinking is. To suggest that they ought to subtend some end beyond themselves would be to profoundly misunderstand what they are. The whole regime of purpose is only possible because there are spheres relieved of all purpose extrinsic to themselves. They alone make possible the schema of purpose, an insight that was intensely apprehended by the Greeks and one that even we moderns have not been able to wholly obliterate. The point of life is not mere life but the good life, for life can only serve that which it carries within as the possibility of exceeding itself. The supererogatory is the imperative that drives beyond all imperatives.

There are hints of this overflowing of nature continually interrupting the rational schemas we impose on it. All of the excitement of science, the breakthroughs that shatter the most firmly held paradigms, are generated by the discovery that the reality we investigate is even more marvelous than we had suspected. This is the fascination so well known to all true explorers. Why else would we build in Switzerland, at enormous expense and effort, the world's largest particle accelerator?[28] We are led by the intuition that it might yield an even deeper initiation into the mystery of matter, far beyond the stale and stable theories so far reached. Even what seems so elemental, the basic components of all materiality, still contain unsuspected secrets; there are yet further wonders we might behold if we strain our minds to glimpse them. The thrill of discovery is not just a subjective viewpoint. It is almost as if nature itself conspires to lead us on with the prospect of ever more enthralling possibilities hidden within it. Our minds are equipped to pursue the deeper structures beyond the surface visibilities, but it is not simply a capacity from our side of the relationship. There is an undeniable allure from within the world we investigate, almost as if mind and nature were made for one another. A mutual reflection makes it possible for mind to find its own rationality present within nature, but there is also the movement in the opposite direction. Nature not only embodies the order of mind, but also moves toward the same transparency by which it becomes ever more than it is. The delight of the scientist who discovers unknown dimensions seems inchoately echoed by nature itself. The joy of knowing is somehow faintly shared by the joy of what is known.

"Nature loves to hide" is one of the memorable fragments from Heraclitus. It perfectly captures the outburst of surprise by which the investigator is recurrently seized. The hiddenness of nature is one that wishes to be
found, although always in such a way that it overflows the boundaries that
thought had set for it. Like the game of hide-and-seek everything builds toward the moment when surprise overwhelms the participants. No matter
how rationally they may have anticipated the event there remains something irrepressible about it. Sheer gratuitousness bursts upon them. To ask
what purpose it serves would be to misunderstand the transcendence of
purpose entailed, for surprise exceeds all that could be anticipated within
the economy of purpose. The gift of disclosure ruptures the boundaries of
closure. New boundaries will then be assigned but we know that they too
will be overwhelmed in the surprise that is the unanticipated in all discovery. Routine, the predictable rationality within which we live most of the
time, does not endure forever. Periodically it is shattered by what cannot be
predicted or anticipated because it lies beyond the purview of the merely
useful. Uselessness finally has the last word, as what cannot be superseded
because it is the very possibility of all supersession. Strictly speaking, however, that possibility remains confined to the world of persons. They alone
can be surprised. But nature too seems to yearn to break free of the routine
in which it finds itself. It seems to virtually require the presence of persons
in whom that rupture of disclosure, of which nature alone is incapable, can
take place. Only persons can be surprised, for they alone can be captured
by a routine in such a way that they fail to be captured by it. Their mode of
being present as not being present is an invitation to the gift of disclosure
that nature recurrently furnishes.

This means, of course, that persons are the point at which the sheer
immoderate exuberance of nature is displayed. It is through persons that
nature discloses more than it can disclose. They are the point at which it is
definitively carried beyond itself. Without persons the surprises hidden
within nature would remain locked within expectancy ever ready to overflow expectations. Left to itself, however, nature provides only the barest
hints of the excessiveness within it. We sense it in the profligacy with which
nature has dispersed itself throughout an ever expanding cosmos, but we
intuit it most directly in the capacity of all living things to leap over the
merely expected. The restless inquisitiveness of all animals is the refutation
of their mere existence. They are never simply what they are. This is why

we can relate to them as if they were persons for they have some element of the capacity to astonish. It is not just the obstinacy of living creatures that they refuse to remain within the laws of behavior assigned to them.[29] There is an inescapable excess of creativity that will probe the limits of the possible. It is in this way that they become individuals, each with their own "personality." By deviating from the norm they establish an identity that says that the unique I is always more than the universal constituents comprising it. They do not of course change their natures in the process, but they proclaim that they are always more than the nature imprinted on them. This is why I know my dog better than the vet who sees him once a year for, although the vet has a far deeper grasp of the biology, the dog is always more than can be captured within the science. He loves to play. From it he undoubtedly derives many biological benefits but they would hardly be available unless he were prepared to be driven by more than biology. Is there not a metaphor for the whole of nature here, nature that loves to hide? This is not to personify nature as another presence within or behind it. The point is not to read personality into it but to appreciate the extent to which nature can only be read within the horizon of personality. To accept this, however, we must be prepared to acknowledge the provisionality of all scientific explanation. Every account of the state of affairs merely awaits the astonishment that overturns it.

The prospect may seem, at first glance, to turn science into an exercise in futility. But closer inspection suggests that it more deeply confirms the trajectory of science itself, which operates within the paradox of avoiding success. It has long been noted that the one thing that retards the momentum of science is the advent of a grand theoretical settlement of fundamental questions. Even worse would be the acceleration of progress to the point that no further questions remained to be investigated. Nietzsche loved to invoke Lessing's observation that scientists are not really interested in truth, they only care about the pursuit of truth.[30] For all who share this love of science, as opposed to its results, the discovery that science is never able to attain its goal is surely welcome. Accepting the provisionality of all that science has uncovered is no mere concession to the limits of our investigative power. It is rather a blessed release from the burden of completion and an opening into the limitless possibility of wonder from which, in Aristotle's observation, all knowledge flows. We ought to be heartened by the realization that nothing that science knows is really known in any definitive sense. Every explanation adduced is only one step away from the astonishing discovery that upends it and, even when the explanation stands, we are often painfully aware that investigators too are subject to the same necessities. The reason for this is that the scientist is ultimately not outside of the reality he or she investigates. He or she understands it from within, knowing matter as one composed of it and of life as one who lives. We are not outside of the categories of our thought but find ourselves within the very things we investigate. The "explanations" at which we arrive therefore are not really explanations in any ultimate sense. They are merely glimpses of the mystery by which we are held. Science, despite the hubristic cloak in which it is often wrapped, has no more been able to pierce the mystery than philosophy. Every genuine scientist knows that the more he or she penetrates into the subject matter the more the mystery deepens, rather than dissolves. But that in itself is sufficient reassurance. Nature that loves to hide does not close itself off from us but rather draws us ever deeper into the romance of understanding that is the surety of its lasting. In the end it is only because we too are part of nature that we are capable of the adventure of deepening understanding that yet never achieves its goal. Science is an inescapably personal activity, possible at once because persons are within nature and at the same time beyond it.

Persons alone can contain what cannot be contained, the movement of nature by which it discloses itself as always more than it is. The supererogatory, the miracle of the personal, pervades reality. It was something of this insight that prompted Nietzsche to suggest that science converges with art.[31] We will have more to say about art below, but for now it is sufficient to note the parallel with science. They each live within the paradox that the means employed to convey what is behind them are in principle insufficient. The difference is that art makes the paradox thematic while science merely exemplifies it in its unending practice. What makes that unattainable odyssey possible eludes the attention of science, even though it is the most intimately involved aspect of it. Forgetting to ask where science itself is contained, we blithely assume that it is present at hand within the world that science examines. The reality is that science is contained only in persons who cannot be contained in anything. It is itself an activity that always exceeds what it is about and is therefore quintessentially attuned to the endless self-disclosure of nature. The fact that the laws of science never quite capture what they aim at capturing is not a defeat but its salvation, for it ensures that science can continue its endless unfolding. All that is needed to realize this self-understanding is the transparence achieved by art. That is, the recognition that art proceeds not from the artist but from the idea that lays hold of her or him. Science too is a process in which it is not so much the case that the investigator seizes reality but rather is seized by it. Science arises only when being has disclosed itself to the scientist who, in turn, cannot fully comprehend the disclosure in which her or his own being too is disclosed. What scientists can grasp, however, is that they are within that movement of disclosure by which they become ever more than they are. It is within this movement of the supererogatory that science lives as the apprehension of the same movement within reality.

CHAPTER FOUR

God as the Seal of the Personal

Persons, as we have seen, are preternaturally inclined to overlook what is closest to them. We can roam through the universe and penetrate the infinitesimal but we cannot grasp what is more intimate to us than ourselves. It is the elusiveness of the mystery by which we are held that renders the sense of being lost in the cosmos so unshakeable. We cannot quite drop the impression that what is most important has escaped us. This is what Nietzsche and Heidegger talked about as the "uncanny" (*Unheimlichkeit*). Their genius was to have brought to our attention what cannot be brought to attention because we are so thoroughly immersed within it. The metaphor we apply is that of the blind spot. For every observer the only point that continually escapes observation is the position occupied by the observer himself or herself. Yet consciousness is not quite like observation. We have learned to distrust all metaphors as incapable of capturing what is sui generis about consciousness, for it is precisely the capacity of consciousness to intuit the limitations of its own standpoint that is most distinctive. The uncanny is not as uncanny as initially we are prepared to concede. *Unheimlichkeit* is premised on a *Heimlichkeit* that is yet more intimate still. In bringing reality to our attention we are simultaneously aware of our incapacity to bring what makes bringing to attention possible. This intimation of what is most crucial has always been there, but it was Kant's insistence on the incapacity of knowing to grasp the condition of its own possibility that brought about the modern philosophical revolution. From now on philosophy would have to grapple with what it could not quite grapple with directly, while sensing that therein lay the source of its own deepest intuitions.

Thought thinking itself, the challenge hurled forward into the centuries by the Greeks, has hardly been taken up, let alone addressed, by the vaunted superiority of science. We might even be inclined to suggest that we are further away than ever from the understanding of thought, suffering as we do from the "scientific delusion" that everything can be understood by reducing it to something more elementary than it is. I use the term "delusion" advisedly here since science itself patently refutes the reductionist paradigm. Thinking does not incline to collapse into what it knows but to shift beyond itself into what it does not yet know. Far from being captured by the material it investigates, thought is a perpetual reaching beyond itself to discover the horizon within which it might grasp what it seeks to know. The affinity of thought is thus less with the content of its reflection than with what it senses is transcendent yet immanent as the very possibility of its becoming what it seeks. While holding the content of its investigation at a distance, thought is itself held by that toward which its thinking aspires. Thinking seeks the truth but simultaneously lives within it. There is no way to understand thought but in relation to what makes it possible. Thinking cannot step outside of that by which thinking is. Truth is not just a label we can affix to the content of our thoughts. It is rather what surpasses thought because there is no thinking outside of it. What cannot thus be comprehended must nevertheless be named. Its presence is simply too overwhelming to be ignored. Before deluded moderns stumbled into calling it the uncanny, human beings already knew it as God. The problem is not that we cannot prove the existence of God but that proof means something quite different when it entails that which undergirds all possibility of proof.

All the great philosophers have understood this predicament, yet they have not succeeded in articulating it so clearly that non-philosophers could be sufficiently dissuaded from overlooking it. This is why the "God question" recurs with such notable regularity. It is the preserve of philosophic amateurs precisely because the unheeded presumption behind it has never been fully exposed. To do so is the task of the present chapter, which builds on the more deliberately personalist language we have undertaken. The tendency toward pseudo-objective modes of discourse, a temptation consummately inappropriate in reference to God, has already been removed. Persons can only be talked about from within the relationship by which they are known as persons. The faithful in every age have always known that it is this oversight that has been the principal impediment to knowledge of God in either theology or science. He reveals himself only in prayer. Even that profound intimation, however, has not been enough to forestall the inclination to dismiss it once the debates begin. What has been missed, as we will see, is the realization that nothing we do stands outside of the God relationship. There is literally no independent vantage point. God is the seal of all that is personal, containing and dispensing all that is possible for persons. Our point of access to the question of God is the realization that it is not simply one of the possible questions we may raise, but the one from which our whole existence arises. It is the very possibility of questioning as such.

To stand within the question of God is to stand within what is beyond being, the very meaning of what it is to be a person who cannot be contained within what is.[1] That is why we begin with the question of God, not simply as one of the possible questions we may choose to raise, but as the question from which all possibility of questioning arises. To stand within the question of God we must begin to see how it is possible for each of us to be the one who embraces the whole of reality in the openness of questioning. We can be persons, beholding all, only because that which is personal has shared its being with us. But this means, second, that persons can only be called forth by a person. Only a love that is the very source of love, that which gives wholly out of love, can sustain the possibility of persons called to love infinitely. We see, third, that love is the source of others for it loves for the sake of the other. As the love that yields completely to the other, we glimpse the trinity of persons within God. To be a person is, fourth, to participate in the freedom of self-creation as well as in the fall from it that calls forth the redemptive expiation of love. Fifth, this brings us back to the mystery of what it means to be a person, for now we see that personhood is not ours but is most properly the being of God. We have thus been able to glimpse more than is possible for human beings to glimpse. It is because we live within self-transcendence that we can receive the revelation of God who becomes man to give himself up utterly for us. Revelation is transcendence.

The Question of God as the Possibility of Questions

"Set me as a seal upon your heart" (Song of Solomon 8:6) perfectly expresses a relationship that is sealed and yet remains to be sealed at the same time. At the core of the person is the question of who I am, which arises only because I know that I do not belong to myself. Even before I know myself I know the other who is even closer to me. I am known before I know, as St. Paul formulates it (1 Corinthians 13:12). But how do I know that I am known when I do not even know myself? This is the question that points out the obliqueness of the Pauline formulation of the dynamic within which we find ourselves. The notion that I am known before I know somehow does not fit within the subject dominant model of knowing. Yet the formulations have endured, for they evoke enough of the resonances that glimmer at the margins of our consciousness. Our whole existence, we intuit, is contained within the tension that cannot be resolved between what we possess and do not possess. To have reached either pole, complete loss or complete gain, would be to abolish the possibility of existence, for we live within the movement that can be neither evaded nor completed. All that is outside of the movement remains inaccessible to us, although we are continually borne aloft by those presences that can never become present. The elusiveness of the Pauline flash is not, therefore, a merely incidental dimension, one that we might someday expect to overcome, but the very condition of our existence. We live within the questions that cannot be resolved because that is what questioning requires. Neither sealed nor unsealed, we live within the prayer.

The question of the ground of our existence is not just one question among many. It is the question from which our existence arises to the extent that it is shaped by the opening of questions. All men desire to know, Aristotle reminds us, as they begin in wonder. But we do not wonder aimlessly or haphazardly. Wonder is already structured in a specific way for it heads toward that which is the source of all, including wonder itself. Questioning is not the same as idle curiosity. In wanting to know the way things are we are already committed to the quest of their ground. Inexorability is already built into the first faint stirring of interest. Otherwise the search would lack seriousness. It might even lack a beginning since its extent would already have been determined. A questioning that does not reach beyond all limits is hardly worthy of the name, for any arbitrary assignment of limits is surely the most questionable of all. It is this unlimited trajectory of the desire to know that prompted St. Thomas to conceive of it as a natural desire to know God by his essence.[2] To the extent that God is the ground and truth of all things then they can be properly known only as they are known in him, while God can only be known as he is in himself since he alone is the source of his own being. All questioning therefore moves toward God as its end and already knows God as the source from which it arises. To preconceive limits on questions is not only an arbitrary inhibition of the process but a derogation of what it means to pursue questions at all. Science cannot so easily shake its theological adumbrations if they are already embedded in the inquiry from which it itself emerges.

However strong the inclination may be to leave God out of the picture the connection cannot be completely severed. Perhaps this is one of the reasons why scientists and popularizers alike cannot resist peering over the edges of their inquiry. Even their resolve to remain firmly within the confines of the empirical cannot quite suppress awareness of the trajectory from which they have diverged. At the very minimum they know that their self-restriction to the factual separates them from a more comprehensive mode of knowledge. Contraction is premised on a wholeness from which the contraction has been made. That greater amplitude may remain ill defined in relation to the newly demarcated discipline that has emerged, but it does not cease to exert an influence of its own. It might even be that it is precisely its absence that renders its presence more palpable. What could be more fascinating, more unshakeable, than the half-remembered we have forgotten? It is this peculiar twilight of the absolute that hovers in the background of modern science. We are familiar with its deleterious impact in the forms of scientism that pervade both militant and moderate brands of ideology. But the more interesting remnants of the numinous are subtly evident within the extra-scientific horizon within which science actually operates. We have seen in the preceding chapter that science, despite its nearly total inadvertence to it, functions within an interpersonal frame of reference. Now we begin to see a more specific, and crucial, dimension of the horizon in the personal relationship of scientists with God.

Before we reach that full accounting and, indeed, acknowledge God as personal, we must begin with a more inchoate awareness of the involvement of science with "absolute knowledge." The term was minted by German Idealists, especially Hegel, and is their contribution to the Aristotelian-Thomist meditation on wonder. Despite the fact that this later term was hammered out in reference to modern science, it has so far not succeeded in establishing its validity within our science-monopolized world. We have still a considerable distance to go before we can understand Heidegger's reapplication of it in his observation that no science can provide its own principles.

The notion of givenness must be enlarged to include not just the data science investigates, but the theoretical principles science brings to bear upon them. Those principles include the inarticulate, and barely noticed, dispositions within which science itself stands. We have already noted the major negative disposition in the admirable modesty that forswears any claim to absolute knowledge. But there is more than parsimony involved. Positively, science still bears a relationship to that absolute horizon from which it has unhitched, for it stands even more intimately within its luminosity. What, for example, is the status of the resolution to set itself apart from absolute knowledge? Does that not, of necessity, partake of the same absoluteness? A laudable confinement to the empirically verifiable cannot itself be grounded in empirical verification. It already stands outside of it, within logic more primordial. Indeed, there is something absolute in the severance from the absolute, in the same way that probability is derivative from certainty. One has to know what absolute knowledge would be like in order to concede that one is going to fall short of it. We do not arrive at the infinite by negating the finite since we cannot have a conception of the infinite that would be adequate to it. The case is rather the reverse. What makes it possible for us to focus on a world of finite things is that we can apprehend their finitude, a possibility that is available to us only because we do not fully occupy finitude ourselves. The dimension of the limitless continually with us is not a mere poetic fancy. We know it as what underpins the openness of our existence. In the same way we know that nothing remains outside the possibility of our thought, nothing so inaccessible that we cannot project our access toward it. Thinking takes its stand within the absolute whose reach is infinite. This does not mean that we are able to think the absolute, since we are not absolute, merely that our thinking occurs within the absolute.

What makes it possible for us to think is that we are not like all other beings. We are able to stand outside of them. Our location is that of being itself, that which cannot be in the same way as beings. This does not mean merely the dependence of beings upon being, a perspective that tends to overlook the "ontological difference" between them as Heidegger insisted.[3] That which contains all, making all appearance possible, cannot itself be contained or appear in the same way. Overlooking this profound difference has been the bane of metaphysics ever since its Greek inception. Dependence is thus far more primordial than we might be inclined to conceive; it is so encompassing that it is independence that is the problem. The latter arises, however, only when being has been conceived of as God, as we will see below. For now we need only take note of the first small step in that direction in reflecting on our ability to grasp the distinction. Have we stepped outside of the status of mere beings to assume an identity with being? At least in thought we seem to have slipped into the position of being, capable of containing all beings. It was this insight that prompted Parmenides to formulate the most famous sentence in philosophy, that thinking and being are the same.[4] He did not of course mean that our thinking creates being but merely that it occupies the same position as being. In other words, we do not think being but being is the possibility of our thinking. That is the great pivot, outside of science, on which science itself turns. Heidegger made this the focus of his intensive meditation, but that does not mean that he necessarily grasped all the implications of his own realization.[5] In particular he hesitated to take the final step, no doubt because of reluctance to obscure the ontological difference he had labored so much to clarify, toward the recognition of being as personal. Readers of the present work should not be surprised at the suggestion, given that we have so much emphasized the irreducibly personal character of thinking.

Only persons can occupy the vantage point of thinking. When we ask ourselves what it means to be in the mode of always not being what one is, the only model that suggests itself is the person. It is because we are persons that we are able to glimpse being as the very mode of our own thinking about it. Heidegger understood this affinity with being as what is "ownmost" about human being, but he was not prepared to admit the staggering implication of the converse. That is, that personhood is what is ownmost about being. Being is a person.[6] The concern that being is then reduced to a mere being, one among many and not in any sense the grounding horizon of all beings, is misplaced. What is characteristic of a person, we have seen, is that each is not one among many but somehow the whole that can contain all others. A person does not compete for space with all other beings because in the most fundamental sense the person is not in the mode of presence that characterizes beings. It is because the person is not, that he or she is open to all other beings. Yet to say that being is a person implies a particularity with all of the localization and specificity attached to uniqueness. How can a being be being if it is assigned such exclusivity? After all, one person is not interchangeable with another. The hesitations evinced by Heidegger may have had a point. But the point quickly disappears once we reflect on how the particularity of the person cannot contain him or her, for he or she continually overflows the boundaries in the direction of the whole. This is why one person is not replaceable with another, not because they are specific particularities, but because each is the whole.[7] All of existence, the universe of particularities, is contained in each one. That is the affinity with being that makes of each person a center of meaning and value that surpasses all that is. It is in such a realization that we behold most clearly the inextricable relationship between being and the personal. What makes possible a world of persons, a whole of wholes, is that their particularities are personally subsumed in the whole that is God.

God's Love as What Makes Possible a World of Others

To say that God makes possible a world of others is not to claim that we know God personally. That disclosure awaits a very special moment of personal revelation that has not yet taken place. Before revelation there is only the diffuse background of readiness that is no different from our knowledge of any other person. When we reflect on how it is possible to know another person we are inclined to concede that it is only possible because in some sense we have always known him or her. This is not in the sense of concrete detailed knowledge but in the sense of an openness within which we "recognize" the other. It is almost as if we are deeply predisposed to the other in all of his or her particularity. Our inwardness is already a listening for the voice of the other. In the case of other human beings the encounter with the other is episodic, a rupture within the steady state of our own consciousness and its preoccupations. Almost unnoticed within this drama of interruption by which the other is more present to me than I am to my-self, is the background of a presence that never wavers in its accompani-ment of every meeting. In its constancy and intimacy that presence can scarcely be detected but we are left in no doubt concerning its approval. To say that this is the voice of conscience that is the voice of God is to assign a specificity that initially is not there. Such designations are indeed only question begging for they merely postpone what needs to be explained. How is it possible for us to hear the voice of God if we have not already heard him and can therefore know who it is? Access to God, to the tran-scendent, is far from obvious and unmistakable, a condition that makes it possible for most of us, even believers, to go through life as practical athe-ists. In this sense atheism is not an unusual modern phenomenon, but the everyday experience of human beings who live in forgetfulness. What pre-vents it from becoming a permanent condition is that the question that overturns it nevertheless lingers at the boundary of our consciousness.

This is not simply the awareness that we did not make ourselves and must seek a source beyond us, a quest that drives inexorably toward that which itself has no source as its resting point. Missing from the meditative unfolding toward the ground is what makes the meditation possible and, more importantly, what makes it possible for us to recognize its goal when we arrive at it. Dissatisfaction with praying to an unmoved mover is not simply incidental; it speaks to a fundamental lacuna within all speculative formulations. They do not explain how it is possible for us to know God, as opposed to knowing about him. Speculation leaves the observer on the outside, never exposed to the vulnerability intrinsic to knowing the other person. But what then is the point at which we are most personally open to God? The speculative impulse is sound in beginning with the realization that we are not God, but it is mistaken in not carrying that awareness deep enough.[8] We must ask, not simply how it was possible that we came into being, but how it is possible for us to be in the present. The question is asked not just from an individual perspective but also on behalf of a whole world of persons. Each of us knows that we are not the whole and yet we know that each one of us is the whole. It is not in need, and certainly not out of fear, that the question is asked, but primarily out of love that we need to know. How is it possible for each to be loved infinitely when all must be loved infinitely? The complete and irrevocable love demanded by each one is hardly compatible with a plurality of individuals.[9] At the most elemental level God is intuited, not as a first cause or a watchmaker, but as the indispensable guarantee of the possibility of a universe of persons. This is why it is in loving an other that we gain the deepest assurance of God. Atheism is impossible within love. Of course, it is eminently possible for atheists to love, it is just that they must suspend their atheism in a practical sense while they are loving. One can affirm this other as the most lovable person in the universe only if one can overcome the contradiction embodied by the equal claim of all others to one's love. To love another exclusively one must be prepared to exclude all others. Each must be loved as if he or she were the only person in the world, a requirement of love that requires God.

It is only God who can love in such a way that each is valued exclusively without the exclusion of all others. Without God love would not be possible, not in the sense that we might say that it is utterly impossible, for there might be a heroic defiance in the name of love, but in the sense that love could never overcome its own inner contradiction. It would have to be a form of love that had already accepted the necessity of becoming untrue to itself. Love compelled to betray itself can hardly be sustained, for it exists through affirming what it is. We may still be able to perform many good deeds for one another for externally nothing has changed, but love is rendered impossible when it is removed from the faith that underpins it. How can we believe in love if it has become impossible? Can love offer anything when it can no longer offer itself? This is why the question of faith is so crucial. It is not that faith tells us whom to love or why we should love, but that faith makes it possible to love. Conversely, we may say that love is the affirmation of faith, made all the more remarkable in the pre-reflective way it pours forth. We do not make a decision for faith as if we were just as free to choose it or to walk away; rather, we find ourselves buoyed by a faith that arises from we know not where. Faith of this type is not subject to examination because we are incapable of stepping outside of it. It can only be noticed in passing as the horizon that sustains the most fundamental dimensions of our existence. Love is in this sense not simply an act of faith in its possibility on a small scale, within the immediate relationships of our own lives. It is at the same time a metaphysical declaration about love as such. Being, we affirm, is radiant with love.

Or, rather, it would be more correct to say that being affirms our love. Nothing originates with us, we merely constitute a moment of transparence within the whole. Just as we are capable of thinking only because we stand within being so we are capable of loving only because we stand within love. It is love that makes love possible. If everything depended on our capacity to love, then the insufficiency would soon become manifest. When we love we know that we do so, not by virtue of ourselves, but by means of that which is love, that which is capable of containing all because it has already reached out in embrace of all. At this stage there is no need to assign pronominal specificity to what is only an inchoate assurance of possibility. We have not yet encountered God who is love, but already we catch the presentiment that it is love itself that sustains all. Our point of access is the simultaneity of persons worthy of infinite love. Past, present, and future, they constitute a vast host and yet they are not such an endless number. Each one is a whole, a whole universe in himself or herself, outdistancing everything else in all existence. This is a truth we can feebly acknowledge only through marriage by which we affirm that the only relationship worthy of the other is an exclusive lifelong commitment. Yet we cannot marry everyone, or marriage would not mean very much if we did. So how can we relate to them as if they were all equally deserving of such supremacy? Somehow love must have already accomplished what remains for us to accomplish only imperfectly. The possibility that they might be disvalued, that their infinite worth could turn out to be a hollow aspiration, is impossible, for they already exceed everything else. Their worth does not await confirmation from us. It is because of them that love exists at all.

Somehow the affirmation of the worth of each person already precedes our arrival on the scene. Our love does not make the other lovable for it is rather the reverse. We love because the other is lovable. The question of whether the other is really deserving of such affection is moot since the question arises only because we have been seized by the imperative of love. Even to ask such a question is to acknowledge its hold on us. How then is it possible for us to be captured by love? Surely it is because we live and move and breathe in a medium in which such interruptions can break forth at any moment. We live within expectancy. That is, there is an openness to love before love is manifest, for there would be no coming to presence of love unless we already existed within its presence. But how then is that movement from absence to presence to be explained? It can be reduced to neither pure absence nor pure presence since either would preclude the possibility of movement. The mystery is strangely inaccessible to us who live within it. We perceive only the glimmering of a luminosity whose source can never be grasped since light cannot illuminate what precedes its shining. Even metaphor can only underline the inaccessibility rather than resolve it. To apprehend the process we must leave language behind to reach that which is its source. Heidegger offered a suggestive formulation of such an effort in overhearing as "the voice of the friend whom every Dasein carries within it."[10] Before there is the voice there is the hearing that is the readiness for it. This insight remained peculiarly undeveloped in Heidegger because, despite everything, he remained tied to a metaphysics of being as presence. The impasse can be resolved only by shifting toward a notion of being as personal since it is only the person that can be within the mode of coming to be that never is. This is the horizon within which love emerges from what never is and always was.

To be a person is thus to exist within a mode of being that is personal, not in the sense that it belongs to each of us personally, but in the more radical sense that we belong to it. We are like fish that navigate a medium so permeable that we are scarcely capable of becoming conscious of it. On the one hand we are open to all, present to everything and everyone, and yet on the other hand we are absent from all, incapable of losing ourselves within them. The only moment by which the shock of awareness of who we are breaks through is in the encounter with the other. Then we are thrown back by the realization that the other is a whole too. The personal as the horizon of our existence bursts upon us. But that is not to resolve the mystery of our permeability in relation to one another; it only deepens it, for now we must confront the multiplicity of particular wholes. How can each of us be the whole, the surpassing center of meaning and value in the universe? Love that outweighs all other reality impresses itself upon us so deeply that we see that we no longer live within space and time. Such are only the externals of an existence far more profoundly anchored in an eternal openness from which we cannot turn aside. Each is a whole and yet open to all other wholes. We are capable of including every other within us. The only possible way of giving an account of this possibility is that our wholeness does not necessarily exclude other wholes. Indeed, the reverse seems to be the case. Each is a whole perpetually prepared to put itself aside for the sake of the other whole. Multiplicity of wholes, far from constituting a challenge, is in the very nature of wholes that are personal. Each is a transcending, a pouring out of self, that makes possible not only the openness toward others but their very being. Otherness is grounded in the gift of self.

In this way we begin to catch a glimpse of what can scarcely be glimpsed. The encounter with the other has abruptly immobilized us. The other is the whole before whom we must give way, while we cannot close ourselves off from his or her appeal. I am the particular that must set itself aside for the sake of the other only because the other is capable of regarding me in the same way. Our openness is a vulnerability toward one another from which neither of us can recede and, in that heightening we become aware that the vulnerability is not primarily our own.[11] We merely participate in vulnerability as such. What makes it possible for us to set ourselves aside for the sake of the other is that setting aside is already our innermost possibility. It does not arise from us, we merely find ourselves within it. We can love only because love has made it possible for us. We know that our love is not sufficient, that it falls short of the call of love and, in that recognition, we see that we are not the source of love. However, we have been permitted to love only because that which is the source of love has withdrawn to yield the place of love to us. Our love is made possible by the absence of love itself which, we now discern, is the deepest expression of love. Love is in that sense not just one possibility of being but that which being is itself. Love sets everything aside, including itself, for the sake of the other so that the other might participate in the being of love. It is a sharing, not merely of what it possesses with the other, but of its very self. What love communicates above all is itself.

Even before the encounter with God has occurred he is present as the silent partner within every meeting of persons. Nietzsche disliked the idea of God as an omnipresent observer of all our private affairs, but this was to mistake him for an anonymous third party.[12] The opposite is really the case, for no one is more deeply concerned about the relationship with the other than God. The other is not an other for him but the one and only for whom he has given all, just as I am not an other but the one through whom the other is loved. It is a relationship in which no third parties are present for none can participate in the mutual encounter of persons. Only persons can be present to one another in that indispensable mode by which they yield presence to one another. It is a meeting that always requires the possibility of absence, the transcendence that makes possible the becoming presence that is never fully absorbed within itself. The meeting of persons is thus always made possible by that which they are not. They cannot even claim it as their own, for the possibility of setting oneself aside in order to become present to the other cannot be derived from the self. Indeed, the very core of the self is this possibility that is not its own. As a pure gift the openness of mutuality points beyond the immediate relationship of persons to that from which they themselves have been given, a source that can never be anything less than what it has provided. Personal encounter cannot arise from what is merely impersonal. We meet because somehow we have already met as the condition of possibility of mutual recognition. This is why the other cannot be indifferent to the greeting of others but must be more deeply entailed as the wellspring of concern.[13] We love because love has made it possible for us to love, for we are not the source of the love by which we are opened in vulnerability toward one another. More than the love we bear is the love by which we are borne. This can only be inexpressibly personal.

There is no such thing as love in general, no matter how often we invoke it as an abstraction. Love *is* only as the opening toward an other that is incapable of becoming a universal. Even when there is yet no recipient of love the beloved is still contained more inwardly than love itself. Just as we cannot love human beings in general but only in their unique specificity, so love cannot exist except within that mode of utter specificity. Love is not a common noun. It is a proper name. The love that arises within us from we know not where does not emerge from anonymous darkness. As love it can only exist through the person who is capable of containing the other within. Love is a holding of the other in love. To the extent that our love is a participation in that possibility it has received, it is an opening that has been made possible by the love that is the other. If love is a unique bearing of the other within it is made possible by the love that uniquely bears all others. The personal reality of love can only come from the person who is love. Even to think of it as a gift is to think of it as the fruit of a personal giving. Only persons can give and only persons can receive. But it is the reality of love that is the most unique of all. It can only be proffered by persons because it is never really a gift that is separate from the giver. In love what is given is the self of the giver. Only persons are capable of giving themselves. Animals can give things, but they can only fleetingly suggest that they have thereby given more. With persons it is of the essence that every giving is a giving of the impossible. The giver gives himself or herself. How we might ask is such an impossibility possible?

That is finally the question that the reflection on love elicits. How can we give more than we possess? Since we never really or fully possess our selves, how can we bestow the same upon an other? Can we give more than we have? Love seems to require as much of us. One has only to reflect on the impossibility of making a lifelong commitment to love another when we cannot guarantee emotional permanence. It is difficult to reconcile this unconditional pledge with a world of rational limits. Is it possible to love beyond reason, as marriage would seem to suggest? Surely it is, but only if love is not something we possess but something that possesses us. Yet it must not be a temporary state of possession from which we might recover. Possession by love must be the ineluctable condition of our being. We are possessed by that which possesses itself so perfectly that it is capable of giving itself completely. The problem with Aristotle's Unmoved Mover is that it entirely overlooks the moral dimension. It suggests that God would exist in unapproachable self-containment, rather than recognize that it is precisely from the vantage point of such perfection that love must arise. Without the need to share itself, divine being most of all shares itself out of love.[14] Only that which contains itself most completely can give itself most perfectly. Love is the primordial divine movement. It is most of all what God is. Before there is creation or revelation or redemption there is the love that is before the beginning, and that is the innermost life of God. Our love too is a partaking of the originating divine life. We can give what we do not possess, ourselves, because we have been given the gift of giving that is love itself.[15] Indeed, we only approach the possibility of possessing ourselves in giving ourselves to an other. It is a possibility that can only be comprehended within the life of God.

We gain ourselves by giving ourselves. This is the paradoxical law of the personal reality we inhabit. From the perspective of finitude it makes no sense, only that which is infinite can render it intelligible. The spiritual is the infinite because it exists through the sharing of itself without limit; it is never more itself than when it is giving itself away. This is why spirit is the source of all that merely is. Everything else exists by remaining locked within the confines of its existence.[16] Spirit is the opening toward otherness that is capable of including others within itself. For us that is always an achievement since we are not spiritual through and through. We aspire toward spirit, an aspiration that of course can only begin in spirit, albeit only by beginning. As yet we do not fully possess ourselves and can only glimpse that status as we move toward the outpouring of self that spirit is. The imperative of loss and gain is paradoxical only from our inconclusive grasp of spiritual reality. From the perspective of that which is Spirit the paradox is resolved; there is nothing that seeks to retain itself within it. Love has no other object than love. Our love invariably falls short of that utter perfection but it is love only because it is derived from love. We could not love if love had not made it possible for us to love, for it is not we who love but love that loves within us. Speculatively we know that it is that which *is* that enables everything that comes into existence to be in that diminished sense of what is and yet is not fully. But we do not have to await such deliberations to know what is most personal. That is, that we are most ourselves when we have become least ourselves, in the way that God is. The possibility of becoming a person, of becoming ourselves most completely, is provided by God who is most fully a person.

God Is a Person Who Is More Than One

A person, we have emphasized, is one who makes room for the other, who carries the other so inwardly that nothing can separate them. To be a person means to be already in community with the other. Even before there is an other, the embrace has occurred. Yet there is nothing of subordination, of the satisfaction of need or interest implied, for otherwise there would only be extension of the self and not the opening toward the other. A person is defined precisely by the capacity to set himself or herself aside in relating to the other as other. Autarky, supreme self-sufficiency in itself, is not just not in conflict with the movement of love; it is indispensable to love. Without consulting the self, the other is loved for his or her own sake. Vulnerability is rooted in invulnerability. Only that which either has no need or has forgotten its own need can see the other as need. Without need of the other, the need of the other is heard. Selflessness is not just an avocation but also the very being of the person. Yet independence of the other is not in any sense indifference to the other, for it is rather the premise for relating to the other as other. Not just an other self, the other is other only for the self that has no dependence on the other. But what then is the basis for the relationship to the other if it is not need or even mutual dependence? The only answer is that the relationship must be rooted in the freedom by which the other remains other. Love alone provides such a bond that one can be contained in the other without the slightest incorporation. Love alone is the union that preserves separation. What cannot be contained within the embrace that would effect a conjunction can be held more deeply within inwardness. That is how God is.

As a person he is glimpsed in inwardness but it is also through that glimpse that we perceive what inwardness is. We see that a person is the container of all things in love that yet does not seek to incorporate them into itself, but rather allows them to become free. Love is creative. Without being driven by necessity it overflows into the otherness that it loves even more intensely. The logic of love is inseparable from the logic of liberty and they are equally impenetrable except through the light of love itself. What does love seek in going beyond itself? It cannot be itself since that would not be love. It must rather head toward the other as other. Love is in this sense bound up with an other even before there is an other. No explanation in terms of self is possible for it is the deliberate leaving of self behind. The mystery of love can be grasped only by love itself. All that one can say is that love overflows, a metaphor that better captures what cannot be captured because it gives itself up for capture. Love, as Kierkegaard insisted, cannot be deceived.[17] Only the deceiver can be deceived. Love has entirely relinquished the calculus of self. There is no self for it, only the opening through which it departs. Even before there is an other there is the other that is beheld more deeply than the self. St. John's formulation that God is love has become so familiar that its strangeness has not been allowed to sink in. What it really means is that God is never really himself because he has always given himself away in love. But what then is God if he is not this stable center of action within being? What then must he be if he is merely this movement that is so inexpressibly deep that it is all but invisible to itself? Yet somehow this is what he must be if God is love. We do not say that God has love but that God is love, a love that is more with the other than it is with itself. The metaphor of overflowing implies too much of a center from which the action takes place, while love has poured itself out to the point of its complete self-emptying. Love does not merely overflow; it gives itself away. This is how God is.

To whom can God give himself if it is not to himself? Since there is no other before God, otherness must somehow be present within God. The love that he bears contains its other within it as the very meaning of love, for it has placed the other before itself. How can love persist in unapproachable remoteness? That would be to cease to be love, that which ever lowers itself that it might come nearer. Already love has made the other more real than itself. It must count for nothing, the other must count for everything. Even if love were alone it would still not be alone for it would not even allow itself to think about itself, thereby attesting to the impossibility of its being alone. We of course can be alone and are often intensely aware of that state, but then it is only because our love is not so perfect as to reach utter forgetfulness of itself. With God who is love it is very different. Then love has removed itself so completely that it has begotten its other, except that the other always remained hidden within love. Begetting is yet another metaphor for what always escapes metaphor for it is merely a way of saying that love cannot be without the other. The being of love is the other. Even apart they cannot be apart. So it is not so much that the metaphor of begetting fails us as that the metaphor can only be understood in the light of love. Love explains begetting, not the other way around. To think begetting is to think the love that cannot be without the other. What for us is separated in the time of generation is for God the simultaneity of truth. Love lives for and in the other. It has no other life than in the other for it is wholly given to the other. In the end we cannot even think of a person as solitary for otherness is its innermost being.[18]

What that means can only be appreciated when we compare it to the more ordinary kind of self-expression. We are familiar with the need of the self to become more intensely aware of itself by bringing forth what it generates within itself. Works and deeds express what is within. They bring inwardness into the outer world and thereby return it to inwardness more deeply. But this is still not a full expression of the self. It is merely an expression of what is contained within the self, not an expression of the self itself. For that it would have to bring forth an other, a self other than itself. As an exercise in semiotics it would mean that the signified has supplanted the signifier. The begotten has surpassed the begetter. This is the very meaning of begetting. It has nothing to do with the expression of self, for on the contrary it points toward the erasure of the self. It is only in God that we see clearly or, rather, mysteriously, what love is. "He must increase,

I must decrease" (John 3:30) is the law of paternity. Love does not await the other; it generates him. The very possibility of otherness is buried deep within love as its innermost truth. Love does not arise from otherness for it is the reverse. Begetting cannot be explained in terms of love; it is love that must be explained in terms of begetting. The other reveals love to itself. Strictly speaking love cannot be until there is an other since love of anything else is merely love of self. It is the begetting of an other that makes love itself possible. Emmanuel Levinas, who thought deeply about the priority of the other to the self, singled out paternity as the most crucial moment, the point at which the self sets itself aside utterly for the other who is yet not a reflection of the self. [19] But even Levinas did not transpose the relationship to the eternity of God. He remained tied to the analogical path of Western metaphysics by which the human becomes the way toward understanding God. The problem with all analogy is that, for all its valuable contributions, it overlooks a crucial limitation. Analogy cannot account for its own possibility. How is it that the human provides an analogue for the divine?[20]

Surely it is because the divine underpins the analogy imputed to explain it. This is what we have sought to do in thinking of God as the possibility of thinking. We can of course think of God as a person and this is what the revelatory traditions have taught us. But can we think of persons without thinking in terms of God? What if the most decisive aspects of personhood are only revealed within the three divine persons of God? This is the great question broached, even if inconclusively, by the German Idealists who taught us that philosophy could no longer think without including the horizon of its own thinking within itself. We could no longer operate on the unquestioned assumption that the human viewpoint was a self-sufficient starting point. It was Jacobi who first pointed out the presumption within this astonishing naiveté.[21] How could a part understand the whole, or finite being infinite being? The possibility arose only if the finite part at some point managed to gain something of the perspective of the absolute. But this meant the definitive overturning of analogy. Now it had to be conceded that it was the supra-analogical perspective that explained the possibility of analogy. When analogy itself is as much in need of explanation of what it aims to explain, then we are compelled to admit that the former must be understood in terms of the latter. There are not first persons and then from them we build an understanding of God.

Instead, it is from God that we perceive what persons are. If they are analogues of God, then God is the source of their analogical reality. This is a decisive limitation of the "analogical imagination" which may work tolerably well on intra-mundane applications but dissolves before the challenge of its own grounds of possibility.

Paternity is not an analogue of the relation of the Father to the Son because it is that relationship that provides the analogue for paternity. The merely human father discovers only slowly and imperfectly that the son is an other who does not belong to him but, rather, that it is much more the case that he belongs to the son. He carried the potentiality for the son who was invisible even to his heart. The question of how human parents can love the child who has not yet been conceived looms larger with the advent of technologies of reproductive design, but the fundamental structure of the question is rooted in the limitations of the human condition. We must love the children we do not know, just as we must love all human beings we do not know. How is this possible? Somehow the other must be present before he or she is present. The analogue of paternity, with its at best fitful envisaging of the other, is not quite adequate to a situation in which the son makes the father. Fatherhood is a possibility because we are already fathers of one another. This is what it means to be a person. The other is always carried within as our ownmost possibility. We do not merely give way to the other or yield to him or her after the fact, for we are defined by the priority of the other. It is in the other we discover who we are. The problem is that paternity cannot explain how it itself is possible. How is it possible for me to generate an other before whom all my own interests must be subordinated, an other who is not an other self? We can explain the biology but the personal eludes us. This is the great lacuna within our so-called mastery of reproductive technology. What can account for the unmastery of the parents by the baby? There must be some way of making it clear that it is precisely that complete sacrifice of self for the sake of the other that is sought, and sought not in the abstract but with the specificity that heads toward that particular other. Parents love the child they have yet to meet. Even our ordinary language attests to the defeat of the biological explanation, for the begetting of children is "procreation." They cannot be born because they have always been.[22]

There is in other words no analogue for the begetting of persons other than the eternal self-giving of the Father through whom the Son is. Biological generation is left far behind as we struggle to conceive of a relationship wholly transparent between persons. The mystery affirmed in the Creed as the Son "proceeding" from the Father can only be glimpsed because our own personal reality strains toward the same horizon. Human begetting is only a faint reflection but yet one that still manages to overturn the hierarchy of biological descent. Persons are persons through their capacity to give themselves completely to an other. We share in this divine capacity abundantly on display within a world of free persons. But we cannot even begin to understand it until we behold its origination within the Love by which the Son proceeds from the Father. There is nothing that grounds or intervenes within the relationship except infinite Love itself, a Love that is so utterly personal that it must become a third person, the Spirit. The famous icon of Andrei Rublev of the three angels who visit Abraham and Sarah is not so inaccurate a depiction of the Trinity because its most striking feature is the extent to which they constitute a perfect circle of personal attention. It is the supreme instance of analogical self-overturning that has always been the secret of analogical reasoning. The analogy points to the necessity of leaving it behind and in turn makes possible a deeper return to it at the same time. The three divine persons perfectly express the separation that is indispensable to the being of persons and the impossibility of separation that is the only meaning of personal union. Infinite Love is the only form of love; all other love is by virtue of infinite Love. It has no reality other than the person who bears it and it has no object other than the person whom it brings forth, a bringing forth that is so perfect that it cannot be other than a person too.

Love is Trinitarian. This is an insight derived not from revelation but from the logic of love itself. It is in light of the Trinitarian unfolding of love that the revelation of the divine Trinity is possible.[23] As finite persons we possess an intimation of what the being of infinite persons must be. Without the slightest element of self there would only be room for the other as that which the self most truly is. Everything is a setting aside and a withdrawal so that the other might be. The self lives entirely through the other and yet in such a way that it is the other who lives rather than the self. It is through love that otherness emerges because it is only love that renders the other utterly free of the source. All other forms of creation, including the procreation of which human beings are capable, carry some element of reciprocity. Dependence and return may still be transcended in love but only by reaching beyond the conditionality by which they are marked. In itself love seeks nothing for itself. The relation to the other is without ulterior purpose to such an extent that it can only be conceived as a pure overflowing of freedom. There is no compulsion to bring forth the other since nothing is required or sought by the source; the process is animated from first to last as a pure expression of love for the other's own sake. Love generates the other in freedom, while the other can only arise from the freedom of love. The Father can be without the Son and yet he does not wish to be so, not because of any necessity, but simply because of love for the Son who without Love would not be. Contrary to the picture of love as in search of the beloved it has lost, we see that love in itself makes way for the beloved it liberates. Their relationship cannot have the smallest hint of need, even reciprocation, for it must be founded wholly on love. This is why, we realize, there must be a third member of their company.

It is not that the Spirit is vaguely present as their common bond but as the deepest affirmation of what the bond of love is. The love by which they are united is not merely a sentiment, an internality, within the Father and the Son. They love, not with their own selves, but with the force of love itself that is other than them. Love that carries otherness within itself must ultimately be other itself. There is no resting place for love other than with itself. If there is love between the two then it must become so real that it too is other. Only as an other person is the love between them so real that they set themselves aside for its sake. It is in the Spirit that the seal of freedom is stamped on the love of the Father and the Son. They love with a love that is no longer even their own for it has come forth as an other of its own. This is what it means to love, no longer through oneself but through the other who is other than the other. In the Spirit love has become real with a reality that can no longer be displaced to the interiority of either lover or beloved. Each has definitively set itself aside for the sake of the other who is Love. It is neither the Father nor the Son but Love itself that loves within them. To use language we more familiarly apply, we might say that it is at this point that love is no longer subjective. The truth of love is that it is more real than any subject that bears it, but it is only when love has become an other that this is definitively established. The Spirit is loved by the Father and the Son as the Love by which they love one another. To give oneself to the other is ultimately to give oneself to Love, the only other by whom one can love the other. Love itself must be a third person as the only surety that love belongs neither to lover nor beloved.

The mystery of the Trinity of persons in the one God is not thereby dissolved or penetrated. It is rather heightened. To know that the unfolding of love constitutes a Trinity of persons in one being does not explain why this must be so. We only know that it must, not because we have seen beyond it but because we have reached the limit of all seeing. The limitless transparence of the three divine persons is not available to us. Analogy has not allowed us to pierce the transcendent but it has brought us to the source of its own possibility. By dispensing with itself analogy has performed its ultimate service. No one can surpass the horizon of love through which the Trinity of divine persons constitute a common self-understanding.[24] We have become participants in the mystery of the divine life. This is all that is known. Yet in another sense that is everything, for now we see that our thinking is carried over from the innermost stirring of love within the divine mind. Even if the reverberations within us are faint we nevertheless know that they carry an unfathomable depth. It is enough that we glimpse our affinity with a Love beyond all telling. No information or grasp of necessity could surpass the thought of that by which we are held more tenderly than we can imagine. It is not through thought that we pierce the mysteries of things but through love by which, of course, thought becomes possible. Even for God thinking arises within the community of persons constituted by Love. Thinking is irreducibly personal. We still do not know what thinking is but we see that its power is entirely derived from the love that unfolds in the generation of persons yielding all to one another. It is enough to know that this is why we have been called into existence, that we might become participants in the life of perfect Love beyond which nothing more can be thought. Creation is itself an icon of the Love that has no icon.

Creation as the Freedom of Love Culminating in Redemption

The problem is that we have sought to understand creation within the horizon of what is created. We even look for God within the world he has created as if he was one of the entities contained within it. That has been the great misstep of Western metaphysics that, as Heidegger saw, virtually doomed the whole enterprise.[25] We have failed to see that the key to creation is that the Creator must withdraw. This is not merely a logic of necessity, the provision of a space to be occupied by independent creatures, but it is much more a logic of love, the self-concealment that awaits the birth of love itself. A Creator who disclosed himself completely to his creatures would overwhelm them, depriving them of their freedom and absorbing them again into himself. It would betoken a deficiency of love within the Creator, which is impossible. In this sense it is the absence of the Creator from creation that is the deepest testament to the love with which he beholds it. Kierkegaard refers to the example of the prince who falls in love with a pauper. [26] What is he to do? To declare his love would be to obliterate any possibility of love between them, for how could the beloved respond if her freedom has been preempted by the power of the other? The only option is for the more powerful to become the most powerless, to do nothing but wait in infinite patience for the beloved to slowly discover his love. The creature must come to realize that the Creator somehow "needs" her love. This is not in the sense that he cannot do without it but in the sense that love includes the vulnerability of the lover before the beloved. To create an other is to expose oneself to rejection by the other, a rejection that can only be overcome by submitting even more completely to the decision of the other. Love can triumph only through love; it can neither seize nor be seized. Behind it all is the divine plan to raise us up to be persons as well, that is, to be like him overflowing with love. It is not enough that he creates us, but that he wants us to be like him in creating ourselves.

Love that pours itself out without counting the cost can have no goal other than the raising up of others who can undertake the same self-outpouring. It is Love that maintains all things in their separate existence, guarding the precious independence from their source. They are loved in their independence even when they do not know it. But it is when separated beings can know the Love by which they are maintained that Love can truly be shared. This is why persons are the apex of creation. It is in them that the purpose of creation is reached, the point at which the Creator can reveal his love for his creature. This is entirely dependent on the creature possessing the capacity to know what is revealed, to recognize in the Creator the Love that brings him into being. But how is that possible? It is only if the creature possesses the same love as the Creator that it knows the Creator through the same love that the creature bears within himself.

Love speaks to love. We can know God only because we are like God, for God can only be known through himself. It is because persons exist within the same self-transparency that is the life of God that they have access to the mystery of love that merely sustains everything else without their knowing it.

Love has called forth its ultimate creation in creating what contains the possibility of love in return. The gift of self that is love has reached its limit in giving itself. Now the creature is an other creator, capable of giving itself not just in part but in whole. That is, of giving as a person. This is why each person is the center of the universe. In each we behold a whole world because each is beyond the whole world. No matter how limited the power of a person, even the smallest child or the dying patient, he or she can still give all that is needed. They can give themselves. Even God does not do any more for when one has given oneself one has given the whole world. This is what it means to communicate for, over and above what is said or even what is given, is the giver who is given with the gift. But for this to occur the giver must somehow contain his or her own existence. We cannot give what we do not possess so that the condition of possibility of giving ourselves is that we are the source of our own being. We are free. Nothing and no one in all the universe can compel us to do what we have determined not to do. Even when we have been physically constrained to act contrary to our will, there is still the inextinguishable and unassailable core of freedom to give or withhold our consent. Nothing can coerce what cannot be coerced, the self that can only be given freely when we put ourselves into the action that is the very meaning of human action. Only the awesome possibility of freedom alone cannot be given away. Freedom as what makes all self-giving possible cannot itself be given away. It is the pure gift given before all giving. We cannot get back to a point before there is freedom since all going back requires the exercise of freedom. As a consequence we can never really know what freedom itself is. Despite the familiarity of its invocation freedom is irreducible. Before all beginning, it is. Ultimately we can know freedom only as the gift of the inner life of God who gives himself to us, not just in the way that he gives existence and life to all other things, but also in the way that he gives his very own life to us. We are like God in our primordial freedom.

The difference is that we are given freedom; we are not identical with it. It is through the exercise of freedom that we discover who we are.

With God freedom is fully actual within the divine being. For us freedom is a process or, rather, the condition of possibility of a process never ultimately accomplished so long as we live. We may have been given freedom but we have always yet to obtain it. Even God, it turns out, cannot give freedom as a thing. He can only bring us to participate in his primordial freedom through the growth of freedom within us. In the beginning we are hardly even free for, at best, we possess only an incipient freedom. To become free, to share in the self-caused life of God, our hearts must be enlarged by the divine love that is the innermost life of God. Freedom, we discover, is self-transcendence, the setting aside of self for the sake of the other most perfectly enacted between the Father, the Son, and the Spirit. Just as freedom is a gift, so also is its actualization. Indeed, there is no freedom other than the freedom to become free. We might even be inclined to argue for the irrelevance of God for this reason, that the giver is obsolete when the gift can only be taken. It cannot be given. There is much in this suggestion that resonates in the modern world. It is not that we cannot believe in God any longer, but that we cannot find any use for him.[27] The secret of the modern appeal to our own unsurpassable independence arises from a profound intuition of freedom behind it. God can do nothing to help us in our freedom. The perception is so true that God himself agrees with it. He has left us free.[28] All that is omitted is the self-concealment of love by which our freedom becomes possible. Before that mystery has been glimpsed we have not yet attained the inwardness of freedom. This is the great question that confronts the modern world erected on the outward conviction of freedom yet unfamiliar with its own condition of possibility. Our freedom is different from the freedom of God because we do not understand whereof we speak when we invoke it. Ours is the freedom of discovering what freedom is.

At every turn there remains the possibility of turning aside from the invitation freedom extends to us. We can respond with love to the unsurpassable gift of love, but we need not. This is the possibility of evil that is inseparable from a gift as dependent on the recipient as on the giver. A freedom that is given is a freedom that has yet to be taken up. Nothing predetermines in advance how it will be received for that is what freedom is. It is the freedom to reject freedom. Love has submitted to its greatest risk in bringing forth free beings who might not love. Yet that is what love entails. It can neither coerce nor be coerced. It must be free. Without prompting or compulsion it must freely deliver itself up to the other, just as it too has received that possibility from Love. The sharing of self must be supererogatory for that is the only self worth giving. A gift incentivized by a reason, a gift that is not free, is hardly even a gift. We have been given nothing, while all we have longed for is the nothing from which all giving arises. A widespread misperception is that freedom is in this sense empty, a formless possibility of assuming an infinity of forms, but this is to entirely overlook its transcendent source. It is to mistake the immanent content of love for love itself. The mistake hardly occurs when we look upon the gift as more than what it is, as we must if we are in the presence of genuine giving. Then we know that the actual gift is irrelevant compared to the giver who has given himself or herself within the gift. They have given all. The gift is nothing, while the nothing is all. But that also means that the gift might conceal the absence of giving behind it. What cannot be contained, the freedom of love, might be withheld even more resolutely. It is because love arises from nothing that it might choose to embrace the nothing. This is evil, the collapse of freedom upon itself.

For God this is impossible. He has ever and always chosen good. We on the other hand have only that possibility and can never definitively foreclose the possibility of rejecting it. God's freedom has been fully realized; ours remains to be. This is why evil is impossible for God, while it is always possible for us. Yet even that is not strictly speaking true, for evil is not a possibility but the definitive turn away from all possibility. Down the path of evil lies nothing. This is why it is such a stark and radical choice, or rather a non-choice. How can nothing be chosen? We may of course frequently choose evil under the guise of the good but what makes it evil is that we know that this is not so and yet persist. We cannot even explain evil to ourselves. Certainly we cannot explain it to God who, as St. Thomas suggested, cannot understand evil.[29] This does not in any way betoken a defect in the divine intellect. It simply underlines the absence of anything to understand. Evil is nothing. It is only because God cannot make us God but instead creates us to become like him that it remains possible for us to turn away from him. The freedom we have been given is the freedom to obtain freedom, a freedom that at every moment might yet turn away from itself. Creation, especially the creation of free beings, sets in motion the possibility of its rejection. This does not mean that the outbreak of evil is inevitable, let alone that it is necessary. It is only to concede that the risk of evil is inseparable from a process in which God makes us participants in his primordial freedom. What for God is eternal self-creation is for us a possibility from which self-destruction cannot be excluded. We live perpetually within the moment of decision and therefore of non-decision. This is the only way that we can become participants in the freedom that is identical with the good. We must choose in time what has been chosen from all eternity as we begin to perceive the aweful responsibility that has been placed upon us. It has been left to us to determine whether creation is good or evil and, even more fundamentally, whether there is a creation or not.

The freedom to choose not to be is the price of a creation that includes freedom. Yet the choice of evil cannot defeat the good from which being is, for even the possibility of its choice derives from what is left of being within it. Evil has no reality of its own; it can only masquerade as the good. Being that turns away from being still depends on being. Love cannot be defeated for it has already surpassed the vulnerability of that which merely seeks to preserve itself. Having given itself away love cannot lose any more than it has surrendered. Everything else can suffer loss, but not that which is loss as such. Love that gives itself away has affirmed a being that is beyond the loss of being. Nothing that happens can touch it. The revolt that turns against the gift of love has already been forgiven by love. Without that, the revolt itself would not be possible. It is love that sustains the possibility of its own rejection, cherishing the freedom that is the innermost heart of love. Refusal of the invitation of love does not negate the unconditionality of love. All that it accomplishes is the self-closure by which freedom collapses into itself. Love is not negated, only the negator is. The invitation to participate in the life of love is the invitation to go beyond what merely is, to enter into partnership with the self-outpouring source that is always more than all. It is this life beyond being that is lost in its rejection, an inestimable loss to the individual who pursues the containment of self that is the annihilation of self. Nothing can compensate for the contraction that eventually leaves nothing behind except an inexhaustible sadness. Hell is a choice that not even the unlimited power of Love is sufficient to prevent. It is this depth of sorrow on behalf of the lost one that is the ultimate suffering of Love. Even when it is broken the bond of Love is not broken but becomes, instead, the substitution of self for the other by which Love seeks to repair the loss.

The one thing Love cannot do is abolish the freedom that is indispensable to Love, even if it permits the possibility of its rejection. What Love can do is demonstrate that Love is deeper than hatred. Through love it can overcome the rejection of love. Evil and its possibility cannot be eliminated but it can be as if it were not. The non-reality of evil is affirmed even more deeply by the suffering of Love that puts itself in place of the other who is in danger of being lost. That which is more than being puts itself in the place of that which is less than being. The Love that pervades all of creation, as the tenderness that preserves all separation from the source, now radiates even more intensely through the Love that suffers on behalf of the other. The suffering of Love discloses the love by which the other has always been loved. It is at that point that Love reveals itself as a person. Only as a person can Love put itself in place of the other, of every other. Substitution cannot be symbolic. Animal sacrifice always fell short for that reason, for it was never sufficient to repair the rupture. Love must finally sacrifice itself if it is to restore love to itself. That cannot occur unless Love is fully incarnated within a person. Creation entailed a sacrifice by Love but it had not yet required the sacrifice of Love, although that full measure was hidden in the heart of Love from the beginning. Love is unconditional. Once it had brought forth the other then it had exposed its vulnerability to the other, not in the sense that it could be injured by the other, but in the sense that it could be affected by the self-inflicted injury of the other. From the beginning it had taken the place of the other. Expiation is an imperfect way of thinking about the imperative of Love. To whom is expiation owed, if not to Love itself? Love does not make expiation; it is expiation. We cannot understand expiation except as the mandate that love is. When the other has rejected love, then love rushes to put itself in place of the other, not in order to satisfy an external requirement, but simply to affirm love. The self-destruction of evil is suffered even more deeply by the Love that loves the other more than itself. There is no greater love, nor any greater being.

The answer to the question, as to why God permits evil to occur, is that he does not. Even before its unreality is manifest, his love has already forgiven all. Love covers over a multitude of sins, not by concealing them, but in the more radical sense of having covered them with love.[30] They are no more when love has taken their place. Not even the refusal of love is permitted to mar what love has created. Instead, love itself repairs the breach by revealing what love is, the surpassing of all possibility of rejection. Love is the victory of love. There is no point at which love might not be sufficient, no moment in which forgiveness might fall short. Love has always reached the limit by ever exceeding it. Love cannot fail. Having poured itself out love never arrives at a stage in which it has still more to give. It is consummated. This is why love is the restoration of all that is lost, the repair of all that has been injured, and the resurrection of all that has perished. Within the arms of love death is no more. The love that comes from beyond being, yields space to the possibility of being and its impossibility, draws all beyond the fatality of being. In love there is no more being because it has already given itself away completely. We recognize that being is possible through the self-erasure of love but now we discover that love has invited us to enter into its own transcendence. Mere being was never the intention of Love for us. Now we discover that Love seeks to make us participants in Love itself. It is not enough that it wishes to share being with us, but that it also wants to share itself. In giving itself up utterly on behalf of fallen humanity, Love finally reveals the depth of its Love. We enter into a personal relationship with Love and learn what it means to be a person.

Personhood Revealed Only in God

The mystery of the person deepens. What we thought was familiar, as familiar as the persons we know, turns out to be more profound than we imagined. We do not know what it means to be a person until we have encountered that which is personal through and through. The revelatory encounter with a personal God had made the discovery of a personal source irreversible. It was no longer possible to think of the ground as other than personal. The difficulty was that the language of persons was applied without sufficient awareness of its externalist character. A pattern of assuming persons could be known other than personally began to deform the discourse. The Nicean and Chalcedonian formulations of dogma did little to resist a hardening of terminology that they in principle endorsed.[31] It was only in the prayer life of the Church that a very different understanding prevailed. There the interpersonal emphasis initiated by St. Paul endured. It is not possible to pray as if to a third party. Prayer could only occur if we entered into the mind of God and that in turn was not possible unless the

Spirit of God prayed within us. It was in prayer that persons discovered the enlargement of the heart by which in being lifted beyond themselves they found themselves.

Momentous as that discovery was in practice it has yet to find appropriate linguistic recognition. A notable beginning was, however, made by Meister Eckhart who not only succeeded in voicing his speculative mysticism but, in preaching to nuns who knew no Latin, also endowed the German vernacular with an astonishing philosophical reach. Perhaps it was no accident that Eckhart furnished one of the strands that fed into the single greatest flowering of personalist philosophy in the modern era. German Idealism marks the point at which the mystic's self-understanding within God becomes the project of a philosophy of the person articulated in the language of the person. They saw that what Eckhart had glimpsed at the boundary of experience, the self-constitution of the soul through God, was neither rare nor inaccessible. It was rather the very core of what it means to be a person. That is the realization that personhood is not ours but is derivative from the person that God is.[32] We participate in a reality we do not possess so that if we want to understand ourselves we must be prepared to reach beyond ourselves to the One who is the ground of possibility. Our inwardness is a possibility because God is inwardness. Yet the penetration with which the Idealists saw what had not been seen so clearly before did not save them from the misunderstandings that had similarly befallen Eckhart's mystical glimpses. Man had either identified himself with God, or failed to recognize the distinction. Almost inevitably the charge of self-divinization was hurled against them. The irony, that this is precisely the opposite of the aspiration to think of human persons in relation to divine persons, was not permitted to impede the accusation. Such misunderstanding is a powerful warning for any personalist philosophy that, like the Idealists, is not sufficiently personalist in its formulations. Only by thinking of God within inwardness can we avoid the danger of distorting implications.

We are not the truth, all of reality seems to say, for the truth lies deeper within truth itself. Everything else can be seen in the light of truth but truth itself eludes us for we cannot behold it from outside, from beyond truth. We live within a truth that can never be present or, rather, it can only be present in the mode of not being present.[33] As such a disclosure truth is inextricably personal, arising from the person who directs it toward me personally and received only personally. There is no impersonal apprehension of truth. It is mine and, yet, not mine for it is of the other. What does it mean to say that God is truth? The words trip off our tongue with a familiarity that almost completely obscures their meaning. This is all the more reason to hold firmly to the glimmer of transcendence they contain. God is truth, not the truth or a truth, but truth that is known only through truth. We do not know truth for we know through truth. How can we know that through which knowing is possible? It would be to go beyond possibility, to grasp the impossible. It would be to see what personhood is, as that which is truth because it is ever more than truth, truthfully. To be a person is to go beyond truth by having always already arrived at it. It is to be at one with the recognition that there is nothing more truthful than truth. The question is how can we, who are on our way to truth, know truth as our destination? It was the question that bedeviled Plato and through him the history of philosophy because he had not yet seen how this impossibility is the possibility of the person. God is the resolution of the contradiction; we are the movement of resolution. The only question is, how can we as persons understand personhood as such, that is, that which is beyond us as persons?

How can we know God? The casualness of our everyday discussion of God masks a layer of difficulty we have scarcely begun to suspect. St. Thomas understood that to understand God we must be God, but even he did not press the insight to inquire how it is even possible for us to glimpse who God is. Even to have a sense of God we must somehow have a sense of what it is to be God. That is how we understand all other things, for we are capable of putting ourselves in their place. With God it is the same except that he is the very source of putting oneself in place of the other. When we think God we do so by virtue of God himself. We can put ourselves in the place of God because he has put himself in our place so completely that we participate in the being by which he yields place to himself. The closest we come to this divine being is, not just in putting ourselves in place of the other in knowledge, but in giving ourselves to the other in love. How is this possible? Who or where are we when we have given ourselves in this way? What is left over when nothing more is left? We do not know what this being is that freely gives its being. All that we can say is that it is not being or, as Emmanuel Levinas phrases it, it is "other-

wise than being [*autrement qu'être*]."[34] Personhood remains the unsurpassable mystery of our existence because all else is surpassed by it. Nothing is more real. Yet we would be inclined to overlook it, to take for granted
what would thus not be taken at all, were it not for the Person who calls by
recalling us to ourselves. Persons are a revelation of God, but a revelation
that can scarcely endure without an even deeper revelation of God. We are
persons, not just because we share in the nonbeing of persons, but also because God reveals himself personally to each one of us. As persons each is
a unique recipient of God's self-revelation.

CHAPTER FIVE

Art as the Radiance of Persons in Reality

Persons disclose by not disclosing. They can be recipients of the divine self-revelation because they are like God in their transcendence. It is as persons that they can know God as a person or, more accurately, as the three persons who disclose what it means to be a person. Nothing can contain a person but a person. The only adequate revelation of a person is the person to whom they have wholly given themselves and to whom they in turn respond with the same self-donation. Only the community of persons is the adequate revelation of the love that reveals persons. Nothing external to persons can express what the person is for the person has always evanesced behind the self-expression. Persons alone can glimpse persons in that meeting place outside of all space and time that is the region of the personal. Greeting occurs only when persons meet as persons, otherwise it is a mere going through the motions in which nothing happens. The surprise, the rupturing of all boundaries, the exceeding of being, is the personal encounter. For millennia we have struggled with the meaning of the *imago Dei*, a formulation whose importance has been continuously sensed yet whose indispensable meaning has constantly eluded us. The metaphor of image has hardly assisted us in grasping what it says, for persons are an image of what cannot be imaged. Nor has the narrowing to the faculty of reason that persons possess illumined what it means to possess what cannot be possessed. It is only slowly and, in part, under the threat of looming instrumentalization, that it has begun to dawn on us that thought does not provide the horizon for thinking of persons. The case is rather the reverse. The personal is the horizon of the disclosure of persons for there is nothing higher, not even God.

Given this inscrutably personal character of revelation one might be inclined to suspect its impossibility. But as we know persons, including God, reveal themselves all the time. They avail themselves of the medium of the non-personal, whether it is signs or words or objects, which they find to be more or less adequate carriers of what can never be carried. Almost any externality will do when its purpose is not to reveal but to convey what has already been given directly and completely, the gift of self that is the only adequate mode of communication between persons. As a consequence mere tokens betoken a universe beyond their possibility. This is the radiance that now pervades the whole of reality when each blade of grass, each sound, each smile, comes to stand for the vastness of the person who intends it for us. Enchantment envelops the merely external environment in which we find ourselves because we know we are not alone. Nature, that realm accessible to cold analytic investigation, manifests a quite different aspect when read as a love letter. Even scientific objectivity is not sufficient, as we have seen, to obviate the horizon of enchantment within which it is conducted. The realm of I-It investigation is contained within the more embracing arc of the I-Thou. When nature no longer addresses us as an immediate presence we are in many respects closer to the mode of address by which absence discloses presence. This is why the truth of science is not science but the quest for what cannot be attained, the glimpse of what cannot be glimpsed because it ever remains beyond the possibility of the merely material. Enchantment is no stranger to the world of science, as any practicing scientist will attest, but it cannot be conceptualized within the realm that it makes possible. In what realm then can enchantment be acknowledged? Where can enchantment be contemplated as enchantment? That is the peculiar prerogative of art that explains why, although we live in a scientific age, we have never ceased to be captivated by art.

It is through art that matter is rendered transparent by means of a radiance that seems to attach to its very materiality. The special status of works of art, that which gives them a capacity to surmount the degenera-tion to which all material realities are subject, derives from this interpene-tration of spirit and matter. Of course, they still remain material and can be destroyed or they may even be so opaque that we fail to recognize them as art. But generally they manage to impart a luminosity that compels their preservation. They seem to leap out of time to become the timeless expres-sions of what constitutes time. Long after their creators have disappeared from history, works of art endure with an imperviousness that defies mor-tality. More than the transcendence that opens in any act of communica-tion between persons, art seems to retain transcendence within the very medium of its expression. This is what makes it such a precious realization of the inwardness accessible in all reality. Matter can become the means of self-expression for what cannot be contained in matter. Art is the event that calls attention to this potentiality because it has so perfectly actualized it. Transparence so utterly pervades the medium that it completely over-comes its finitude. We forget that notes are only sounds, words are only marks, and colors are only paint. The interpenetration of spirit and matter is so complete that nothing is left over. In the spellbinding event the whole-ness of reality is disclosed. More than the sacrament of meeting between persons, art is the sacrament within which the sacramental effect has fully taken place. The radiance of persons is for the moment made to appear within the non-personal. That is the miracle of revelation that art is.

Through art beauty stands apart from the person who apprehends it, as a permanence available to all other persons. Art provides therefore a unique avenue on the person who stands outside of all saying and yet is disclosed within that very saying. Through art we see that persons are not simply marked by the evanescence of their presence in time but that they also aspire to the permanence of truth that radiates beyond the persons who glimpse it. Beauty is the shining of truth that defeats time. It is because the struggle to bring forth beauty is of necessity in the service of truth that art can provide such reliable access to truth. We begin with the recognition that even when meaning has been lost and certainty has ebbed we are never without the guidance of art. Art is first a path of truth. This is surely why art has attained such eminence in a modernity marked by the loss of faith in the traditional symbolisms of truth. The privileged access of art depends neither on divine nor human authority but only on a readiness to trust its own inner hearing. Art rests on the faith that reality discloses itself to those who have ears to hear. It is a faith that is confirmed in the truth at which it arrives and nowhere outside of that resplendence itself. Art shows, second, that even the material elements of reality disclose the truth of beauty and the beauty of truth. Like science, art discovers that reality lies open to the person. But this means, third, that persons are the unique point in being in which mute material says what it otherwise could not say. In many respects the art required for matter to gain spirit is what art is about. The correlative is that the overhearing of what the world has to say is, fourth, made possible by its metaphoric predisposition. It is not simply that the artist reads in a personal perspective unconnected to the subject matter but that the latter is already prepared for the leap into the personal horizon. Metaphor is the confirmation that reality itself is metaphoric. Art is not apart from nature for it is nature reaching its self-conscious culmination.

Art Shines through the Loss of Spirit

It is no accident that the category of "art" is a modern development.[1] Prior to the opening of the modern world most artists were anonymous and their creations generally served the larger purposes of religion and power. All of that changes when artists acquire names and step forth in the authority of their own voices. No longer subordinate to institutional overseers, artists obey only the imperative of their own inspiration. The process of this change is of course gradual as artists continue to serve the Church, the state, and patrons, but eventually their emancipation is so complete that they fill commissions entirely at their own discretion. We no longer instruct artists what they are to create; we simply await their instruction of us through art. Such is the extraordinary stature acquired by art in the modern period that we might well regard it as a parallel to the astonishing independence gained by science. Both art and science have been released from all oversight but their own. The astonishing progress of science resulting from this liberation is a familiar staple of our world. But art too has demonstrated a prodigious inventiveness through the same autonomy. It is simply that "progress" is not an appropriate category for a field defined by the goal of producing what is timeless. What is not in doubt, however, is that art has established itself as an authority answerable to no one but itself. It is a differentiation worthy of being ranked with the greatest modern achievements, for we now see that art provides unparalleled access to the mystery of the whole in which we find ourselves. Prior to this modern elevation art was merely an auxiliary in the service of other paths of spiritual truth; it was not a path of truth of its own. Thus it is from the modern perspective that we can reconstruct the history of "art" before there was such a thing as art with its own autonomous authority.[2]

It is also from this modern differentiation of art that its philosophic recognition begins. Aesthetics and philosophy of art are modern innovations for, while Plato categorized the beautiful and Aristotle wrote his *Poetics*, neither regarded them as the core of their philosophic reflection.[3] It is in the modern era that aesthetics, like art, emerges as a separate field. One might even suggest that it was the openness to beauty that provided an answer to the epistemological straitjacket in which philosophy itself was held. Kant had concluded that our knowledge reaches only the phenomenal world accessed through sense intuition, never to reality as it is in itself. Locked within the categories of his understanding, the subject had no avenue to truth as such. It was only in the moral life that truth imposed itself in the form of duty uncontaminated by merely subjective perceptions, although this did not lead to any cognitive consequences. The latter would have to await the turn toward judgments of beauty in which we seem to simultaneously hold a subjective perception and assert it as universally valid. How was it possible for my personal taste to register truth? This was the question with which Kant's great *Critique of the Power Judgment* begins and, in the process, opens up a rich vein of reflection that would be extensively mined by his Idealist successors. For Kant it was enough to discover that at least at this point the wholly subjective coincided with the wholly objective.[4] Judgments of beauty are possible only because we already bring to bear criteria that cannot be derived from an enumeration of instances, no matter how exhaustive. Truth is not something at which we arrive, it is the very possibility of arrival. The step Kant hesitated to take was effected by his successors in reflecting on the possibility of Kant's own self-perception here. Judgments of beauty are possible because we are already constituted by the openness to beauty. Beauty is transparent to us because we are transparent to beauty. That still may not "explain" our access to beauty, as Kant and his followers insist, but it does begin to account for the impossibility of explanation. That, as Socrates was the first to inform us, is a mode of explanation.

The real response to Kantian hesitancy is to suggest that explanation is a misplaced category. We do not explain our apprehension of the beautiful for it is that apprehension that explains us. This was the move initiated by Schelling and Hegel, and made memorable in the latter's identification of art as one of the forms of absolute spirit.[5] What that designation means is of course still debated, but we do come close to its core in seeing it as an acknowledgment of the horizon within which our thinking of beauty occurs. Art is an access to the beautiful that accounts for itself. If there were a more fundamental mode, then art would not form a limiting horizon but rather be subsumed into what does. Sometimes Hegel has been taken as holding that art and religion, as two forms of absolute spirit, are eventually surpassed by the third, philosophy. But that reading flies in the face of the attention Hegel lavished on all three in his extensive lecture courses. It was in that context that he really demonstrated his conviction that each remains an irreplaceable mode of participation within the transparency of spirit. What is most notable from our point of view is that it is with Hegel that art gets its designation as a third dispensation, equivalent to the long-standing ones, of philosophy and revelation. The authoritative truth of art is validated, as befits the status of its emergence in the modern world. We should not be surprised to find, as Schelling and Hegel suggest, that art is a mode of religion or that religion is a mode of art, or that philosophy, as Kant was beginning to discover, finds its confirmation in art.[6] Each is a unique mode of saying what can only be said within its respective discourse. Philosophy merely enjoys the advantage of explicating after its own fashion what the other two have been able to convey in their equally incomparable way. It is an advantage in articulateness, not in authoritativeness.

In many respects it is art that possesses the greater force of truth since it steps forth without authority. What it has to say radiates without need to question its credentials. This is why Dostoevsky could assert through several of his characters that "beauty will save the world," a conviction made all the more compelling in an age in which faith has drained away and reason has undermined itself.[7] Art needs neither predispositions nor presuppositions. Its impact is direct, for it can find its way straight into our hearts. Without explanation, art simply is. That is its power. Faith and reason have frequently clothed themselves in its radiance for they sense its surpassing hold on us. One might even say that their truth can be revealed only through beauty, for it is only then that it has been revealed as the beauty of truth that is identical with the truth of beauty. Can truth be if it does not radiate? That is the question from which art springs, brushing aside the question of whether there is truth at all. Even what truth *is* is a question that hardly concerns art since the only truth it cares about is the truth that shines. Unconstrained by the anxiety that it might not even find its way toward the truth, art knows that it cannot guarantee a goal that can be reached only by arriving at it. Just as it requires no authentication after the fact, neither does it seek any assurances before it. Art lives within its own supreme self-confidence, even when the individual artist may be riddled by doubts about his or her capacity to accomplish the task. Doubts concern only the artist, not the validity of art itself. This is why even when the whole world is shaken, even when the faith sustaining civilization erodes, art nevertheless prevails. The death of God and the death of metaphysics cannot encompass the death of art.

It is this intimacy with the life-sustaining force of life that prompts art to assume leadership of the spirit.[8] Where previously it had been content to subordinate or coordinate its efforts with its more exalted partners, especially religion, now it is compelled to assume the mantle on its own. This is surely why art in the modern period has been propelled into the forefront of cultural leadership. Cult has become culture for that very reason. In the absence of a public cult that unites us art, both high and low, shapes the symbolic universe we inhabit.[9] Whether it is mass culture or art more self-consciously conceived, the power of sound and image and word is abundantly on display. The most notable aspect is that all of this occurs without superintendence, either political or spiritual, for the most part. We might say that modern society is the first thoroughly artistic civilization, that is, one in which its creativity is allowed almost complete liberty in constructing the world we inhabit. We may think of ourselves as living in a scientific age but science, despite its enormous impact, extends to only a very narrow elite. For the most part we remain as susceptible to superstition and irrationality, especially in our judgment of the results of science, as ever before. Art alone is capable of providing a semblance of that global rationality so indispensable to existence as a whole. Nowhere is this more evident than in the convergence between art and politics, the self-understanding of art as a force for social and political change. Art is in its essence a dissident movement, not merely through the accident of artists who become dissidents. Whether this assumption of political responsibility, including the unchecked liberty of expression implied within it, leads to great art remains a matter of debate. There may be good reason to conclude that art flourishes within more tightly constrained forms. Indeed, dissent is itself a moment that can only be sustained as long as the oppression lasts. What is not in doubt, however, is that art contains within itself the capacity to play such a leadership role. By its emanation from truth, art is singularly equipped to invoke the truth of a common public order.[10]

Art, if it is true to itself, speaks only with the voice of truth. This is why it is infallible. Art is incapable of subterfuge for when it puts itself in the service of an external power it ceases to be art. It can become propaganda but only at the cost of its art. To be true to itself art cannot permit even the slightest accommodation that would rob truth of its luster. Even the form or style it employs must remain within the truth at which it aims. Art cannot afford to clothe itself in a mode of expression no longer consistent with its content. Form and substance must be united within a luminous whole. This is the very point of the radiance at which art aims. It is what makes artists the most sure-footed guides to what in any historical epoch can be said; they know that the meaning of what is said cannot be separated from the means by which it is said. Truth can only radiate truthfully. That is the struggle at the core of the artist, to find the most honest means of saying what can only be said honestly. This is why art is a moral enterprise. In their lives artists may still be subject to as many, or even more, moral failings than the rest of us, but in their art they cannot countenance the slightest infraction. To do so would be to obviate the whole effort. This is why composers cannot simply write piano concertos in the manner of Mozart any longer, no more than poets can write epics along the lines of the *Iliad* or the *Odyssey*. If they attempt to do so the result is a pastiche that says nothing, for they must so thoroughly internalize the received forms that they have made them their own. They are no longer the forms of historical convention but their contemporary transformation. Even the low art of mass culture must remain consistent with the world in which it finds itself. Television programs cannot slavishly emulate models of an earlier era but must find their own distinct style of communication. Artists both low and high are the infallible barometers of the age, not simply because of their acute sensitivity to shifts of milieu, but much more because of the imperative under which they labor. If it is not true, then it is not art.[11]

The search for truth is undertaken in truth. That is the formidable source of artistic authority. It is why, as Solzhenitsyn announces, writers are entrusted with a global mandate more profound than any appointment or election can issue.[12] Speaking, not in the name of party or cause, artists must take their stand on the transparence of truth. This of course should not be confused with the political interventions of artists when, no longer practicing their art, they step forward to offer expertise they may or may not possess. Simply being an artist does not guarantee possession of the information, perspective, and insight required for social or political advocacy. It is only in the practice of their art that they possess the unerring sensitivity to truth that is their real public contribution. They testify to truth as such, thereby opening the space of the political. A common good, a public order, exists only because we are bound together in truth. What distinguishes great art is that the artist is prepared to set aside his or her own predilections in obedience to the truth mandated by art itself. The public space is illumined by a light that subterfuge cannot stand. Untruth, the lie that seeks to conceal the common world, cannot endure when its falsity is exposed by truth resplendent.[13] Art makes it impossible to lie because art cannot lie. That is the great contribution of art to the political, one that political actors themselves often feel compelled to recruit even at their peril. Art can be a dangerous quantity within the political world since it carries the possibility of exposing the loss of reality. Artists are in a certain sense the founders of states for they continually attest to the possibility of a re-founding within the dissolution of the present. The symbolic universe of the nation creates a common world only because the symbols emerge with the imprint of truth already stamped upon them. That work of distillation of truth is the work of art. It could not be further from the conventional picture of the mere production of cultural artifacts that in any case cannot be made but only revealed. Culture is, like cult, a revelation. Artists are its seers.

When culture ceases to be transparent it becomes the dead incubus that weighed so heavily on Nietzsche.[14] The burden can, he saw, become a danger to life, especially within modern societies that have for centuries elevated art to the status of a third testament. The irony is that this indifference is the polar opposite of what art is, as Nietzsche demonstrated by calling for an artistic renovation as his response. A rebirth of tragedy was intended to retrieve cult from culture. He asked his contemporaries to consider that "we are already images and artistic projections for the true creators of art, and that our highest dignity lies in our significance as works of art—for only as an *aesthetic phenomenon* is existence and the world eternally justified" (183).[15] Greek tragedy was the historical moment in which the transparence of human existence for the cult that underpinned it shone forth and might do so again, if the appropriate aesthetic vehicle could acquire public resonance. Wagner's music dramas proved inadequate to the task as they lapsed too readily into mere spectacle, no longer evoking the living truth that inspired them. Nietzsche's idea of the mutual penetration of life and art was the project that now defined his whole life. Disappointment with Wagner did not constitute disillusion with art, for art endured beyond its own disappointments.[16] Even in its failures art proved to be indispensable. We cannot think outside of art because art remains one of the fundamental paths of thinking. Its distinctive feature is its transparence to the truth from which it arises, for art is the radiance of truth. That is the beauty at which it aims and from which it emerges. As such art always retains awareness of its own genesis. Science is premised on the forgetting of the self that reaches for the touchstone of objectivity. Art is the more embracing mode that is capable of comprehending itself, at least to the extent of knowing that it arises from what it is not. The work of art is other than the movement that gives birth to it, yet it preserves the trace of its self-conscious gestation. This is what marks it as a preeminent epiphany of the person. Art is not only a revelation of the person but is simultaneously a disclosure of the process that constitutes the person, a process that even then cannot be fully fathomed. Hegel was right in announcing art as one of the supreme moments when consciousness becomes self-consciousness.

The Demonstration of Being as Personal

What is notable about the emergence of self-consciousness is that it is not simply an event within consciousness. Contrary to the impression that even Hegel's language seems to leave, self-consciousness is not the fruit of introspection. Rather, as in the process of artistic creation, self-consciousness is glimpsed in the struggle to liberate spirit within matter. Michelangelo's statue of the *Prisoners*, a group of figures left in an incompletely carved block of marble, captures what art is. The artist does not have a conception in advance that he imposes on a passively receptive medium. Rather, he works on the material in order to discover what is contained within it. Or conversely, as Michelangelo seemed to suggest, it is the material that is engaged in a struggle to disclose what is inward, a struggle that can only reach its goal through the cooperation of the artist. In this sense the artist serves the material, rather than the material the artist. As servant of a medium that cannot find its own voice until it is made to sing, the artist bears responsibility for the inchoate possibility of disclosure hidden within it. Yet the artist does not know in advance what the content of that disclosure will be. He or she may start with intimations, may indeed be led by them, but it is only in the final denouement that disclosure occurs, a disclosure that could not occur in any other way. That is the moment of recognition that seems almost a mutual recognition. While the artist recognizes in the fully formed work the inspiration that drew forth his or her efforts, there is also a sense in which the material might be said to recognize what was contained unbeknownst to itself. The prisoners are set free; matter is transformed into spirit. This is of course a metaphor and, like all metaphors, is endlessly revealing and concealing, but it does call attention to the continuity between the realms of spirit and matter nowhere more closely demonstrated than within the artistic process.

Science attests to the miracle of mind grasping the intelligibility of that which is unintelligible to itself. In that sense mind can easily infer its own superiority over brute inertness. Our prevailing materialism is merely an eccentric oversight prompted by the very success of our material penetration. Physical explanations have become so powerful that we have difficulty resisting the tendency to reduce explanation itself to those terms. We are uncomfortable accepting the evident superiority of mind over matter because we have no way of holding them together within a unity. Without a divine creator we lack the surety of our own divine status in the order of things. Dualism, as the opaque coexistence of mind and matter is called, is the kind of tortuous position that only philosophers could love. Common sense cannot abide such a disconnect. For art, however, an unbridgeable duality is impossible since the mutual penetration of mind and matter is what it proclaims.[17] Science may not make thematic its own condition of possibility, the mutual openness of mind and matter, but art is engaged in its perpetual demonstration. The condition of its possibility is drawn into the foreground of art, while in science it recedes into the background. This is the metaphysical significance of art as Kant and his successors made clear. Almost as soon as Kant had established the impossibility of metaphysical knowledge, art began to emerge as one of the paths (together with the moral life) along which a more expansive perception of the whole is possible.[18] But Kant hesitated to take the next step needed to resolve the duality of mind and matter that still blocked the way. It was Fichte, Schelling, Hegel, and others who took the bold step of declaring that reality could not be resolved into either its mental or material manifestations but had to be viewed as the unity that underpinned both of them. They knew that the condition of the possibility of mind *and* of matter could not be grasped simply in terms of either one and for this reason they were content to admit its unknowability, variously designated as the "I," "identity," or the "absolute."[19] As a consequence their brilliant speculations were destined to languish under a reputed impenetrability, occasionally pierced by an equally brilliant reader, but only now coming to be viewed as the seminal achievement they are. It may be worth noting in passing that one of the factors responsible for the notorious density of German Idealism is an inability to settle on a language appropriate to the intuition from which it drew. The Idealists understood the centrality of the person to the metaphysical dynamic they tried to elaborate but, without a personalist language, they fell back on the terminology of a reified metaphysics they intended to replace. It is this formidable linguistic deficit that the present study aims at remedying.

The one exception to the reputed obscurity of the Idealists and, thus, a path often recommended for piercing it, is their treatment of art.[20] More clearly than anywhere else, it was art that demonstrated the truth of their thesis of the continuity between mind and matter, a continuity that could not be adequately perceived from the perspective of either one. This insight is so thoroughly exemplified by art that it was not surprising that Schelling made it the centerpiece in his first mature formulation, *The System of Transcendental Idealism* (1801), and Hegel elevated it to a status equivalent to philosophy and religion as a mode of absolute spirit. In a sense, art so perfectly exemplified the thesis that it rendered its metaphysical formulation almost redundant. Art is the continuous demonstration of the mutual permeability of the material and the spiritual. The interplay between them is a profound inexhaustible dynamic in which the initiative can never simply lie on one side to the exclusion of the other. Sheer inert matter seems to be straining to reveal what it cannot reveal, just as it does when it yields up its secrets to the probing of science. The difference is that the relationship is even more intimate, for the artist could hardly know the direction to follow before the promptings reach him or her. To speak of a yearning to reveal itself even within the inorganic is a metaphor, but it does call attention to the extent to which metaphor forms the boundary for art's own self-understanding. Ultimately there is no non-metaphorical analysis of metaphor for the same reason that art represents the limiting absolute of spirit.[21] We cannot step outside the boundary constituted by art, nor understand it in terms of anything other than itself. The straining toward self-revelation, no matter how metaphorical, is not just an inescapable dimension of the artistic experience. It is an indispensable condition. Without the stirring of imagination initiated by nature, inorganic as well as organic, there would be nothing to draw forth the creative adventure. A bicycle seat could suggest the head of a bull to Picasso, just as a few notes could prompt the "shepherds farewell" from which Berlioz elaborated his oratorio "L'Enfance du Christ." The resulting work can neither be attributed nor reduced to one side alone. Far from mind merely imprinting itself on matter, it is just as much the case that matter absorbs mind into itself.

The event is a revelatory overflowing of the boundaries assigned to spirit and matter. Radiance demolishes their fixity, as the material medium is released from gravity and the elusiveness of spirit acquires maximal presence. Nothing accounts for the event but the event itself, which is just as much of a surprise to the artist as to any other observer. Preparation of the material is as indispensable as the self-preparation of the artist. But the epiphany, when it occurs, exceeds all expectations, rendering the finitude of its ingredients incommensurable to their transformation. The often-invoked analogy with divine creation is not without validity. God creates the world out of nothing, while the artist creates a world out of what is apparently nothing. Perhaps the "nothing" in each case is not so totally bereft, perhaps a secret bond unites it with the fullness that can be revealed in no other way. What is clear is that the revelation in its flash establishes the nothingness of the material substratum. The value of the paint or stone or paper or the labor expended cannot be compared to the beauty that shines forth from them. Solid materiality is no longer as inert as it had seemed, once it becomes the vehicle for the shining of the immaterial. Neither spiritual nor material, the conjunction powerfully attests to the non-ultimacy of their separation. The mystery of our existence as spiritual beings inhabiting a material universe is not dissolved but deepened through the glimpse of their integration. Whether it is necessary to have recourse to the overarching metaphysical concepts favored by the German Idealists is hardly the issue, for art itself definitively establishes that toward which mere speculation limps. To gain a more consonant articulation of the event that art is, it is necessary to draw closer to the revelatory opening at its core.

Art is ineluctably a disclosure of the person. Terms like "spiritual" and "material" are still at a remove from the elusiveness of art and thus from its concrete actuality. To see this we have only to ask how it is possible for colors or sounds or marks on paper to "say" anything. In themselves they are mute. But to respond that mind "recognizes" itself within them is to beg the question of how that is possible, precisely what is at issue.[22] Only the horizon of the person begins to point the way, for it is the mark of persons to become present in that which cannot contain them. The paradox of the inexpressible is routinely surmounted. To call this the activity of spirit is already to endow it with more presence than it has, as if it was a slightly more rarified version of materiality. The language of persons helps to avoid this misplaced concreteness because it reminds us of the intimately familiar evanescence within which we live. There can be no mistaking the non-presence of what we grasp as non-presence. At the same time it enables us to see the material world differently than from a strictly materialist point of view. Now the realm of opaqueness is replete with the possibility of enchantment that is indistinguishable from the enchantment that art so powerfully affirms. We do not live in a world of fixed quantifiable objects but in a medium of remarkable fluidity for the disclosure of mysteries beyond and within it. Mere matter has been personalized. In that realization matter has been transformed for it is no longer "merely" what it seemed to be. Now even the physical world partakes of the fluctuating movement of a presence that becomes present by way of its absence. Nothing can be drawn into the world of personhood without being touched by the dynamic of revelation within non-revelation. This of course does not mean that we personalize the world of nature with individual presences, as in the magical world of myth, but it does mean that even when we depart from the mode of myth we can never sever ourselves from the astonishment of revelation in which myth begins. Art is the form that myth assumes when there is no myth. This is the source of its shamanistic power.

We still live in an enchanted universe as the continuing appeal of fairytales, legends, and heroic exploits attests.[23] In the earlier consideration of science we had occasion to stress that it is a similar capacity for enchantment that drives its ever-deeper investigations too. Disclosure is the drama equivalently enacted in art and science. Nature does not reveal for it "loves to hide"; it will only yield up its secrets to one who probes it more deeply by going within it. Both art and science are different modes of that going within, putting oneself aside to put oneself in place of the other. A reading of the natural, whether analytic or metaphorical, enables it to say what it otherwise cannot say. The operation is emphatically not a reading in, but a letting be and a letting say in which the inquirer is more midwife than observer. In the quest for truth the last thing one wants to do is to impose a truth, for then it is no longer true. Rather, it is the obligation of both the artist and the scientist to be true first of all to the material that draws her or him into its disclosure. Her or his work is to give voice to that which initially has no voice, although such a work would be impossible if the natural world utterly lacked a voice. A hidden nature ultimately wills to be found. The finding is therefore not a merely objective event outside of it, but intimately connected to a drama of self-revelation deeply embedded within it. The disjunction of matter and spirit against which German Idealism struggled so valiantly, and which has wracked the philosophic tradition since its Greek inception, begins to fall away. The separation between the two simply ceases when they are seen as indissoluble dimensions of a revelation that can only occur through non-revelation. A nature that loves to hide proclaims it loves to disclose.

Within that engagement science is notable for its remarkable lack of self-consciousness. In contrast, art is distinguished by its incomparable sensitivity to the process that makes art possible. One might almost say that that is its principal theme or, at least, the prevailing background to all that it foregrounds. For art reality is inescapably metaphoric. Science may give voice to the silence of nature, but art is made possible by the address that it receives. Each is an overhearing, although it makes all the difference whether questions are asked of nature, as science does, or one simply opens to the self-questioning of nature, as art does. The latter is the more intimate relationship. It is why poetry can say more than physics about the universe in which we find ourselves. There are no preset restrictions to the trail of evidence available; instead, there is the reaching further to where the trail begins and to what is there before there is a beginning. Science too is not immune to such aspirations but its discipline requires a firmer resistance against them, a resistance that for that very reason means that science can never quite suppress the poetic undertow. When the questions of science have been answered there is still a hunger for the something more that cannot be disclosed in its terms. It is, in other words, the process of disclosure that is fundamental. The difference is that science is incapable of relating to it at the personal level to which art responds. The capacity for a far deeper insight into nature through art arises, not from a superior grasp of evidence, but from its opening concession that no accounting for data can penetrate to the unaccountable.[24] Art can access the inaccessible because it operates within a personal horizon. That is, within a horizon that, far from incorporating the other as object, reaches the other only by submission to the impossibility of reaching it. Art is more self-aware than science because its revelations emerge from the depth of non-revelation.

A non-present presence hovers continually in art. This is the source of its inexhaustibility but, even more, it is what renders art so uniquely personal. Science prides itself on repeatability, art never ceases to be a singular work. Nature that hides does not just conceal itself indifferently, it rather awaits the voice of the unique one who might overhear it. The identity of artists matters in a way that the identity of scientists does not. For the latter the discovery is what counts, for the former the discovery is inseparable from them. The reason has nothing to do with prestige or vanity, but with the highly personal character of the artistic enterprise. Only Shakespeare could write the works of Shakespeare for, even if they were penned by Johnson or Bacon, then one or the other would become the inimitable bard. The artist who hears does so with his or her own unique inwardness, otherwise it would be impossible to hear at all. Just as it is only persons who can know other persons, so it is only the person who can sense what comes to him or her from beyond all sensibility. Acuteness of hearing and sight, dexterity of hand and imagination, are all useful equipment for an artist, but they do not bring about an encounter with the transcendent. For that the artist must be prepared to open his or her whole self. Only inwardly can that which is utterly inward be encountered. The unique one beyond all repetition can alone receive that which uniquely addresses him or her. Singular responsibility arises because of the singular call. But it is because what is said addresses the core of the person, the person as such, that its resonance can also be received by all other persons.

Art is universal. It is universal because of its singularity. Each is addressed in his or her utterly irreplaceable inwardness. We cannot all become scientists but we do all have the makings of artists, even if we are relatively untalented. The unmusical can still "hear" the music. Kierkegaard's puzzling expression that the individual exceeds the universal has particular relevance here. Beyond the universal features that distinguish us from one another there is the pure inwardness that can respond to every other inwardness because each is wholly individual. Each person is a whole capable of knowing all other persons as wholes. Indeed, we do not just know other persons; we live in them and they in us. Above all, this is what is on display in the work of art. The artist may not be there to speak to us but the work does and we are able to hear it in more or less the same way as the artist heard it. One heart speaks to another. It matters far less what is said than that it is said. Indeed, what can be said that has not been said in such a meeting where everything has been said? It is at once a meeting of singulars that is at the same time universally open to all singulars. The meeting ground is irreplaceable personal uniqueness that the work of art brings with it. Hegel was right in thinking of it as universal like religion and philosophy, transcending the time and place of its creation toward all human beings. But it is unlike religion and philosophy in that it has no universal formulation. Each work is unique and attests to the unique inwardness of its truth. This is why, as we noted, art cannot be untrue; it can only fail to radiate its inspiration.

The key to that radiance is that the work transcends its creator. This is not just in the sense that it survives afterward or that it takes on a life of its own, but also in the sense that its depths cannot be fully plumbed by the one who brings it forth. Could Cervantes ever fully explain even to himself all that is going on in *Don Quixote* or Beethoven give us everything that is within his Ninth Symphony? Homer is lost in the mists of time but the *Iliad* and the *Odyssey* are as vivid as ever. This is not just the gift of memorable characterization but of an even deeper gift for the uncharacterizable. What could not be fully captured within the work is nevertheless retained as its inexhaustible source. Even if Homer had been able to write more epics he could never have exhausted the inspiration that drew him. As a man he might have exhausted himself but as an artist he could scarcely reach the limit of what in every work he could never reach. He knew more than he could say. The greatness of his saying is that he nevertheless managed to say it. He said it in the only way that it could be said, as the overflowing that the work fails to capture and, yet, in this way manages to powerfully intimate. He could not understand it fully, nor can we. This is why he wrote, as it is why art exists. As a man he seems overshadowed by his work. This is surely a strange conception since the man is indisputably the creator of the work and he might well have many more tucked up his sleeve or, like Schubert, "unfinished" in his bottom drawer. But this hardly matters for they too point to the same result. They are better than he can create. The presence of what cannot become presence but only personally accessed has become so powerfully present that it glows forever in the work. Art is what has escaped the vicissitudes of existence, not merely by way of the response that preserves it, but in the far more integral sense of what no longer exists because it simply is. This is what Heidegger saw as the event of the work of art.[25] He took Van Gogh's famous painting of a pair of old shoes as his example for they make present a whole world that is nowhere present in the work. Yet Heidegger's assimilation of absence to the disclosure of being still does not quite account for the possibility of our reception of it. Nor does it account for the disclosure of what cannot be disclosed. In both respects art is an ineluctable modality of persons.

Art as the Being of Persons

Heidegger is aware of art as the disclosure of being but he resists the suggestion that persons might provide the avenue toward an understanding of the event. His reasoning is that persons would then be treated as beings apart from being, the mistake he himself had committed in privileging *Dasein* over *Sein* in *Being and Time*. The problem with this approach is that it never returns to examine its original assumption that persons are beings, rather than the point at which being is glimpsed. As a consequence even the event of being begins to take on the aspect of a pure event without any reference to persons for whom and through whom the event occurs. That an extensive meditation can be carried on without any hint of its carriers is testament to the penetration of Heidegger's philosophy. One can develop a fully personalist philosophy without the acknowledgment of persons, but at the cost of obscuring its connection with the ordinary dimensions of existence. The absence of any moral or political philosophy is a criticism against which Heidegger had to frequently respond. His own political misjudgments are the most damning indictment of the philosophical disorientation arising from the exclusive focus on being. A less catastrophic but still notable oversight occurs in the treatment of art when it is viewed apart from the persons who give it birth. While no one wishes to see art reduced to the facts of biography, neither can it be elevated to a status utterly unconditioned. To understand art as the event of being, as that which ever escapes and transforms the conditions of its existence, we need more than a meditation on the pure dynamics of disclosure. We must anchor it in the only instance of the nonexistence of what *is* that we know. Art must be seen as emblematic of the being of persons.

The difficulty is always to ensure that we do not look upon it as merely the product of their activity in the same way that we casually attribute ownership of what they do to persons. Art is different in that it expresses the person more fully than anything else, that is, as the inexpressible person. Neither a sign nor an object, art cannot be defined by its utility since its very purpose is to transcend all purpose as that which gives purpose. This is why the work of art takes on a life of its own. It continues to vibrate with a life beyond the life of the artist. Of all human creations art comes closest to the expression of the self as self, precisely what no expression can accomplish. It is a feat of the impossible, a "raid on the inarticulate," a marvel eclipsing its source. We should not be surprised therefore to discover that Heidegger is not alone in thinking that it can be treated as fully formed from the head of being. To the extent that art always surpasses the artist, indeed, to the extent that that is its central feature, the biographical details of its genesis become irrelevant. Art exists in an empyrean realm of its own to which mere mortals are only fitfully admitted to perform its bidding unknowingly. The problem with this notion of "art for art's sake" is not that it is wholly untrue, for this is precisely the transcendence from which art radiates, but that it is not the whole truth, for the great work is the fruit of a capacity for self-transcendence indiscernible before the event.[26] Frail human beings become the vehicle for an epiphany of truth beyond all that might be expected of them. A great part of the astonishment that art evokes derives from just that rupture with the finitude of its beginning. To the extent that art is housed in the museum of the inestimable it loses its capacity to connect with the ordinary life of mere human beings. How can we be surprised by the genius that has come to be expected? At that point art ceases to be understood for it can only be understood as the unexpected.

Art is the radiance of the personal. It cannot be separated from the personal that radiates. Heidegger glimpsed this but he sought to assimilate it to the anonymity of being, overlooking being as personal. The appearing, the unconcealing, the shining he attributed to being is inconceivable except as the being of the person who is ever more than is disclosed. Art is among the supreme affirmations of this. But it has often been disserved by the very categorization of art. The emergence of art as a distinct category was, we have seen, one of the results of its increasingly authoritative role in the modern world. A consequence of this elevation was ironically a decline in its accessibility. The impact of its truth waned with the waxing of its prestige. Professionalization, ever a barrier to understanding, plays a particularly insidious role when it absorbs the most elementally human. Art is a universally accessible language because it is spoken by every human being. We are all artists even though we do not all create art, especially of the kind that receives official approbation. Artists themselves never tire of reminding us of this in the contemporary proliferation of the art of the found, the ephemeral, and the everyday. Art that shocks attests to the somnolence of art. The conventions of art, the forms and frames in which it has been so neatly deposited, have become a principal obstacle to art as such. Expansion of the boundaries of the permissible, whatever one may think of it as a tactic, is one of the enduring dynamics of art's capacity to astonish. Why should we be surprised by the antics of our contemporaries when Michelangelo's *David* still takes our breath away, as it was intended to do? No doubt this is true of all great art, but we would be even more amazed if we consider it, not as an immortal work, but as a block of marble with the good fortune of receiving just the right touch of the hand. It is the sort of miracle we might encounter around any corner so long as we have not cordoned it off. Art is the event in which matter takes wing. It happens not just in museums but in our daily immersion in the world, otherwise the ineffable would never have been realized.

In many respects "art" is the great obstacle to art. We forget that our history of art is largely a construction retrospectively from the point at which art became a separate category within life. The danger then is that it becomes a category separate from life, and then art ceases to be the flash of transparence. Opaqueness conceals it. No such problems afflicted the Paleolithic symbol makers or the Neolithic cave painters, who were not artists but apocalyptic visionaries of meaning. The images they limned were not intended to decorate but to invoke powers beyond the limits of their mastery. In subordinating themselves to the forces of the cosmos they effected a miracle; the divine had become present within the realm of human access. This is why the positioning of the drawings and paintings had nothing to do with their admiration but everything to do with their sacral function.[27] Often the work is hardly visible from vantage points on the floor. Art has to do with the gods, not with human beings. It is truth that drives their efforts rather than the art displayed in the process. Yet it is the latter that accomplishes their goal. The numinous radiates in the paintings with a luminosity that reaches all the way forward to our own time. We cannot look upon them without being touched by their power. Their fears and longings are not our fears and longings, but both of us have been released by the ascent into the supererogatory that has happened. Through beauty we too have been saved. We might even be forgiven for thinking that our cave artists aimed at contact with the beautiful as our conventional history of art suggests. Art may not have been differentiated but art was powerfully embedded in life. To miss this encompassing setting by making of it only an aspiration for beauty is already to rob it of the raw vitality from which the discernment of beauty is possible. A disconnected beauty may still work its charm but it does not strike us dumb with the force that it might. Living beauty is the truth at which art aims as it ever runs the risk of affixing it as the beauty of art.

What saves art from the slide into the mundane, what preserves it as the radiance of the more than can be contained, is that it exists within the mode of the personal. In that sense it scarcely exists at all, just as persons elude the parameters that seem to contain them. Art overflows in the same way. It is a resounding declaration that materiality at its apex, subsumed within the non-utility of spirit, partakes of the same liberation from presence. For that reason art, if it has been reached in the work, has slipped the surly bonds encasing it. That which has failed to reach the radiance at which it aimed falls back into the gravitational pull of the merely useful. The secret of Haydn's music as he labored in the employment of the Esterhazys, a shrewd investment in the prestige calculated to advance their political ambitions, is that it bears no relation to the conditions that sustained it. This is why when one visits Eisentstadt today it is not the memory of the Esterhazys that receives prominence but the glory of the house musician they retained. It is the Haydnsaal that now is featured where the Esterhazys sought to endow their familial eminence. One would scarcely even recall their name if it had not been linked forever with that of Haydn. It is the music of the latter that escapes time and place to deepen and delight the human spirit in ever-widening circles of diffusion. The influence of art reaches far more than the influence of politics. Haydn has more divisions, not because he commands material forces, but because he does not. The danger that the music might lapse into the silence of the instruments that produce it is hardly a great threat since the music does not exist within such tangibilities. It is what has escaped them.

Not even the sounds encompass the music. Certainly the music cannot be explained in terms of the specific frequencies in all their variegated multiplicity. Notes on the score cannot contain the music even though they are the most effective means of recalling it. This is obvious when one considers how the music is composed. It does not begin with annotations but with itself, the music that is heard inwardly before it can be made by any instruments. Not of course that the inner hearing is sufficient, for it only takes on a reality when it is made in the air and heard with the ears. But the hearing is still not within the external organs. They are only the vibrating media through which the inner hearing recurs. The music that cannot die, that lives eternally, is born again in the physical space we inhabit and yet it cannot belong within it, any more than we do. Art is not just the aspiration toward immortal creation. It is a possibility for beings that are mortal immortals. Art is the being of persons and it brings the character of that being more fully into view. Without art we would not know who we are. If we think of persons as disclosing themselves by way of what does not disclose them, then art is their supreme instantiation. Art, we may say, is the highest possibility of self-disclosure precisely because it does not disclose a self. Rather, art discloses the beyond from which the self acquires definition. Great art is thus selfless, the outpouring of self through which the self reaches its utmost. In the end there is no self but only the beauty that it loves so intensely that it forgets itself. What is glimpsed inwardly is not really inward at all, but the container of all that we know inwardly. We are not adrift in existence without direction as if we had been cast free to wander aimlessly through time, for in every moment we are held fast by what is more real than we are ourselves. But we do not know this until it has been discovered. Art is the event that illuminates what makes art itself possible. This is its epiphany. John Paul II, in his nocturnal wandering in the Sistine Chapel, sees the convergence of Michelangelo's vision with the vision of God in the beginning of Genesis as the path available to every person.[28]

Existence as Metaphor

Plato was probably the first to think through the encompassing role of beauty. In the *Symposium* and elsewhere Socrates reminds his interlocutors that we can recognize the many beautiful things in existence only in light of the beautiful as such. They participate in beauty without possessing it completely, just as we too have a partial grasp sufficient for apprehending beauty within them. Neither from the side of the known nor the knower does beauty come fully into view, yet it remains the indispensable condition for anything to be or to be seen as beautiful. Such a formulation might well have been sufficient to distinguish the situation in which we find ourselves in regard to the beautiful, the true, or the good. The ceaseless fluidity of the dialogues did much to preserve the necessarily elusive qualities of a reflection that grapples with its own limits. Along the way, however, a concession was made with fatal consequences for the unfolding of the history of philosophy. The form or idea of beauty was pronounced, and seized upon as the indubitable fixity within the dynamic of thought thinking itself. Metaphysics got under way as the construction of what could not be constructed because it was presupposed in the endeavor, while the transcendence of what could not be reached gained the solidity of transcendentals. What was lost was the process by which Plato had arrived at his insight into the beautiful as such. He had failed to anchor it in the horizon of the person through which he had received it. Without a personalist language it is difficult to retain the dynamic of disclosure that ever reaches and recedes from its goal.[29] Beauty is then what is found in objects by means of an idea we unfailingly carry around with us. Good and truth are both subject to the same unexamined assertion of competence that, as soon as it is scrutinized, begins to fall apart. We realize that there would be no possibility of finding unless what is sought could be neither lost nor found. It is within the oscillation of closure and disclosure of the human person that beauty is revealed.

What is sought in every instance is already known but not in such a way that it can be held firmly before us. It is only through the holding before us that beauty is beheld, although that beauty always falls short of the beauty that draws our seeking. Yet we would not know the beauty by which we are guided if we did not yield to its promptings to fashion its image. Art is the expression of a self that surpasses the self with which it begins. Thus, it is indispensable to the disclosure of who we are. There would be no possibility of disclosure unless what is to be revealed is already present, but there would be no need for disclosure if we already knew what it was. Persons, we have emphasized, reveal themselves by not revealing themselves in what they say or do. At the same time they seek to approach more closely the fullest reflection of who they are, that is, as persons. For God this is the creation of other persons. He gives himself in creating an other person; the work of redemption has its beginning in the first moment of creation. We cannot pour ourselves out so completely as to create an other person, but we do give ourselves completely to other persons. Art is the gift of self-giving somehow made permanent in material. Unlike the work of God it is not a living, breathing creation, but it does vibrate with the spirit from which it originated. In this way it is sent out into the world with an independent existence. Who we are as persons has become a little clearer to us; we are reflected in the work produced. From almost complete invisibility we have become slightly more visible to ourselves and to others. Transparence has been advanced, not completed. With God the situation is different. He begins with transparence; he need not create to discover who he is, yet he does for the sake of those others who emerge as a consequence. To say that he seeks to reveal his love to them is not quite accurate since it is his love that has placed them beyond even the reach of his love. They are free.

Art thus aspires to what only God can accomplish. That is, the creation of free beings impervious to the wishes of the creator. For us the works remain too close by and too dependent on their originators. We cannot withdraw so easily behind them. The best we can attain is the relative independence of a work whereby it seems to say more than the author intended or, perhaps, was even capable of saying. Then a genuine revelation has occurred, a rupture with all that might have been expected, and we see how much the creator is dependent on the creation. With God the revelation of himself to himself has already fully taken place. Nothing more is left for everything is present. For us the transparence is only partial and, thus, all the more necessarily incremental. We do not live in the divine transparence but we do live within its metaphor. Indeed, metaphor is the luminosity that can only be rendered metaphorically. The halting steps by which we disclose in creating and create in disclosing are contained within an illumination shining behind a glass darkly. We do not see the light, yet we are unmistakably led by it. That it is not ours is evident by the surprise of what emerges under its guidance. Looking back we cannot explain how we brought forth what we had scarcely envisaged in advance, and discover that we had no full or proper conception of the inspiration under which we labored. We felt and fumbled and fashioned our way toward the creation of what now astonishes us and that, as its creators, we cannot fully comprehend. Art is the indispensable path for us to articulate what cannot be fully articulated. The guiding thread had been the line of metaphor that points beyond itself.

Transparency, the self-revelation toward which art leads, cannot be grasped. It is rather the case that we are grasped by it. God is transparency, we grapple toward transparency by means of the transparency that draws us. This is why God's creation is a shining forth that need not return to its source, while our creation is a reflection of the source back to itself.[30] Yet even that small revelation could not have occurred if we were not led by a luminosity greater than ourselves. In many respects this astonishment, the "greater than," is the central theme of art. It is the path along which art unfolds as it glimpses what it had not glimpsed before and labors to bring forth what it had not brought forth before. We have already mentioned the promptings that come to the artist from the material on which he or she works, a dimension so prominent that it often seems that the artist struggles to uncover what has long lain buried within materiality. The figures imprisoned within the block of marble cry out, but how does the artist hear them? He cannot even see them for they have not yet appeared. Yet he does see them inwardly as a possibility that eludes the fixity of the material substrate. He grasps them before they are present through metaphor or, rather, it is metaphor that makes present that which is not present. This is its indispensable role in art. Metaphor is the pivot around which the life of the person revolves, the means by which art is definitive of the person. To reveal what cannot be revealed metaphor steps forward. The prisoners that are not prisoners are grasped by the leap of analogy that bridges impossibility. It is by means of metaphor that the impermeability of matter is rendered transparent. No longer is imagination blocked by the solidity in which it is located but instead roams with abandon. Metaphor is the very possibility of art. Before we are artistic beings we are first and foremost analogical beings. Through metaphor we possess the key that opens reality in all its multiply variegated directions.[31]

We are borne along by the intimations that reach us before we are even aware of them, although they could not affect us unless we had already carried them secretly within. Human beings are inveterate symbol makers. As far back as we can find our earliest ancestors they are engaged in the creation of images that are not what they are.[32] They stand for something else. What this means is not just that the earliest humans lived in relation to a space and time other than the one they occupied, but that they had simultaneously elevated their environment into a realm other than it was. To live in relation to an "environment," we have suggested, is to be no longer contained by it. Heidegger made a great deal of the different affinities with the world effected by living beings, concluding that it was only man that properly had a world because he was not simply in it.[33] What Heidegger did not elucidate was the depth beyond the possibility of human detachment, for it is not a mere standing over against that defines the relationship. It is rather an immersion in which what is hidden is brought to light, an illumination that does not just consist of the subject shining a light. The process is one of self-disclosure of the world that yet lacks a self. The person becomes the voice of the world, not in terms of some mysterious mandate, but in the sense that the world actually does speak. Indeed, the person would hardly have anything to say unless the world spoke through him or her. Certainly it is never a matter of reading in what is not there but of reading what is. What else can reading be if it is not a reading of what cannot simply be read in? We do not instruct the world but are rather instructed by it. This is the whole point of the exercise in which it is the world that discloses what it cannot say because it merely points.[34]

Mute physical presence is, in other words, no longer mute. It partakes of the radiance of the person whose own radiance is enhanced by it. That which points is no longer simply present in the same substantial fashion;

its significance has evanesced toward that which is not present. Metaphor is thus the participation of all things in the being of the personal as that which is not what it is. The only difference is that the metaphoric does not recognize itself as such. Persons are distinguished by their transparence. So the participation of the metaphoric lacks only that last degree of self-consciousness, a lack that renders its disclosure all the more poignant. The intimacy of the connection of persons with the non-personal reaches its culmination in this moment of mutuality short of full mutuality. The otherness that is lacking in the other is supplied by the artist who personifies the forces of the world. This is no mere device of art, dispensable once the occasion has passed. It is an enduring feature of metaphor in which all saying presupposes a speaker, not as a logical necessity, but as a personal imperative. That which points without saying already speaks from a depth that cannot be plumbed. The impersonal is the personal in its purest utterance. The line between the two begins to be obliterated as we reflect, not just on the incapacity of bare physicality to speak, but even of the self-aware to finally declare himself or herself. Communication, as the miracle by which heart speaks to heart, is not limited by the impossibility of the means to convey what is conveyed. The self that is beyond the self is as fully proclaimed by the silence of the natural world. Indeed, it is more fully proclaimed because it bears no claim to adequacy for the task. Poetry is the transmission of the ineffable. This is why Shostakovich could conclude his last symphony, a series of songs about death, with an affirmation of art as the only sure path toward immortality.

It is made possible by the poetry that is disclosed before any poet arrives on the scene, otherwise there would be no possibility of arrival. The advent of poetry is sustained by the intensity of the urge to communicate prior to the poet's own inner prompting. Love is called forth by the sheer self-effacement of the merely present. But how do we know that this is not a projection of wish fulfillment? How do we know that it is not just a metaphor? Whence does metaphor derive its truth? These are the questions that arise particularly when the event is viewed from the outside. These are the questions of those who wish to have answers before they have entered into the conversation, that is, before they have really been asked. Their obliqueness is sufficiently evident by the extent to which they are precisely the questions that art itself seeks to answer. Art, we have emphasized, carries no verification within it other than the truth of its self-evidence. It is in the authentication of its metaphor that the issue is engaged. Why is it not a reading in rather than a reading of? Certainly nothing in nature establishes that the sun is the benevolent ruler over the whole of space or that the moon governs the passage of time through which we live. Nothing says that the sky is higher or the Earth is lower, for all is relative to one's viewpoint. Science has already disabused us of our heliocentric prejudice as well as our evolutionary self-importance. What then can the human power of symbol making say that is any longer true, that is not just the vapor of sheer egocentrism? We may say that we still live within the rhythms of the cosmos, its cycles of birth and death, as well as its demarcation of qualitative differences in space. But the kind of answer given by such a great comparative religionist as Mircea Eliade still begs the question of that primordiality.[35] Why are we susceptible to the experiential pulls that are as archaic as those that formed our earliest ancestors? It is one thing to assert such continuities, it is another to perceive their irremovability. Art surpasses symbol making in carrying the source of its validity within it, a force that renders such reservations irrelevant.

Art is not about life. It is life. That is its truth, as Nietzsche understood. The point is not merely to symbolize, to hold at a distance in the mode of representation, but to enter into what is symbolized and represented. This is the point at which person knows person, or there at least hovers before us the dim presentiments of otherness. Either way the encounter is by way of indirection and, thus, can only take place by way of metaphor, whose constants must be continually lifted up from the inexorable lapse into the routine. This is the role of art. It makes symbols live and, therefore, must continually explore and expand and invent new variations. The fecundity of metaphor is its principal resource in this great project as it demonstrates that metaphor continually lives off of what is beyond metaphor. Indeed, the key to the inexhaustibility of art is just the impossibility of metaphor reaching a state of adequacy. Ever unstable, metaphor testifies to the personal horizon that makes it possible. In this sense the shortcomings and limitations of metaphor never present a fatal objection, for they are the secret of the perpetual vitality of its process of continuous of self-replacement. The cosmic analogues that furnish the stuff of myth, as well as their limitless elaboration through the history of art, attest to the metaphoric imagination that resists all imaging. More than the constants of symbols is the constant of metaphor that stands behind them. To understand the former we must place them in relation to the latter. That is, in relation to what is not constant because it is not anywhere. As the non-reality of the person it has no metaphor, for all possibility of metaphor presupposes it. When we ask about the validity of the contents of metaphor we ask about a process that continually overturns and revises itself in light of its own inexhaustible quest. The vitality of art, the apex of our symbol-making activity, derives from this inexhaustibility. As such, metaphor has no resting point but lives continually out of the impulse to surpass itself. Metaphor is the instability of metaphor. That is its life, as it is the life of the person.

Metaphor is unthinkable without persons. Objections to the limitations of metaphor are beside the point for they have already been incorporated into the leap it endorses.[36] Inapplication is included with its application. We can hardly grasp the metaphor without grasping its metaphoric status, that is, the extent to which it falls short of its target. We can relate the sun to the Good, as Plato does in the *Republic*, because we also grasp their dissimilarity. When we ask then how the grasping occurs at all we fall back on the capacity to grasp what cannot be grasped. The glimmering of metaphor is parallel with the self-transcendence of the person. It says what is not and thereby says more than it can. In the end this is what the metaphoric imagination calls attention to most of all. It calls attention to itself as that which cannot be grasped, cannot be submitted to metaphorical identification. Only what is immune to metaphor, the irreducible reality of persons, can grasp metaphor in all its irremediable deficiency. That which simultaneously hits and misses its target is the special preserve of persons, but that unique derivation does not simply remain there. Somehow the wavering of metaphor reaches out to its putatively stable contents. It is not just persons that point without saying but, derivatively, the whole of reality over which their metaphoric grasp stretches is touched by the same instability. Nothing is what it seems and, in acknowledging this, we realize how much reality colludes in its own metaphoric comprehension. It is not just persons who are open to what is not, but the whole of reality is pervaded by a mutual openness by which any one part can stand for any other.[37] Art and the symbol making that lies behind it arise, not just from imagination, but just as much from the levels of reality that metaphorically disclose one another.

How do we grasp what cannot be grasped, what can only be intimated through metaphor? The astonishment we experience at the discovery of the metaphorical openness of reality, just as we sense when confronted by its intelligibility, is the same that Kant conceded when he contemplated the starry sky above and the moral law within. He was, he said, filled with "wonder and awe." A similar and equally striking confession is wrung from him when he admits to being "disconcerted" (*befremdend*) at the thought that the individual exists only to serve the cause of historical progress.[38] Such concessions are precious in human life because they bring into view the personal horizon of thought. They arise from the innocent assumption that we can think about our condition without thereby transcending it and without thereby reaching the greatest insight that such revelations can provide. That is, that we are not what we are and that everything about us derives from that inescapable feature. Knowledge is possible because there is in the world a point at which reality can hold itself at the distance of contemplation and therefore can hold itself more closely than ever. This is the person, the point at which reality most truly is by not being. Art is possible because there is in reality a point at which the metaphoric openness of its layers can be grasped by what utterly escapes the possibility of metaphor. The person is where reality discloses most completely by not disclosing at all. For reality to disclose, for metaphor to work, there must be hiddenness as such since only what cannot be disclosed can grasp what is disclosed. All of reality is therefore one gigantic metaphor of the person, the disclosure of what cannot be disclosed that can nevertheless be glimpsed with the eye of love. The astonishment before the cosmos is the same as the astonishment before the human heart, for they are continuous as the astonishment within which the person dwells.[39] Art lives within that irruption. It attests to the life beyond life that is the source of life.

CHAPTER SIX

History as the Memory of Persons

The notion that history may be like art, in the sense that persons are the ultimate judges of the truth of what happened, may strike us as strange. Echoes of the uncanny that we have met before seem to resound. Kierkegaard's pronouncement, "truth is subjectivity," looms large, even though its precise meaning continues to elude us.[1] How can a purely subjective perception define the truth of historical events? Does this mean that there is no truth at all, and that everything is a matter of opinion? But why even bother to drag in the connection with truth? Something more is at stake than mere subjective assertion if the question of truth is invoked. History is not a spectacle indifferently unfolded before a subject who may impose his or her preferences upon it. It is rather a realm in which truth is constantly at stake as an existential imperative, for both the actor and the observer. Even when separated by the distance of time and space, they are bound together by an inexorability not so easily ignored. The truth of existence as it emerges in history is as valid for the inheritors as for the initiators, and the lines of responsibility flow in both directions. What is received by one human being is of relevance to all others who, in turn, have an obligation to preserve and pass it along to their successors. Before it is a field for objective investigation, history is a community of mutual collaboration. There would be no possibility of investigating the past unless it was related to the present. The preservation of memory is not only the goal of history, but its possibility as well. Historiography is so intimately connected with history that the terms are used almost interchangeably.

Narrative, the story that is identical with *historia*, is a possibility because it has always already occurred. We narrate what we live within. In this sense, truth is given as the possibility of narrative. Subjectivity, in Kierkegaard's sense, does not construct truth but finds itself responsible for it. There is no truth apart from this relationship we bear toward it. Historians can often give the impression that truth is something outside of them, that at which they aim, but they can only do so by forgetting that it is they who engage in its pursuit. Like scientists they are capable of omitting themselves but they can only do so because they are so good at the task. Truth can become objectified but then it gives rise to the troubling questions about its status, reliability, universality, and, ultimately, truth. Practicing historians are no better situated than practicing scientists to resolve such conundrums, although the resources lie no further afield than their own unexamined practice. If they were to reflect on what they do, they would discover that truth is not a fixed quantity but a relation, one that underpins the possibility of fixing any quantities at all. The past can be known only because we already stand in a relation of knowability toward it. At the most elemental level we know the past as past. Without that there would be no possibility of investigating the historical details, details we know are embedded in the past. Our task is clear because the very notion of a past firmly defines the realm of inquiry. We do not establish the past by means of the investigation but presuppose it as already given or, more accurately, as pre-given. Foraging through the past is subtended by the knowledge that it is past. Before it is known in any of its particular features, the past is known as past. We stand in relation to it as the past we know and, for that reason, seek to know ever more adequately. Historiography is a possibility provided by historical existence. We do not acquire historical knowledge and then construct an historiographic account of it, for neither facts nor their narration are separable from the history in which they arise.

Narrative is made possible by narrative. We do not narrate history but are, rather, narrated by it. It is because we are embedded in an historical narrative that we undertake the historiographical investigations needed to clarify it. History is known before we initiate the deeper delving into what, we discover, is virtually bottomless. How, then, do we limit the field of investigation and, more importantly, how do we know we have arrived at the truth of what we seek within it? The answer in each case lies in the horizon of relevance that spans the movement back from the present, a relevance that emerges in the present only because of its dissemination from the past. To the extent that a moment in the past gave rise to a publicly accessible truth, then it constituted a bridge into the present opening of truth. Only what is true can be accessed in the past. Even when we are mistaken about events or their meaning we can only be mistaken against the background of not being mistaken. Truth is the condition of error. What we apprehend as true about the past we apprehend within the resonance of truth in the present. This is what communication with the past means. We do not connect with other human beings on the basis of utterly distinctive private worlds but on the basis of what has become common because it arises from the commonality of existence. Such others would not form a bond with us if there were not a continuity more enduring than the subjective individuals who happen at any given moment to bear it within time. What really authenticates such continuity, however, is that it at root transcends its purely historical manifestations. History is the openness of persons to one another as the possibility of stepping over the vastness of space and time as if they were nonexistent.[2]

It is the mutuality of persons that underpins the mutuality of past and present. The past can be accessed from the present because it is never really past; it forms part of the eternal presence of persons to one another. Their mutual presence is, as we have seen, made possible by the mode of non-presence that distinguishes persons. They cannot be lost by the passage of time and they cannot be found in it either, for they ever escape the vehicles by which they made themselves known. The past that we know before we begin its investigation is that of the persons whose non-presence renders them more present than any of the traces they left behind. We know them before we have come to know them. That is the bond that history establishes between us before we have even become acquainted. Our mutual responsibilities toward one another, and toward the truth of one another, flow from the preexisting community of persons. It is because we are persons that we have history, that is, an openness to one another that is prior to our chronological intersection within time. Persons who are not in history bear history as their mutuality across time. In a parallel fashion, which we will investigate in the following chapter, politics is the openness of persons to one another across space. It is because persons are not present in space that they can be present to one another in the political realm. To say, therefore, that the narrative of history provides the possibility of historiography is to affirm that the voices of our predecessors are already heard before we have begun to listen to them. It is possible for us to hear what they have to say because they are already present in our memory, for it is in memory that persons can be present who are not present. Far from constituting a defect, this non-present presence is the way that all persons are present to us. Without it there would be no possibility of sustaining the conversation across time despite the ravages of time.

Historiography is possible, first, because persons are never contained in what they have left behind. The distance that separates them from us is one that has already occurred within their own lives. History is the space in which not only we, the historians, but also the actors themselves can contemplate what has been said and done. It is for this reason that the opening of history is at the same time the discovery of the person. But this second dimension only arises when the person has emerged as the one who transcends history. Initially it occurs in the immortality of memory but then it becomes clear that it is the immortality of action that confers the immortal memory on them. Heroes transcend their existence. What this means can only become clear in the revelation of God, who is transcendence as such. Just as history cannot contain the heroes who live beyond it, so it cannot contain the God whose self-revelation is the turning point within it. In every moment history is surpassed by the inwardness of those who behold it in going beyond it, and who go beyond it by beholding it. But now history assumes its third feature as the maximum danger that threatens the person. When history has become the horizon of reality, then it is all too easy to subordinate the person to the pattern of its culmination. Only in our own time has the scheme of historical progress been shattered by the individuals who found within themselves the means of resisting its totalitarian oppression. The person bore witness to the transcendence of history, thereby saving history from the closure of a culmination. The openness of history cannot be separated from the transcendence of the person who continually exceeds it. The problems of the historicity of truth, of solidarity in the midst of contingency, and of the reconciliation of nature and history, find their fulfillment in the person who is the pivot of history. In every instance the person has already transcended in the direction of a whole that could not be without him or her. The person is the apocalypse of history.

History as the Record of Persons Not Contained by It

The record has been left behind while the person who generated it has disappeared. In this sense the historical record is, like the trail of artistic creations, mute testament to its creators. But it is unlike art in that the reliquaries are far less deliberate. They are not consciously fashioned to achieve a radiance that might preserve them from the vicissitudes that daily assault them. Even when the record is deposited, such as through institutional transmission, the content is far less intimately connected with the expression. We can do with a copy of the Constitution, provided it is faithfully rendered, but we cannot do with a copy of the *Mona Lisa*. For the most important documents, the Gospels or the works of Plato, we have only copies. Art, in other words, puts us more directly in touch with its originators because it is in each case a unique irreplaceable singularity. Those art forms that rely more on historical transmission, such as music through its system of notation, fare less well. We do not really know what Greek music sounded like and are left only with speculative reconstructions. Art too, we are reminded, is ephemeral even though it may attain an amazing historical persistence. For the rest of the human record we are usually left only with a copy, not an original. That this is generally not too great a deficiency is no doubt due to the derivative character of even the most primary sources. All documents fall short of what they record since they exist precisely to preserve what they are not. They are not the original events themselves. All records merely record what they cannot contain. The distance through which even the participants begin to distance themselves from what has happened is the very possibility of remembering.

Artists may be more fully present in their works, indeed they aim at this peculiar intensity, while historical actors ever flow away from them. It is only with effort, often difficult effort, that we can regain a sense of what happened. The situation is not markedly different for those who come much later than for those who were originally present. Distance already intervenes within the moment of the event itself. Otherwise there would be no possibility of remembering. We can remember only because we have forgotten; we are no longer there and must recall what it was, what it was like. The story can be told because it no longer is. But there would be no possibility of telling and retelling if the participants had been fully actualized in what happened. History is the time of existence because it is the time of persons. At no point are they wholly absorbed by what is, so that even the events of their lives do not fully contain them. They have always begun to view them historically, that is, as if they themselves were merely derivative from what actually happened. It is not of course that everything is simply mimetic and nothing is original, but that the process of derivation is already embedded within the original. There is nothing so original that it contains the whole reality of the persons involved. Even in the events the modulation has taken place. This is why it is possible for the participants to think about how their actions will be viewed in historical perspective. History is a perspective that does not await historiography. On the contrary, historiography is only a possibility because the events themselves do not wholly define the participants. They live their lives as if they were not fully their own. What else does the sense of historical significance mean? The events and actions that are singled out for remembering are so regarded because their bearers see them in the same light. Only persons are capable of historical significance because they exceed their historical moment.

Their deeds are their record, while they themselves cannot be recorded. All that they leave are the deeds and words that at best express their uncontainability. In such instances their lives attain the durability of works of art although that was never their primary intention. Individuals may become famous in history but never by simply aiming at it. Elevation to the stratum that is worth remembering hardly ever drives their actions, although there are many ways in which such a goal might function as an ancillary motive. Ambivalence infects the relationship of actors to history in much the same way as that of artists to their work. Actors, like artists, are likely to become so identified with their accomplishments that they cease to be regarded as persons of unfathomable mystery in their own right. Or they have given themselves so completely to the task that it does indeed take on a greater reality, a reality more precious to them, than their very own selves. In that sense they are perhaps rightly identified with what they have done. But then the worm of self-examination rears its ugly head to remind them, and us, that there is always another side to even the most selfless human accomplishments. Perhaps there is some unnoticed corner of self-regard whose stain begins to spread through all they have endured, including even the glimmer of hope that their deeds might yet garner endless adulation. It would be far better, if one wanted to enact historically memorable action, to have done so in such a way that history cannot possibly remember. The endless vacillations of conscience are not a mere afterthought, the product of the more leisurely distance afforded historians, but the very fabric of historical existence itself. Ambivalence is the horizon of human action. We can be examined by all who come after us because we have already lived within the moment of self-examination.

The point of such self-reflection, however, is not to effect the paralysis of human action, although it can, but to surmount the ambivalence by means of an even deeper sacrifice of self. Human action on this account is, as Nietzsche demonstrated, impossible. It cannot efface the self that is its source. Hegel too thought about this problem of the relationship of the individual to world historic action, and he arrived at a formulation that perfectly summarizes the conflict. No man, he declared, can be a hero to his valet. The reason is that the valet is so intimately familiar with the small world of the self that it is incredible that his master could attain anything more than the veneer of heroism.[3] It is easy to dismiss the perspective of the valet as one truncated by its confinement to the world of appearances, although it does contain its own undeniable truth. The words of Christ, "no servant is above his master" (John 13:16; 15:20), may be more aptly quoted. It is not a question of who possesses the superior insight, if there is nothing to be grasped before the ungraspable has occurred. The hero is the one who not only surprises the servant but himself as well. Action becomes historically memorable when it is out of the ordinary, when human beings manage to do something that is in itself or in its consequences greater than they had any right to expect. Its miracle is that it achieves something more than that of which it is capable. If it were something fully predictable, then it would be routine, hardly worth recording or recalling except in the most routine way. What renders it memorable is that it achieves the impossible. Frail, self-obsessed human beings, who can hardly minister to their own physical needs unaided, have accomplished the impossible. They have given more than they can give. They have given themselves.

The device that Homer utilizes when any of his heroes undertake such an astonishing train of events is hardly less effective than the later psychologization of the impulse to action.[4] He depicts the occurrence as an intervention of a god who prompts the whole thing. To give one's life for another is hardly more astonishing than if the voice of Zeus thunders in one's ear. Such actions cannot contain their meaning. They overflow meaning as testament to the overflowing that is the non-reality of persons, as always more than they are. We can apprehend the event, or rather the non-event, for it is incommensurable, because we too are persons. Externally the life of a biological entity has been arrested, but to describe what has taken place requires us to reach outside of the limits of space and time, the world of measurability as such. The incommensurable is that which has no measure, transcending all finite scale of reference. For good or bad it is only the person who is capable of such madness in which the whole of existence is contained in a single moment. By sacrificing oneself, or sacrificing the other, a choice is made that inexorably affects the whole of reality. It is not, of course, as if one single person possesses such unlimited control over the cosmos but that it might as well be since each one is a whole unto himself or herself. Greater than the sum of all finitude, the infinite of the person gives or withholds what cannot be so assigned. At stake is giving or withholding as such, the very pivot of existence. History itself hangs in the balance of every human action. There is no need to wait for an apocalypse at the end of time for time has reached its culmination in every human action. The revelation of what it *is* is being proclaimed in every instant.

History is the history of what in every instant exceeds history. It partakes of the paradox of the person who cannot be contained in what is said or done and for that reason must be so contained. Communicating the incommunicable, historiography is the means of preserving the imperishable. All other vehicles merely emulate imperishability, they do not attain it. They are still too much located within history and, for that reason, cannot contain history. Motives, incentives, interests may be the stuff of history, the warp and woof of its fabric, but they are not the cloth itself. That is visible only from outside of it. The tension between history and historiography reemerges. Historiography is possible only by transcending history, comprehending it from its conclusion, but such a perspective can be attained only by persons who have already reached it. That is, by persons whose own existence has attained the luminosity of the end. This does not necessarily mean that they have gained the vantage point of an actual end, although that is often how such a principle has been interpreted. But what it does mean is that historiography is a possibility only for persons who have transcended history from within it. History can be written only by persons who can make history. Doers are, of course, not often the writers but they must share a common perspective so that they converge on what Eliot coined "the point of intersection of the timeless with time." Living neither in the timeless nor in time, they exist in the intersection. That is the opening of history from which its discourse can be written. When we ask where that mysterious intersection is located we are at a loss to account for it, just as we are for the whole possibility of discourse that cannot be contained within it. There is no point, it exists nowhere, and we have no access to it except that it is that out of which we live. Persons live from that inaccessible point. They are its reality. This is why the discovery of persons is bound up with the discovery of history. They mutually illumine one another, but it is the writing of history that is the most definitive demonstration of the accessibility of what is inaccessible.

All human beings live in history but consciousness of history, the moment at which historiography emerges, is specific. Eric Voegelin has correlated it with the ecumenic expansion of empires by which space becomes enlarged beyond limit, or at least to the non-limit of the globe, and the spiritual outbursts by which the utter transcendence of God comes into view as what cannot come into view.[5] History is the opening of time in which the accomplishment of such impossible feats becomes possible. Just as the expansion of space, first through conquest and then through exploration, cannot reach a limit, or at least none that can be regarded as anything more than an invitation to further expansion, so time cannot be contained within the limits of narrative but must be continually enlarged as the very condition of narrative. We think of the infinities of space and time as consequences of their empirical exploration by science, but we cannot separate their virtual infinities from the event by which transcendence is not so much experienced as glimpsed as the condition of experience. Voegelin's own historical research called attention to the coincidence of these three factors, ecumene, historiography, and revelation, but he could do no more than point out the convergences between them. Spatial and temporal enlargement seemed to prepare a world in which transcendence could be glimpsed. What he did not do is push his own reflection to discover the inner relationship these events bear within them. Voegelin still clung to the convention of the historian who could objectively map the materials of his investigation. He held on to this convention even as he sensed its untenability, for he had already abandoned the standard chronological framework from which he had begun. It was as if Voegelin could not yet see why such a logic was thrust upon him and, if it was, why its further unraveling would prove irresistible. Historiography, even for Voegelin, had not yet fully absorbed the person through whom historiography is possible. This may be the great intellectual challenge across the disciplines, as we have suggested in the case of science, but it is more likely to be taken up within the field of historiography that depends on just such an acknowledgment.

In this respect Voegelin pointed the way in his groundbreaking account of *Israel and Revelation*. History in the full sense was the fruit of the Israelite encounter with the God who reveals himself as beyond all revelation. The term "history" may have come from the Greeks but its reality, existence within the full openness of history, is a distinctly Hebraic achievement. Only the people of Israel could conceive of themselves as living within history, that is, within a horizon that would not be brought to a conclusion with the establishment of a particular form of community. Where the Greeks lived in the polis, the Israelites lived within the unending struggle of fidelity to God. This did not mean that the Israelites were not inclined to look toward settlement within the Promised Land, of kingdom or empire, but that they never failed to perceive the unreality of such an alternative. It would have meant a turning away from the call to become the people of God, the call to become what they could never fully become. This is historical existence. Its only answer, they eventually came to recognize, is apocalypse, the transfiguring divine intervention that brings history to its conclusion. In itself history is the expectation of what cannot be expected. The shocking impact of transcendence is hardly captured by confining its significance to the introduction of linear history, as if there was any other. But such standard pronouncements are not easily displaced since they serve the undeniable function of rendering the unmanageable manageable. It is as if we have sought to comprehend history from some perspective outside of it, neglecting to notice that none such are available from within it. History is the perspective from which history can be glimpsed for it is the possibility of glimpsing as such.

Even Voegelin's estimable willingness to abandon the chronological framework with which he began, ultimately characterizing it as a form of mytho-speculation termed "historiogenesis," did not confront the extent to which linearity has nothing to do with history.[6] The collapse of narrative history in our own time, largely as a result of its overwhelming by sheer empirical profusion, is not unrelated. This too had been a factor in Voegelin's retreat from chronology. But what has remained unexamined is narrativity as such. If narrative is no longer possible, then should we not raise the question of whether it ever was? Or are we so dependent on narrative as the rejected other that we cannot afford to do without it, most of all in the moment of its greatest obsolescence? Fascinating as such questions are they can hardly be addressed without taking account of the impossibility of narrative, including its own point of narration. History cannot be linear if it is at every moment the point of intersection of the timeless with time. Rather than rendering time as linear, historiography abolishes it through the leap into the eternity from which it is apprehended.[7] Linearity is in this sense purely an historiographic construct that surpasses temporality in its illumination. Historiography compresses time within the time of its narration, ultimately approaching the point of mutual simultaneity that is its inwardness. Outer history, the history of events, scarcely exists except in an empirical manifold awaiting the arc of their comprehension. Apocalypse does not happen within history; it is the point from which history happens. From the perspective of history it is unthinkable that it could be comprehended from within. But that impossibility is what the person is, the whole within a part because it is not even a part. The advent of historiography proclaims the person as apocalypse.[8]

Historiography is a possibility because history is the possibility of persons. In their existence they already live beyond themselves; they are never simply present in what they say or do. The participants in the Peloponnesian War might have been surprised to learn of this characterization of their experience as a unity but they would not have been shocked by it. Even in the more immediate clashes that occupied them there was still the possibility of an enlargement of perspective. At no point had they been wholly subsumed into the course of action. To say that their actions were historical does not just mean that they could be comprehended within the perspective of later historians, as if the whole purpose of their existence had been to play a part in some grand narrative utterly beyond them. This may be an impression historical narration often conveys, but it is only as a result of the peculiar forgetfulness by which historiography overlooks its own historicality. The writing of history is itself an historical action that is made possible only by historical existence. We can write the history of the past only because we live in relation to a past that we are not. But this is not simply true of the writers; it reaches all the way down to the events themselves. Human beings can write history because in their existence they make history. The first interpretation of words and events is that which is assigned to them by their authors. To be an originating author does not mean that one definitively controls the meaning of what is said or done, but it does mean that one is first in the line of meaning-giving that stretches forth from that point. The transmission is possible and, thus, the writing of history, because it is carried forward by persons who are never merely what they are in the moments that constitute history.

Participants are not simply confined to their time and place. They always possess the possibility of seeing and being more than they are. It is for this reason that they can be partners in the emergence of a truth beyond their immediate grasp. The truth of history is the history of truth.[9] What is true within the later historiographical perspective is of little value unless it is consonant with the truth of historical existence. The litmus test is in every instance whether the predecessors would recognize themselves in the characterizations formulated by their successors. It is not the historiographer who assigns truth but he has it assigned to him by the subjects of history. Validity is confirmed as the truth recognizable by the participants. This, of course, does not mean that nothing new has emerged, that there is no historical change, but it does mean that development has occurred within a continuum. History is thus the emergence of truth ever more fully explicated in historiography. But there would be no truth to explicate if it had not been present from the beginning, albeit in the mode of a truth that is not present. Conversely, there is no emergence of truth that abolishes the emergence of truth. History has neither a beginning, a point of impenetrability, nor an end, a point of maximal disclosure. The underlying unity, that which provides the possibility of continuity and change so essential to the very notion of history, is this tensional structure, between ignorance and knowledge, as Voegelin characterized it. Even this Platonic metaphor of the between, however, with its imaginative projection of poles beyond the between, does not quite get at the personal reality involved. The between is not the condition of the possibility of persons but rather the reverse. It is persons who give rise to the between because they have ever ceased to be what they are. That is why they live within history.[10]

What they have done, the record they have left behind, does not contain them. They must continue to seek its meaning and its truth, and the unattainability of meaning and truth is the guarantee of the continuity of seeking. Whatever advantages flow to those who arise later in the process are not so decisive that they supersede the attainments of those who came before. Deference to ancestors is almost built in since it is in terms of the relationship to them that the descendants understand themselves. Even departure from forebears bears their mark. Yet there would be no understanding at all if it did not constitute a break with what is, for difference is the pivot around which history revolves. What is decisive is that the pattern of beginning anew is the constant that underpins the possibility of beginning. There is no privileged point of history, no absolute beginning or end, because every moment is saturated with that possibility. History is the possibility of beginning that is indistinguishable from ending. This is why it is one vast collaborative enterprise in which no one is lost to all and no one surpasses all. The new beginning that each person is takes on a unique significance when it is viewed through the lens of history. It is because each person is outside of all history that each one contains all of history and is therefore the still point of the turning world. They enter into history as not being in history, and it is this transcendence that enables them to reach one another through history. We can come to know them by what they have left behind because they themselves have not been left behind. As persons they remain outside of history, which is, therefore, the way they can be without being present.

We take for granted the mutuality of all persons within history but this is its most striking feature. We can hold in mind and in love persons long dead and they, in turn, can hold us in mind before we are even born. This is not just a matter of inner imagination, although that certainly is involved. Imagination is not enough, for we do not hold or behold them as mere images. The whole point is their reality. Historiography is not a parlor game constructing figments of imagination. Fiction is perfectly adequate for that and we have no difficulty telling the difference. We do not seek to reach an image of Plato or of Augustine but seek them as they really were or are, apart from everything else about them. They too did not merely spin out thoughts for their own entertainment but earnestly struggled to communicate to all they might be able to reach. Behind it all is the constancy of persons who seek one another out. The mere passage of time is as irrelevant to that as mere separation in space. Their openness to one another leaps over the distances because they have never lived in space and time. To demonstrate that history is the arena in which that mutuality is disclosed is the task of historiography. Narration is possible only because the narrator can never be included within it, but it is also the case that the narrator cannot properly be without narration. We are not wholly within history, yet we cannot dispense with history. It is through history that we discover who we are, even though we are always more than we discover ourselves to be. What shifts the odyssey of the person to a wholly other level is the realization that before I have reached out to others, others have reached out to me. History is never a solitary search but the irruption of mutuality in which the bonds of responsibility we bear one another structure time before we become aware of it. History is the history of persons who are in history without being of it. They belong to one another before they belong to history.

History as the Differentiation of the Person

History is the differentiation of the person before the language of the person has emerged. Holding persons in memory, living in relation to persons who are no longer present, is the thread of memory in which persons live. But while this is characteristic of persons at all times, it acquires a peculiar salience when the lifting up into memory has become explicit. Deeds sung in memory raise up the person to the immortality of the gods. Death is no more when the hero lives in the memory of the gods who are deathless. A vista of infinity has opened upon the person although there is as yet no language that names it; only the welcome of the gods in the song of memory evokes the transcendence of the person. The poet has not yet stepped outside the poem. There is only the poem itself as the evocation of immortality, without the inclusion of the poet within the horizon of attention. All that is needed to express the realization that a person cannot die is fully present, although there is nothing that accounts for that realization itself. This is the compactness that the differentiation of history begins to loosen, for those who live in historic memory can never quite be contained by their historic setting. Everything is being readied for the momentous discovery of the person who is never contained by what he or she is. Their words and deeds have already borne witness to their self-transcendence. It is not we, the historiographers, who have conferred immortality upon them, for they have rather claimed it as the birthright of persons who have been prepared to give their all. The mystery of those who can give what they cannot give and who, therefore, must give themselves completely, has not yet come into view. But its reality has become unmistakably manifest.

In the opening of history we discover that we too are constituted by the same pull to self-transcendence as those whose self-transcendence has differentiated the horizon of history. Historiography is premised on historical existence, that is, existence that surpasses itself. In that sense it is an account of what cannot be contained within history and which, therefore, brings that impossibility into view. History acquires the peculiar status of what is by not being what it is. To us this is familiar as the unique mode of personal existence, but in its historical manifestation it is an unnamed tension toward what cannot be reached. All we can say about it is that it is the tension within which we live, for we cannot even think outside of it. This is why historiography does not comprehend the events that constitute history. It recognizes and remembers them, ultimately conceding that it too is formed by the same pull it recalls. Even the most resolutely objectivist accounts can still not quite avoid a shudder before the mystery of the historical perspective as such. We may think that we have shaken free from the mythic reverberations embedded in it, the notion that great deeds elevate mere mortals beyond the banal limits of their condition, but we remain enchanted by the enlargement of horizon that history nevertheless provides. Somehow it remains the realm of the momentous. Myth may have been wiped from history but history has not been sanitized of myth. By virtue of its construction history unfolds a reality beyond the quotidian present. The exotic is exotic, we know, only because it is unfamiliar, but it could never become familiar unless it withdrew us from familiarity. We long to be other than we are, and it is this that draws us toward the memorable that compels us to remember. Despite the distance insulating the historiographer there is ultimately no barrier to the flash of transcendence that attaches to the historical figure. There would be no historiography unless we were touched by the same fascination. Exploration of the past is driven, like the exploration of space, by the intense awareness of our trajectory toward a beyond. The big difference, however, is that time travel is entirely constituted by the encounter with the others whose own encounters have blazed a trail. Space travel may be underpinned by such an inchoate longing for others, but historical research is rooted in a meeting that has already taken place.

It is for this reason that history renders time visible. The so-called linear conception of time is entirely the fruit of the reaching backward and forward from the moment in which history is constituted. Apart from history there is no linear time. We do not first contemplate an extent of time and then ask about the history of what happened in it. There is rather the outburst of what is memorable, transcendent and transcending at the same time, and from it we begin to consider the course of events that led up to it and wonder about the consequences that unfold from it. Time is already structured by meaning. It is not an indifferent expanse like space generally is, although even that is not so homogeneously the same. We go home and we can never return without being affected by the deepest significance of place, as that in which we are sheltered and embraced. Crossing the threshold always evokes resonances of the passage we go through. Even there, however, the reverberations are carried as much by the temporal dimension of our lives. It is in time that meaning is disclosed; space is merely the setting that gains its radiance from that event. Memory harbors us far more intimately than place, although they are in fundamental ways inseparable. We live in time because the event of transcendence is what discloses it to us. Meaning and time are coincident. Heidegger's conjunction of "being and time" yields many different interpretations but surely one of the most pivotal is that time is the horizon in which being is glimpsed. That is the advent of history. The epiphany in which we grasp the possibility of participation in the impossible, being or the immortal, furnishes us with the memory through which time is apprehended.

It is through memory that being is apprehended. That is, as what cannot be apprehended, except through memory. This is why time and history are so completely bound up with the discovery of the person. It is not just that only persons live through memory, but that it is this that defines them most profoundly. They understand themselves as ever not being what they are and this can principally be glimpsed in the retrospective turn to what is no longer. As a process of self-transcendence the person is equipped with memory. It would be impossible to go beyond if we did not remember what we had left. Leaving behind takes place by way of recalling what is past. Of course we can always undertake that odyssey without paying much attention to it, without remembering, and then it is almost as if we are sleepwalking. Going through the motions, we seem to sense, hardly counts as a mode of self-transcendence. The result is a mere shift of location, while a journey implies our awareness of traveling. We cannot give ourselves without knowing that we do, for there is nothing to give but the possibility of self-giving as such. When we give ourselves we do not give something; we give what cannot be given. But that means that there is no gift without the intention that is the source of giving, that stands outside the gift or, rather, stands nowhere but in the memory of the giver. The recipient receives the gift, not just by taking possession of it, but by receiving the intention behind it. They are united in memory more fully than by any tangible expression of it. Loss of memory is such a burden because it drains away all that constitutes the person in his or her relationship to others. This is why we struggle so much to hold on to memory for everything in our lives is constructed on it. Even the relationships most rooted in nature, of mother and child, depend on the capacity to remember. Persons we see are not rooted in nature but in memory as the precious treasury of their personhood. Without memory we are wholly deposited within time. It is history and memory that enables us to transcend it.

The ascent, however, does not take place under our own steam. No matter how much we are inclined to feel that we hold on to memory the truth is that memory holds on to us. This is why we can lose our memories although memory continues without us. In order for us to hold something in mind there must first be the something that holds our minds. Memory is created through the advent of the memorable. Without the memorable, that which ruptures the present, there would be no memory. This is why we cannot remember an indifferent jumble of facts, as if an empty repository were equally available for all kinds of information. Even computers can only retain what has been reduced to the code in which they read information. Our infinitely greater susceptibility to nuance still does not permit us to record sheer chaos. Only what is already structured by meaning can enter memory for we can scarcely hold on to the merely random. What we hold in memory is meaning and therefore must itself be meaningful.

Historiography does not contain the events of history; it distills and retains them in their meaning. This is why the emergence of historiography is entirely bound up with the emergence of meaning in history. Without an advance in meaning there is nothing by which history may be constituted. What is must be ruptured by what is not, an event that is irreducibly personal on the side of both the giver and the receiver. Only persons can interrupt the status quo, disclosing the transcendence that is the self-disclosure of the person. And only persons can recognize what has occurred as what cannot be seen or quantified because it exceeds all boundaries. The event that constitutes history exceeds history, and historiography is the recall of what cannot be recalled. Meaning in every respect overflows its own boundaries because it is inseparable from the horizon of the person. It is the person who creates memory and thereby gains memory.

History contains the uncontainable. It is the revelation of what cannot be revealed because it is the revelation of a person. Everything that is has been surpassed by what is not, as the superabundance beyond the event. Meaning is tied to the disruption that overturns expectations. The new beginning that each person represents has become definitively manifest as the beginning of time. History is thus a series of beginnings, of points of intersection, and not in any sense a flow or line along which individuals can be located. Punctuated outbursts more accurately denote the ruptures involved, for what is memorable in each instance is the overflowing of limits. The pivot of meaning is the person who lies utterly beyond it. The hero, the prophet, the leader is the one who in each instance does more than he or she does. Memorability is the impossibility of containing it in memory; this is why it must be continually remembered. Such a rupture in time, constituting a before and an after, is possible only through the disclosure of what cannot be disclosed. The person stands outside of all of history and within it at the same time, but always in the mode of absent presence of the person. Even when historiography devolves into a recounting of the routine, there still hovers over it the expectation of what cannot be expected because it is the unexpected. When we ask what that is, especially with the hard-bitten cynicism of the professional historian, we are inclined to respond with the observation "nothing new under the sun" (Ecclesiastes 1:9). Surprise must come, therefore, from what is not under the sun because it has transcended all suns. The person who gives and in giving discloses what cannot be disclosed, the person himself or herself, reaches into our hearts.

Even historians cannot surpass the mystery of the person within which they live. It is the unsurpassable.

This is why history is not the story of external events. It certainly includes them, reaching back to discern the first vague glimmerings of what later takes shape, but that vital core always consists of an inner recognition of meaning. If we think of history as the realm in which meaning is enlarged and transmitted, then it is primarily a realm encountered in inwardness. Kierkegaard most famously asked the question of what relevance an event that happened eighteen hundred years ago could have for his life. How would it affect his eternal destiny?[11] Could a merely historical event forever alter the structure of existence? The answer, he found, was that the facts of history in their externality really affected the course very little. One man's death is no different from another's. But if externality is the least significant aspect of it, then the scale of measurement is completely different. Viewed through the gaze of inwardness the obstacles to personal relevance slip away. The one who gives himself for others, for all others, does so in a way that cannot be diminished by the passage of time or remoteness of place. He is as much present with me today as he was to those with whom he talked twenty hundred years ago. A person can overleap separation to affirm a love more profound than we can contemplate. An act of complete self-giving radiates an undying love that reaches from beginning to end. That is why its irruption within history is the turning point of history, never a part but always greater than the whole of history. We can continue to gather information about the external realities, gaining an ever more accurate picture of what it appeared to contemporaries, but we can never claim to be disadvantaged by coming later to what could never be apprehended from the outside. Within the eternal non-presence of persons to one another we remain as near and as far as everyone else. The revelation that constitutes history is, in all its decisive aspects, wholly inward.

For this reason we should not be too surprised to discover that the historiographic opening arises from the event of revelation in its fullest sense. It may seem strange that an event that is wholly inward has the most far-reaching impact on the external course of history, but we know that it is the irruption of the world religions that forms the arcs of relevance all the way into our own present. Even our secular civilization cannot ignore the durability of the spiritual outbursts and may even be compelled to understand itself as a variant within them. What is the secular, after all, if not the withdrawal from the sacred? Our difficulty has always arisen from the inclination to think of religion as a phenomenon within history rather than as the event that constitutes it. Perhaps we would be better off if Cicero had not given us a term (*religio*) for what cannot be accessed except inwardly.[12] Then we might avoid the misconception that revelation occurs within history, rather than history within revelation. But the fault is not entirely Cicero's since, once revelation has occurred, it is immediately marked with the time and place of its breakthrough. The tendency to forget that there is no such time or place is almost irresistible. From it arise all the difficulties of historical faiths that must return to their beginnings to make contact with what cannot be found in any beginning, no matter how accurate.[13] This was Kierkegaard's big insight, just as it is of all the great spiritual traditions that understand their transmission through living communities rather than through historical research. It is not that historical research is irrelevant, but that it is propaedeutic to the interior encounter that ever escapes it. Even the narrative of history is no more than a valiant attempt to convey what cannot be conveyed through its narrative and, for that reason, must be conveyed as its source. Revelation is the turning point of history because it is the definitive recognition of the impossibility of revelation. What history reveals is that nothing is revealed in history. Nothing that is, except history as such.

Transcendence is the event that exceeds history and thereby renders it visible. From this point on history is overshadowed by what it cannot contain and yet contains a durability it is incapable of comprehending. Even to say that the world religions demonstrate a formidable staying power is already to subscribe to the scale of historical measurement. What should be recognized is that they cannot be eliminated from history because they are never truly within it. How can the deathless be put to death? Its representatives may be liquidated at any time but its source can scarcely be touched, as the rejuvenating force of martyrdom regularly attests. The naiveté of Gibbon's attempt to account for the rise of Christianity in the face of formidable obstacles confronting it is, like all such attempts to "explain," rooted in the category mistake of thinking of Christianity as an immanent reality. Christianity may *have* a presence within history but it is not *a* presence within history. Judgments of success or failure can hardly be rendered coherently when their basis has been overturned. To die is to live. That is the momentous discovery of those who realize that they no longer live within history at all. They live within the inwardness of love that transcends any historical scale of measurement. That which is *not* can scarcely be touched by that which is. It is only if it fails to be true to itself that it can suffer defeat in the world, for defeat attaches only to what is within the world. The transcendent cannot be defeated; it can only be defeated if it clings to what it is not. Invincibility is its life. There is nothing left for it to give since it has given all. It is perfect self-giving, not as an occasional outpouring, but as what it is. The world is no more for it has overcome the world. That does not mean that the apocalypse has abolished history but it does mean that history has emerged as what is under its judgment. The judgment of history is enacted by the person whose inwardness surpasses it.

What is decisive is the encounter with God as transcendent. Inwardness is the path of that encounter and, from that point on, establishes itself as the locus of our existence. No more do we live simply in the external world. Now we recount history because we know we are not absorbed by it. The distance by which we contemplate reality, indeed the possibility of contemplation, is established by that differentiation. One word of truth outweighs the whole world, not because truth has acquired the divisions needed to prevail against the world, but because we cannot doubt the inner reality in which truth is glimpsed. Outwardly nothing has changed but inwardly a revolution has taken place. The turning point of history is, fittingly, a turning point that cannot be discerned within history. Revelation has no history for it transcends history. Yet as a rupture it changes history, not by abolishing it, but by imprinting it with the mark of the secondary. The real now lies within. The accent of reality has shifted decisively when the opening to the transcendent has occurred. Mind has established a beachhead from which it cannot easily be dislodged even when, as we see in our own time, its credentials are intensely scrutinized. The priority of the person is not irreversible. But it has proved more durable than one might imagine, given the decline in the notion of the person as a spiritual being destined for union with God beyond this life. Inwardness is so firmly differentiated that it can even survive the decline of the experience of the transcendent in which it emerges. It may well be that, having drifted apart for so long, the connection between inwardness and transcendence is on the verge of an even more profound affirmation.[14]

Instead of thinking of the interiority of the person as contained in solid externality, we now see that the opposite holds. The outer is transcended, not eliminated, in the movement of inwardness that is the whole possibility of transcending. God is the definitive revelation of the primordiality of the inner. The outer is always what is transcended and, in the process, is displaced in the order of reality to what is less real. By his victory over the world Christ shows what is beyond it. To say that each person outweighs the whole of history is not a noble aspiration but the literal truth of what it means to be a person. It means that one is nowhere within history as the external course of events but, on the contrary, contains history within as a transcended moment. The death of metaphysics was inevitable once it became clear that metaphysical structures could not contain the person who comprehends them. In the same way, the death of God flowed from his excessive absorption within immanence. When we ask where God is when he has absconded the answer remains what it has always been. God is present only in God, that is, within the inwardness of God. It is through God that God is known, not through any intermediary. A person is known only through himself or herself. History too, the horizon of the person, can only be known within itself for history is not a factor within history. What we call metaphysics is that recognition. Nothing can contain the person who shares the primordiality of God as uncontainable inwardness. Transcendence is inwardness. That is the truth of metaphysics as it is of history.

The Person as the Apocalypse of History

The discovery of the person as the point at which the whole becomes transparent through inwardness is the pivot of history. It is the recognition that inwardness is not ours but derives from the One who is inwardness. The life of God is accessed in that moment when history is differentiated. When we ask where history occurs, it must be said that it occurs in the inwardness of God who contains and transcends all. The whole of reality unfolds, not as a dream in the mind of God, but as the being of God that he shares with all without being wholly present in it. That which expresses God is other than him while he remains within himself. It is a sharing of his life that stops short of sharing himself. Only persons are drawn within that circle of intimacy to know God as a person. That is, as an inwardness. They alone can stand apart from reality because they have transcended it within the inwardness that is transcendence. The turning point of history is the moment in which history as such is differentiated; it cannot be contained within history. Simultaneously, history is discovered and exceeded in an epiphany that grasps that it could not be discovered without being exceeded. The problem is that the discovery of history immediately imposes a burden on the condition of its discovery. Scarcely has the irruption of transcendence rendered history visible than the focus on history begins to occlude its own transcendence. The instability of the relationship comes to the fore as an instability that cannot be eliminated from history. How can history contain the moment of its own recognition as history? This becomes the great question of historical meaning that stretches all the way up to the present without finding a definitive resolution, but also not without an advancing clarification along the way. That latter process revolves around the relationship of the person to history for, while the inwardness of the person is indispensable to the discovery of history, history as such can scarcely find a place or role for inwardness. If everything occurs in history, where does history occur?

The uncontainability of the person and the uncontainability of history are correlative. As one goes so goes the other and, in most instances, history has been the culprit. This explains why the differentiation of history has become the principal obstacle to the preservation of history. Once history has come into view the temptation to reach its culmination is well nigh irresistible. This has not just been a feature of the drive toward perfection that defines modern civilization, but has marked historical existence from its first emergence. With the Greeks whom we associate with the term "history," the abolition of historical existence had been muted but it was there nevertheless. Their narrative did not reach the transcendence that opened the indefinite expanse of history, for it culminated firmly in the actualization of the polis, the community that fully realized human nature and, for that reason, did not require historical existence.[15] Their differentiation of history was foreshortened by the life of the polis that could not be superseded. So strong was this conviction that it blocked the way toward the full unfolding of philosophy itself. To the extent that no community beyond the polis was conceivable there was no way to acknowledge the community of philosophy itself that could only be constituted historically. Classical philosophy could look back toward its own historical emergence but it could not conceive of history as the horizon in which it presently existed. This is why it remained so heavily invested in the remediation of the polis as the indispensable community for the life of philosophy. An ancillary consequence was that even the beloved polis could not be viewed in its full historical reality. The curious result is that classical philosophy could account for neither philosophy nor the polis, a limitation that impelled it toward less than rational commitments. The life of the polis may not have been the apocalypse that abolished history but it was the apocalypse that prevented it from coming fully into view. Historical success can be as problematic as historical failure in distorting history.

More typically, however, history has come under pressure from its refusal to abolish the tension embedded within it. From its opening in a glimpse of transcendence the demand for transfiguration often sounded with indefatigable insistence. It has been this contradiction between what constitutes history and what history constitutes that has generated the symbol of apocalypse. The unregenerate character of historical reality has heightened the awareness of its tensional character to such a pitch that it can no longer be sustained. A breaking point is reached in the projection of a transfiguring intervention from beyond history. The opening toward transcendence that had differentiated history returns to effect its termination. In this invocation we see that the relationship between transcendence and history is inescapably unstable. History comes into view from the perspective of a viewpoint outside of it, but endures under the shadow of its own supersession. The conflict is ineradicable for it is not the result of a merely historical shortcoming. History is what cannot be incorporated into the transcendent from which it has been separated. The fall is not an event within history; it is the event of history. History is fallenness, the irremediable condition that demands its abolition. Nowhere was this drama played out more fully than in the intractable conflict between the people of Israel and the people of God. No amount of reform could transform the recalcitrance of Israel into the radiance of a divinely ordered community. Apocalypse was only one of the symbolic forms explored in a range of alternatives that also included legalism, redemptive suffering, and transmission into a universal spiritual community. Only the latter was firmly rejected because it would have entailed the obsolescence of Israel as a concrete political society within history. They were carriers of a transcendent message but they could not become a community wholly constituted by transcendence.[16]

That was the option unfolded within Christianity. Yet even there, when the impossibility of history embodying the transcendent had become clear, the demand could not so easily be erased. The only way the transcendent can be present within time is through the person who is transcendent, Jesus Christ. Only a person can access the transcendent for only a person is beyond all that is, but to be the transcendent in history the person must be identical with the transcendent as such.[17] He must be God. This is the uniqueness of Christ that makes unmistakably clear the impossibility of anything else representing the transcendent. History cannot reach its end within time and therefore must point toward an end beyond it. The differentiation of history, correlative with the differentiation of its eschatological fulfillment, is the distinctively Christian contribution. On its surface it would seem to secure history as an openness against all possibility of collapse back into immanence. History has finally emerged as the horizon of the person who knows it through the transcendence of it. We are not likely to be tempted to find our home within it, not likely, that is, until we are tempted. Perhaps it is because Christianity makes the end time such a distinctive element that imagination is drawn toward its visualization. The Apocalypse of John is the last book of the Christian canon and an enduring source of disturbance within the Christian tradition ever since. Of particular importance is the millennium, the time after Christ's return in glory when he rules on earth with his saints for a thousand years. It seems as if the demand for a vindication of transcendence within history was simply too strong to be denied satisfaction. It was only with difficulty that the Church managed to wrest control of the interpretation of the millennium from millenarians who would use it to occlude the transcendent openness of the Christian message. Once the advent of the millennium had become the focus, attention shifted from the event that constitutes history to the history that includes it.

For those who sought to live within the event rather than contemplate it at a distance, this was a fatal mistake. Even the centrality of Christ's life, death, and resurrection begins to recede if it becomes a mere prelude to a final revelation. But it is the change that millenarian expectation works within the life of the Christian that is the decisive factor. In place of living in fidelity to what can never be fully lived, there is the contraction of existence toward a moment of future resolution. Expectation of the millennium does not resolve the imperative of living in light of the transcendent, but it does convey the sense of an even more rigorous dedication to the task. When one has begun to concentrate exclusively on the ultimate victory of good over evil, then one establishes one's impeccable credentials in the struggle. The only difficulty is that this contributes nothing to victory in the present. On the contrary, we have acquired an unimpeachable alibi for neglect. Christ in the Gospels had warned against this deviation, counseling that we "know not the day nor the hour" (Mark 13:32). The point was to live always as if we are in the moment of the apocalypse so that we bend every effort to ensure that good defeats evil. But if we step back from the struggle, to contemplate its final outcome at some future moment, we have already yielded place within it. The differentiation of apocalypse is the great obstacle to living within it. This was why, St. Augustine understood, millenarian excitement had to be countered by calling attention to existence within the millennium. He was the one who has been credited with bringing about the redirection of the symbol of the millennium from a moment in the future to the present moment of existence.[18] The reign of Christ on Earth does not have to await his return in glory but is already taking place through his presence in the Church within history. If his reign is in the future then it is not in the present. That is the great betrayal of the Christian millennium disseminated by Christian millenarianism. It was crucial that the Church regain the meaning of the eschaton to prevent its derailment into the millennium.

As Augustine articulated it the distinction was not difficult to maintain. His success at a time of heightened millenarianism, coincident with the Theodosian establishment of Christianity, demonstrates the relative ease of the adjustment. At its core Christianity remains an eschatological symbolism, as even the intermediate character of the millennium makes clear. Anything that endangers or detracts from its eschatological foundation collides with its inner imperative. Even when more extensive and more deeply rooted millenarian passions stirred, in the twelfth to fourteenth centuries, it was still possible for the Church to mount a successful campaign of spiritual and material suppression, albeit not without costs that were both spiritual and material. In many respects the ferocity of those conflicts attests to the depth of the convictions involved. The Christ of the millennium could not be allowed to eclipse the Christ already within us. Not only would this devalue what he has done, but it would also eviscerate all that he continues to do in the Church. The Christ of the end of history would supplant the Christ of history. His opening of transcendence within which every person lives, each an incomparable epiphany of love surpassing the whole of being, would shrink to the expectation of a future opening, one that could scarcely even be sustained without the opening of the present. To reverse the priority of the fulfillment to the promise is to rob the grounds for the expectation. Imagining the apocalypse may endanger living within it, but the former cannot long endure without the latter. The transcendence that cannot be included within history must not be projected toward a point at which the impossible becomes possible.

Whatever the difficulty of sustaining the opening of transcendence, it is nothing compared to the dead end evoked by its closure. Not even the closure can be sustained when the condition of openness has disappeared. This was the logic of the end of history constructions, as Alexandre Kojève pointed out, for the end could no longer be comprehended when the process that generated it had disappeared.[19] Yet something more than a question of logic was at stake within this impasse. Its perpetrators, proponents of an intra-mundane apocalypse, had demonstrated their low regard for history as such. They had turned their backs on existence in rejecting the imperative of transcending it, the only condition under which its openness could be preserved within every single person. A history that headed toward its consummation was one that no longer had any room for the person who carries it by exceeding it. The transcendence of the person that is the mark of history is declared redundant. No appeal to the imputed humanitarianism of the motives can erase the disdain for the dignity of the human person. Humanity cannot be served apart from the unique irreplaceability of every member. Their aggregation within a history that marches toward its culmination cannot overcome their individual devaluation. Nothing is left of the end or the process when the persons who hold them together have disappeared from view. We suspect all such homogenizing schemas as incapable of grasping the destiny at which they aim. When the person has been eliminated, history itself is abolished, for it is only as the history of persons who transcend it that history has any meaning. This discovery occurred within the same kind of resistance as the Church had earlier undertaken against the collapse of its message into speculation on its end. From within the modern preoccupation with the culmination of historical progress there emerged a powerful opposition to its dehumanizing implications.

The sharpest such expressions came from those who grasped that humanity cannot be separated from the person through whom it becomes transparent. Few offer a more striking example than Kant in giving voice to the astonishment that called a halt to his own unexamined progressivism. In his essay on the "Idea for a Universal History" he allows himself to think about the contradiction inherent in the idea of progress. That is, that the benefits and significance of progress only become apparent to the final generation, while all of their predecessors must regard their own lives as mere stages on the road to that fulfillment. Moreover, it is a fulfillment that seems to carry the uncomfortable implication that it too is a transition toward extinction. Even without confronting the last element of bleakness in the vision, Kant bluntly confesses to being "disconcerted" (*befremdend*) by the whole prospect.[20] The admission is important because Kant fully accepted the idea of historical progress as the framing conception of human existence. If even he with his well-developed Enlightenment sensibility cannot quite shake the unease, then it must arise from a deeper problematic. Could it be that progress violates its own idea?[21] Kant does not allow himself to ponder the matter any further on this occasion, but it would hardly have taken much to dislodge the idea of progress if a passing glance had been given to his moral philosophy. The person who is charged with enacting universal moral law irrespective of the consequences in his own life or the lives of others has already departed from any purely historical frame of reference. Can a contribution to progress justify dereliction of the categorical imperative? Or is it not the case that moral action must be determined within an eternal scale of measurement that transcends all historical considerations? It is testament to Kant's greatness that he does not conceal, but even dwells, on the contradiction that we seek not to expose but to hear in the same spirit.[22] It is the contradiction within which the person as the bearer of history unfolds history.

The issue would become clear only in the totalitarian convulsion that finally overturned the idea of progress. Not only was the scale of dehumanization a shattering blow to all progressivist illusions, but also the very notion of progress stood exposed as complicit in the mendacity. It was no isolated or occasional lapse when moral depravity had taken over whole societies or at least very sizable components of them. Only a more radical blindness could explain the ineffectiveness of the normal inhibitions and a chief culprit lay in progressivist ideologies that regarded individuals as expendable within the collective march of history. Resistance against this abyss of dehumanization prompted a revival of liberal democratic convictions within states that opposed the ideological regimes. A heightened respect for the inviolable dignity of the human person flows from the recognition of crimes against humanity.[23] But it was those who confronted the full totalitarian nightmare who brought forth the deepest affirmation of that imperative. They were the ones who showed through their own lives that they could not simply be reduced to the detritus of history. Some deep inexpungible core still remained after the most extensive efforts to eradicate them. What that core was they could hardly say but they knew that the more they continued to draw upon it the more real it became. This is the formidable spiritual power of the *zek* that, Solzhenitsyn remarks, was the most impressive feature of those who survived the camps without selling their souls. They had learned that even when they had nothing, they still had all that mattered in preserving a purified conscience. Think back over your whole life, Solzhenitsyn had been advised by an old doctor, and see if there is not some wrongdoing that has merited all the suffering you have received.[24] By refusing to turn their back on suffering, Victor Frankl concludes, individuals learned to surmount even the horrors of the concentration camps.[25] The change that was worked within them lifted them inexorably upward, so that they seemed to become like a different species. Their captors were now the ones imprisoned within their own fears, while the captives had soared over fences that could no longer contain them. Remember, one of the prisoners in *The First Circle* declares to the Minister of State Security, those from whom you have taken everything are free again.[26]

This was no abstract invocation of liberty. It was the liberty out of which a whole human life was lived because everything had been compressed into the decision between life and death. Choice is not an empty word when it is the event on which a whole existence hangs. Then it becomes clear that more than existence is at stake. The choice between good and evil is the point of existential transparence. Only those who are beyond good and evil, beyond life and death, can exercise such a choice. We do not contain the whole of our existence but there arise moments when we are compelled to act as if we did. For ever after things will be settled by that decision, an intimation of the horizon that reaches well beyond the confines of my own finite existence. While living in time we live continually in relation to what is beyond it. This was the great discovery of life lived at the extreme, that there is always more than life involved. One could not simply survive at any cost but always and only with a view to what is higher than survival. Kant's designation of the actor enacting universal moral law had received its finest instantiation. The reason why such an individual cannot be subordinated to any movement of historical progress is that he or she exceeds all finite scale of measurement. It may not be easy to say why the part must be greater than the whole, but it has become indisputable when the part has raised itself up to exercise judgment on the whole. The appearance of such individuals within history establishes that history cannot contain them.

In history truth is preserved by its transcendence of history. The problem is that we cannot easily explain how it is possible for the truth that is lost in history, by virtue of its immersion within forms and symbols no longer transparent, to be recovered. Again we see that these notorious questions about history, in this case the historicity of truth, implicate the very possibility of history. If all truth is historical, then there is no possibility of history which, by definition, takes its stand on the transcendence of the merely historical.[27] Conversely, if history is possible, then its truth is not simply historical. We cannot deal with the historicity of truth while prescinding from the challenge it represents. Our very question invokes a truth that is not simply historical since it aims at reaching a conclusion about history as such. In other words, the objection of the historicity of truth cannot account for its own possibility. We cannot give a non-historicist account without presupposing it, but this is precisely what is at issue. Overlooked in this labyrinthine inquiry is the person who walks it and who, for that reason, is never simply in the labyrinth. Persons can be in a labyrinth because they are never simply inside it. In all the decisive respects the labyrinth is inside of them and they are nowhere. Is this not the same with history? History is a possibility for persons who are never simply in it. Just as it is the openness of persons that underpins the possibility of history so it is the same transcendence that sustains the possibility of truth. All of this is overlooked, however, unless we are able to articulate it through the transparence of the person. A personalist philosophy of truth is continuous with a personalist philosophy of history, for history is the realm in which persons can apprehend the truth that has eluded expression.

How is it possible for us to translate truth from one language into another? How is it possible to translate truly what is in one language into another? The questions revolve around one another and the answer in each case is negative. It is impossible, but that is why we must do it. Without being able to apprehend truth perfectly we nevertheless begin to apprehend it imperfectly and thereby become aware of the imperfection, which is already to begin to remedy it. The question then is no longer about the validity of the outcome but of the dynamic that sustains it. Little is to be gained by relativizing the relativizers unless it prompts us to move beyond the futility of such disputes to discern the inner vitality of the person they disclose. We do not establish truth but live in the struggle to reach truth that would not be possible if we were not persons who already live in relation to what cannot be established. They know what cannot be known because they have always eluded what merely is. Nothing merely historical can present a barrier to their power of overleaping. In the texts and effects of history they can always hear the voice of the other who cannot be lost because he or she has never been present in the traces remaining. Transcendence speaks to transcendence across history. That is its truth. Conundrums about the historicity of truth have puzzled us for so long, despite their manifest refutation in all that we do, only because we have lacked a way of explaining the possibility of truth to ourselves. It is not enough to grasp the transcendence of the other, there must be a way of accounting for its possibility as well. Otherwise our faith in the possibility is recurrently shaken. That is why the shift toward a personalist account of the person remains indispensable.

The transition is one that has been under way since the differentiation of history began the erosion of the idea of nature. Some measure of the scale of the adjustment required may be gleaned from the fact that we still dispute whether human beings are defined by nature or by history. Both are concepts that have historically emerged and, as a consequence, have tended to become arrested in the first condition of their emergence, without including the condition of their emergence. We have already noted the inclination of history to swallow up the possibility of events that constitute history, nowhere more completely than in the imagination of the apocalypse that ends history. In the case of nature the issue has sunk below the level of visibility so much that we can only with difficulty recover the duality involved. Nature is what fixes and defines things, while their genesis recedes from view. But the original meaning of *phusis*, as what appears, aims precisely at the emergence, just as history is the recounting of what exceeds history.[28] The tensions, in other words, embedded in our most fundamental concepts all arise from their inability to include themselves. They are concepts that cannot conceive their own derivation. What they lack is the transparence uniquely available only in the person who knows his or her own emergence because he or she has never simply been contained by it. No nature can understand its own nature; it must simply regard it, if it regards it, as the given. The person alone is different for there the question of his or her nature arises and, with it, the transcendence of nature. This was an insight that was already in the Greek discovery of nature but never managed to find a place within the overall articulation of nature. As a result the awareness of transcending nature remained as an unsettling vibration at the edge of classical philosophy. The polis, for example, was supposed to have a nature but yet a great deal of attention and effort was to be put into the struggle to realize it. What is the status of a nature that has not yet become actual and may, perhaps, never be fully actualized? Most importantly, what is the realm in which the struggle for nature takes place? Clearly that is not simply nature.

It is the space within which nature is realized as that which appears from what is beyond appearing. This is the indefinability of history, an openness to possibility that has not been determined in advance. Instead, it is the realm in which the determination of determination takes place and, in that sense, the realm of the unexpected we associate with the realm of the person. The tension of history is the struggle between containment in what has emerged and the rupture that ever enlarges it. The openness of history is dependent on the awareness that it does not yield a final emergence of nature that fixes it forever. Instead, history must be seen as the region in which nature determines itself and, as such, never realizes its nature. Always on the way toward an end that is never reached, history is the point at which nature becomes transparent for its emergence as nature. Such a prospect assails us with a multitude of questions as to what kind of nature it is that requires such an emergence, who sets it in motion and why, without giving us any indication of the direction in which our puzzlement is likely to be resolved. It is only because we are persons, that is, because we occupy the perspective of those for whom nature and history are, that our puzzlement is not disorientation. Instead, we are fully capable of seeing that nature and history are the process of the emergence of the person, about whom we do not need to wonder about his or her emergence. The person is emergence as such because the person is never what he or she is, having already reached that point from which he or she is not. We can ask the question about the source of all because we are that question ourselves.

It is not a question we ask, it is the question we are in all that constitutes our existence. Nature and history are not the fixed quantities we have often taken them to be, but way stations in the emergence of the person who, in the process of self-determination, takes account of that very process of self-determination. Reality becomes transparent in the person because the person is transparence. It is through nature and history that that transparence is articulated and, as a consequence, that nature and history are rendered transparent for the person who transcends them.

CHAPTER SEVEN

Politics of the Person

Politics is the realm where history is transacted. When we think of history we think of it as political history, the history of the events and actions that constitute political reality. Even the writing of history, the preservation of the records on which it is based, is a function of the political community. No more vivid reminder of this can be adduced than the paucity of the Greek historical record. The Greeks were conscious of the shallowness of an historical record that could scarcely extend beyond the memory of a few generations. Lacking an imperial organization they were consigned to the status of perpetual youth, as compared to the ancient lineage the Egyptians and others could call upon to attest their longevity.[1] The link between politics and history is close as their mutual relationship demonstrates. Without politics there would be nothing to provide the subject matter of history but without history the achievements of politics can scarcely be remembered. It is in the writing of history that the two come together, the recollection of event as well as the event of recollection. Politics aims at the establishment of a community that endures beyond the moment of its establishment. In that sense politics provides both the content and the form of history. History, we may say, is the form that political existence assumes once it has emerged. Of course, all of this is only dimly intuited at the beginning. Historiography is little more than the preservation of the records on which it can be based, although that transmission is sensed as indispensable. Only later will the full significance of that service to the past become more apparent as the opening of a horizon that embraces all human beings living and dead and yet to be born. History thereby reveals politics as constituted by an opening toward a community that transcends the particularity of the community in which it originates. Local history is inexorably pulled toward universal history as its only viable unfolding.

It is at this point that the representative significance of political action comes to the fore. What is transacted in politics concerns more than a purely local interest for it is the vehicle by which the truth of existence is gained or lost for humanity as a whole. The political community, as a concrete people organized for action, stands revealed in its deepest attenuation as an opening to the community of mankind as a whole. That is, the political community is constituted by its relationship to the community that can never become a political community. The tension between them is bridged by a history that has no boundary short of universality. Politics has become transparent for its universal significance and history is the narrative of what is gained or lost for humanity as a whole. What had seemed to be matters of purely local import, how Achilles would support the loss of Briseis, turns out to be of far wider consequence.[2] Even what happens to the Achaeans as a result of his pique is hardly extensive enough to constitute the parameters of what is being decided. Nothing short of the epic struggle between good and evil, a battle continually waged in every human heart, fits the proportions of the contest. Political victory, the victory of the particular community, recedes in comparison to the primordiality of the choice being made. This is why the outcome remains of undying interest to us who are indifferent to the fortunes of the forces engaged in the Trojan War. But in relation to the conflict perpetually waged within, we remain deeply affected. Just as history is the perspective that abolishes historical distance, politics is the community that transcends its own particularity. The bonds of loyalty may originate within the ties of affection stemming from our local platoon, but they cannot remain tied to the allegiances from which they arise. The turning point is reached in the realization that loyalty requires more than local loyalty. We must first be loyal to loyalty, otherwise we can hardly be of use to anyone.

The political community exists through this transcendence of itself that constitutes its history. No community can survive unless its members are prepared to die for it, although this is in no way to suggest that their deaths are superfluous to it. We do not simply move on from the death of heroes who found states. They are rather held more tightly and more constantly within the ritual renewal of memory through which the state exists. History remains the truth of politics. And those who have given their lives have not relinquished membership in the community, for now they are enfolded within it more completely. Indeed, we might say that it is not only through death that the political community is founded and sustained, but that it is in death that it is most perfectly realized. The cult of the patriotic dead is not a mere afterthought in the life of the community; it is of its essence.[3] Having given all there is nothing more that remains to mark an interest different from the whole. A greater love no man hath than to lay down his life for an other or for all others. Wherever the community of friends exists he lives, not just in memory, but also in truth, for the community that has been formed consists of those who have transcended themselves. Membership is limited to those who have mutually given themselves. Death may be a boundary but it is not a barrier when it demarcates the fellowship of those who are already dead to themselves. In that sense the political community is also deathless, not just in the sense that it is the whole that endures by means of the demise of its parts, but also in the more profound sense that it is the joining together of those whose generosity has transcended death. Plato's famous anthropological principle, that the polis is man written in larger letters, here receives its highest exemplification. The hero is the idea of the city, without whom the city would not exist and, more importantly, would not even be a city.[4]

But this in turn sets up a responsibility of the community toward the member who embodies its self-transcendence. It cannot afford to treat him or her with anything less than inextinguishable tenderness. Not only must the community never take the self-sacrifice of its members for granted, it cannot afford to expend it in any way that fails to venerate them as ends-in-themselves. The whole has no higher goal than service toward its members. This is what makes the civil association so different from every enterprise association, to enlist the distinction of Michael Oakeshott.[5] In the latter case agreement on a common purpose is sufficient warrant for subordinating the interests of the members to the task at hand. The civil association, by contrast, has no purpose other than the self-chosen ends that the participants happen to have separately proposed for themselves. Yet even that distinction does not quite get at the heart of the matter for it still leaves the unity of the civil association in the background, a unity that consists precisely in foregrounding the inviolable liberty of its members. The great theoretical limitation of liberal political thought, with its foundation in the rights and dignity of the individual, arises from its inability to articulate the relationship between parts and whole when the whole elevates the primacy of the parts above itself. Jacques Maritain's brilliant encapsulation of liberal democracy as "a whole of wholes" virtually cries out for an explanation of the grounds of its possibility.[6] Where in the world do we find a model for such a relationship, one in which the whole willingly sacrifices itself for the sake of the parts? Aristotle evinces a glimmer of awareness of the challenge in his insistence that the polis is prior to its members in the order of nature but not in the order of time (*Politics* 1253a). The source of the difficulty lies in the limitation of our perspective to the model of nature while the person, who continuously surpasses nature, escapes attention. Politics thus cannot be properly understood unless it is viewed within this dynamic by which persons are its self-transcending source and are, in turn, embraced as the transcending purpose of the political. Persons are the origin and end of politics.

This can be seen first in the opening toward truth that defines the public space. Persons are political animals because they can come together within the realm of truth that is the achievement of politics. Yet they never form that perfect union because they are ever on their way toward it as the community that unfolds through history. That is why it is, second, impossible to step outside of the bonds of community that make community possible. Only persons are capable of that unbidden act of generosity by which they put themselves in place of the other. Each is, as a third feature, the founder of the political community, containing the whole inwardly. Persons are the possibility of politics as the community that must acknowledge the transcendence of persons within it. The problem is to find a means of conveying this infinity of the person who outweighs the whole of the political realm. We come finally to the language of rights as the only adequate epiphany of the person, the flash of transcendence within the finitude of politics. It is through the veneration of the person accorded by the whole understanding of rights that we reach a personalist treatment of the person.

The political affirms the inexhaustibility of the person and recognizes that affirmation as its own end.

Politics as the Realm of Truth

The Greeks discovered politics. This is literally true in the sense that they discovered that what concerns the polis was unfolded as politics. It is the public space in which the business of the public is transacted. Unlike government or rule whose decrees can be transmitted in secret, politics requires the visibility of a public realm, a space where all can see what is being decided. The Greeks took great pride in opening the events of the polis to the sunlight, in making what affects the public a matter of public determination, as opposed to the invisible machinations through which tyrannical rule must of necessity reach its determinations. They are the originators of free government, not because they embraced democratic voting, but because for them politics remained a matter of persuasion. Without the establishment of such a public realm there is no *res publica*, no common good, for it exists nowhere that it can be beheld. Limited to the mind of the ruler, the public good that is indistinguishable from the polis itself remains a purely private matter. The good of the ruler coincides with the political good. Only a space that is visible, accessible to all, guarantees the possibility of a good common to all. The polis, as that which constitutes the commonality of their existence together, is of necessity a public event. Inhabitants may continue to live within the same confines but they do not constitute a city until they come together within the mutuality by which their actions render it visible. A city ruled by the hidden decisions of a single individual or of a closely guarded cabal is not properly speaking a city. It is only the private possession of the ruling family, durable only so long as those who are possessed in this way do not walk away from it. Consent is the indispensable foundation of the city and it cannot be transmitted in anything less than a public affirmation. The city then exists through the space that its self-enactment constitutes.[7] Free government is self-government that takes place, not primarily through a specific institutional arrangement, but through the emergence of the political as the realm in which such structures are transparent for their purpose. Voting does not create the common good; the common good is what makes voting meaningful.

In other words, there must be a political realm within which our actions can be displayed before there is any possibility of forming a community. The Greeks were convinced that the optimum setting for politics is the polis because that is the largest community within which the members can meet one another. This explains why they held on to the idea of the polis long after its reality had become obsolete. No more poignant expression can be adduced than Aristotle's masterful account in the *Politics*, reflections that were penned on the eve of Greece's subsumption within the empire of Alexander. The conviction that the polis provided the only shelter for its constitutive mutuality ran so deep that no other arrangement was even contemplated. Politics apart from the community that can meet as the polis is unthinkable. The reason we retain the term to identify the process through which the public business is transacted is that we are still bound by the same logic as the Greeks uncovered. We no longer live in poleis, certainly not within communities in which face-to-face assemblies are any longer possible, but we have not left the inexorable necessity of such encounters. Politics remains the possibility of constituting a public space. As a consequence we are compelled to invent alternate routes toward the same achievement of mutuality even if we never reach its full extent. Citizens no longer meet as a whole but their representatives do within the virtual polis of congress, assembly, or parliament. Meeting remains indispensable to the formation of policy, not because we do not possess other means of aggregating consensus, but because consensus would have no meaning apart from the forum in which it emerges. Politics can still not be separated from the polis. What politics aims at preserving is the polis that makes politics possible. Unless the polis exists somewhere, albeit in the virtuality of a representative assembly, then it exists nowhere. The common good must be manifest for it to be served. This is familiar in the recognition that what unites us in the disputes over policy is the affirmation of the good of resolving them through debate.

The singular importance of politics is that it is the forum in which we are more than we say. Despite the words we may employ to deliver and yet not to deliver our intentions, we cannot conceal our standing in relation to them. Politics is that inexpungible record of who we are. We may think one thing and say another but we cannot conceal what we have done. In the realm of action truth shines forth because it is the realm of shining.[8] It is in the public space that we become visible because it is the arena that is made possible by our stepping out of the privacy where concealment is still possible. In political action who we are is manifest for all to see. This is why for the Greeks the public arena was preeminently the space in which we reach full human stature. Outside of it we can scarcely act, for our actions remain invisible even to ourselves. The notion of private action simply does not make sense. It was not that the Greeks had no notion of a private realm distinct from the public but that it was regarded as so insignificant that it could scarcely be regarded at all. For action to count it had to be publicly displayed.[9] Concealment therefore becomes impossible when action resoundingly declares who we are. It is not of course that political figures cannot dissemble, for we know it as a not infrequent occurrence, but that they cannot evade the display of deception as their action. Their concealment may not be immediately discovered, indeed, it may never be, but it has occurred within the realm in which discovery is possible. Just as we cannot lie to ourselves, we cannot lie when exposure is impossible. Truth is the condition of deception and politics is the realm of truth within which deception can occur. Politics enables self-communication or self-withholding because it makes it possible for us to be within the commonality that makes even invisibility visible.

A more modern view, drawing in part on its Christian background, would think of the moral life as prior to and foundational of the political. It is in the sight of God that we enact the choice of good or evil that stamps the character of who we are. The value of this transcendent perspective is that it renders the correlation between the good and being unmistakably clear. It is through the moral struggle that we ascend toward that which is or yield to the downward pull that falls away from what is. From either perspective we seem to have left the political far behind as of only diminished significance. Overlooked in this reflection is that we never actually live within the empyrean in which God and the soul contemplate one another. Our lives are passed in the untidy urgency of the political community and the whole order of life it renders possible, including the moral life. We do not live within the parameters of the categorical imperative but within the concrete immediacy of historical political society whose foundation is a continuous enactment. It is as the begetters or betrayers of that foundation that the moral life is gained or lost. This is not because there is no such thing as private action, private morality, or private life, but because there is no other community in which we exist than what is constituted by the public good. We may be participants and contributors to the wider trans-political community of mankind as a whole but that universal fraternity has no concrete existence. It cannot be served except by means of action that takes place within the shelter of the political community that makes such action possible. For the Greeks there was no higher service than to become a benefactor of the city, not because they did not have an intimation of universal human fellowship, but because only a citizen would possess the requisite solidity from which a contribution could be made. It is only as a member of a concrete community organized for action, that is, a political community, that one knows what the gravity and the cost of action entail. Nothing serious can be accomplished unless it is undertaken within the openness of political debate.

Only in that forum does it become evident what is at stake. The fate of humanity, the judgment of good or evil, may be implicated in the outcome, but it is transacted within the circumstances of a finite community within its specific place and time. We do not legislate the universal moral law; we only render specific justice in the case at issue. The complex web of adjudication, the intricate unfolding of the common law, is one long testament to the inseparability of justice from its particular application. There is hardly a principle of adjudication as such if it is not responsive to that invisible unfolding. When Aristotle insisted that ethics is a science whose truth lies in the particulars rather than in the universals he was asserting the same thing. Persons, we have emphasized, transcend all limitations of place and time for they are an openness to being that reaches beyond being. But they do not exist outside of the circumstances of their setting in life. Transcendence is a movement that remains tied to what it transcends and, most importantly, never ultimately escapes it. The call to transcendence is taken up by rendering faithful service to the conditions of its own possibility. Like art, it is a radiance that is inseparable from the medium from which it radiates. Never limited to the finitude of conditions, persons can yet never dispense with them without rendering their own movement of transcendence impossible. It is for this reason that the political looms large as the realm in which truth reigns for, even when it is evaded, the imprescriptibility of truth commands the tribute of appearance.

The claim to represent truth is paramount in every political regime for legitimacy is entirely bound up with validity. But this means that politics is the battlefield of truth. A regime can neither expose itself to the charge of untruth nor permit such an affront to stand unanswered. The assertion of a monopoly of truth is endemic to the character of political authority. Unlike the parallel assertion of a monopoly of force, however, truth is not so easily consolidated. The very invitation to contemplate it renders the assertion of truth into an invitation for scrutiny. The truth of the regime is inexorably molded into the regime of truth. Political authority that seeks the backing of truth discovers that it can gain no such support without itself backing truth. It is no accident that the constitutional forms most deeply rooted in truth achieve the greatest stability. Not only is it pragmatically difficult to govern when deception has become the rule rather than the exception, but government itself can hardly survive when it masquerades as an authority that is nonexistent. Without the recognition of authority there is no authority, and there can be no recognition unless it is a recognition in truth. The bond of commonality is a bond of truth. The appearance of truth may serve the same end for a considerable period of time, but it is only a matter of time before discovery exposes its illegitimacy. The tyrant is the weakest form of rule because his support is entirely composed of appearance. Ultimately the objection is not that he has misruled the city but that he has not even ruled it, for he has hardly even constituted a city. This was how the issue was clarified in the first great examination of the truth of the city in the light of truth itself, as that contest was unfolded in the emergence of classical philosophy. It was in this way that the city gave birth to philosophy.[10]

The contest over truth is a contest over rule. But it is not *simply* a contest over rule. What is at stake is more than rule and that is the momentous discovery of the struggle. There would be no possibility for philosophy to question the city's representation of truth if the city had not taken its stand in relation to what is beyond itself. This is the wedge through which an authority that challenges the authority of the city emerges. It is because the city transcends itself in the direction of truth that it gives rise to a transcendent articulation of truth. Philosophy could not render judgment on the city if it did not share the same ground with it. Philosophy is political and the polis is philosophical. Inexorably they move toward the same realization that existence is transcendence. Whether the city can follow the path of philosophy is initially an open question although it is soon resolved against it, thereby separating philosophy forever from the city. That does not detract, however, from their common lineage. The city may not become philosophical but it perseveres in the tension with philosophy because it cannot sever the orientation toward truth.[11] Without becoming philosophical the city remains philosophical in action. The life of philosophy may be more elaborately unfolded beyond the boundaries of the city but the life of the city continues to be animated by its philosophical impulse. Transparence toward truth remains an ineluctable feature of the city that cannot endure as a brute imposition of power. Consent is the ineliminable condition that opens it toward dialogue. The ironic consequence is that the political realm remains open to that dialogue long after philosophy has trailed off into irrelevance. In philosophy truth can become a purely speculative inquiry; in the polis it remains a matter of life and death.

The very existence of the political community is dependent on the attainment of truth for only then is the public realm properly constituted. Not only is consent evoked in the arrival at truth, but also there is nothing to which consent can be given if it is not the common acknowledgment of truth. The public and truth are synonymous when the alternative is the assertion of the private under the guise of the public. Only truth can constitute a public realm. But it cannot impose itself upon the community, for it must arise through the dialogic process by which truth ever emerges. The city in speech is none other than the city in truth. Just as there can be no dialogue unless it centers on the emergence of truth so there can be no city unless the event of truth is the ground of authority. Mere assertion of private perspectives does not frame a dialogue, just as the exercise of power without authority does not make a city.[12] Only truth, as an aspiration and an attainment, can provide the space of meeting. It is truth, therefore, that provides the opening for truth, for there is nothing prior to truth that can function as its ground. Authorization depends on truth rather than the other way around. Whatever might be adduced as standing higher than truth, capable of vouching for truth, lies susceptible to the question of its truth. In a community of persons, each of whom is open to truth, the only viable path to truth runs through truth. There is no possibility of transferring responsibility for truth to some other authorizing source once our own responsibility has become apparent. As that which arises from itself, truth is the exemplification of the political foundation. This is why politics is preeminently the realm of truth. Holding power only through its own sovereign sway, truth is beholden to nothing and no one in a way that converges almost perfectly with the supremacy of the public realm. Truth stands within its own right.[13]

Political rule is the rule that derives from the authorization of truth. Consent, extracted through neither coercion nor subterfuge, forges the most durable bond of community. A society of friends, Aristotle observed, constitutes a formidable power for nothing can disrupt their unity (*Nicomachean Ethics* 1158b5–10). Suspicion and mistrust cannot break the ranks of an association rooted solely in truth; nothing undisclosed can fracture their bond. They are unassailable from the perspective of truth, having anchored their friendship in the conviction that nothing is outside of truth. Yet this is in no sense a philosophically explicated position. It is simply the lived truth of their existence. As such, it possesses more impressive durability than the best-mounted philosophic defense of truth. They exemplify what they do not say and they say all the more powerfully for that silence. This is the politics of truth and the truth of politics. It is truth in action and the reason why all reflection on politics takes its start from the truth that constitutes politics. No more theoretically penetrating first principle is available. Reflection must take its beginning from the reflection that is prior to it and thereby provides the possibility of reflection. The political occupies that kind of role. It is not derived from a reflection on politics but rather makes such reflection possible, a priority that has not always been taken on board by political theory. As a consequence, the philosophical development that emerges to challenge the truth of the city does not always recognize the degree to which it too is derivative from the same source. To conceive of politics as the more primordial realm of truth is to require a corresponding acknowledgment of the inability of philosophy to capture that primordiality. In some sense politics is the realm outside of which we cannot think, or at least not think without thinking within it.

Truth is lived in politics before it is discussed. This is why the discourse of truth, philosophy, has received its impetus from politics and still remains within its ambit. How we stand in relation to truth is more abundantly manifest within the political realm than anywhere else precisely because it is unavoidable. Before we have had a chance to concoct our alibis we have stepped into the witness box. The owl of Minerva comes too late on the scene to be of any help to us, for we have already inscribed an affidavit in life that we cannot retract in thought. Without intending to do so we have assumed a position that now is subject to philosophical examination. It is from that interrogation that philosophy emerges without being able to shed the connection with its emergence. We continue to philosophize within the truth proclaimed by the political inauguration. This is not to say that we remain bound by the form of its establishment, for otherwise there would be no possibility of philosophizing in tension with it, but that we remain indebted to the opening of truth proclaimed within the political construction. In asserting a truth the civil constitution asserts truth as such. One cannot profess a certain order of affairs as right without simultaneously declaring that an order of right prevails. In many respects this is what is dimly intuited in Rawls's famous proclamation that the right is prior to the good.[14] To those who object that an order of right presupposes the good Rawls's defenders might respond that the converse also holds. Their case might be better served if they could explain why this is so, by pointing to the derivation of the good from the right as the priority of the political over the philosophical. Instead, they tend to confuse the issue by suggesting that philosophy might uncover the arguments by which the political is grounded. This is to overlook the extent to which even this way of posing the issue presupposes the political. If politics furnishes the material for philosophical reflection, then philosophy can never stand completely outside of it. Philosophy uncovers what it can never provide.

Even the Kingdom of God derives from the meaning of kingdom as such. The City of God is an eschatological city we would scarcely be able to conceive without the Earthly City. But that does not mean it is a projection of the perfection denied us within the merely political realm. The City of God is rather the definitive judgment of the unattainability of the perfection at which all earthly community aims. Projection is merely the failure to acknowledge that impossibility. In contrast, the City of God is the assurance of our membership within a city that transcends all possibility of breakdown. We are never simply citizens of the Earthly City, so that even when we become stateless persons we do not lose our humanity. The question then is what is the status of that eschatological community to which we also belong? It is the question at the heart of political theory ever since Plato's *Republic* characterized it as the "city in speech." Is the judgment under which politics labors merely a matter of speech? Or does it have any reality? Revelation, even more than philosophy, accentuates the higher reality as the most real. Now the truth of politics exists under the truth that eclipses it. Even while transcendent truth is incapable of establishing a realm within this world it bears witness to the primordial community of love that embraces all human beings. Christ is the head of all, as St. Thomas insisted. The possibility of the political is thus assured by the community that the political can never contain. At best the political community may acknowledge that self-limitation and thereby glimpse beyond itself.

Politics as Its Own Horizon

Nothing can explain the foundation of the political that is identical with its history. What establishes the polity is the pure self-giving that cannot be accounted for by anything other than itself. There is nothing there before the gift has been given, for it is the gift of giving that constitutes a common realm. In order to found a relationship of mutuality there is no resource other than mutuality itself. Where does it come from? We do not know, but we can confirm that it cannot come from anything other than mutuality. It is not like we are building a bridge on which, after it is completed, we can walk across. What we are building is the possibility of building together, a bridge that joins us so closely we have reached the other side. Before any meeting takes place we have already met. Even to work on framing a constitution implies that we are already related in such a way that a constitution is the suitable evocation of our relationship. Communities that succeed in this task of politically articulating themselves often invoke an ancient constitution, a pact from "time out of mind the memory of man runneth not to the contrary," as the appropriate acknowledgment of this primordiality.[15] But this does not quite cohere with the imperative to unfold such a constitution in the present, a necessity rendered all the more imperative by the impossibility of simply basing it on the past. We are required to found again what may have been, although not definitively, found before. Nothing compels us to undertake what cannot be compelled. Invocations of the mists of time are no more than that, confessions of our inability to dispel even the mists of the present. We have no more idea of how to move toward establishing what had not been there before, than of how our distant forebears might have managed the same negotiation.

This is not just the irreducibility of decision inherent in every action, but a far deeper unfathomability that attaches to the actions that initiate community itself. We act not just in regard to others but also with them in mutuality. It is as if the space of our coming together precedes our coming together. In acting we are not alone but are already in relation to others who similarly hold us within their purview. We do not create the political, the political creates us. Who we are and who we are to become is only apparent within the unfolding by which we create a common world between us, a world that does not exist merely as a space but as a space that is organized for action together. A long dormant political world is awakened through its constitutional invocation. We bring about its emergence and, in turn, are brought about by it. How we can be simultaneously its lawgivers and its law recipients is the great mystery we seek to finesse by distinguishing between sovereign and subject. Alternation of roles is not quite an adequate account of the political beginning that revolves within the tension between them. It is not a question of whether we occupy those different roles, but of how. The subject must be sovereign and the sovereign subject, a reciprocity that is only possible if they are indeed interchangeable. Sovereign and subject are the same, an observation that provided Plato with the model of constitutional rule in the philosopher-king.[16] Giving and receiving may be differentiated but they cannot be separated for they mutually imply one another. Even to distinguish them as roles is already to endow with too much stasis the vital dynamic they intend to supply. The source of the difficulty is that we have thought of the political community as a more fixed quantity than it is. Strictly speaking it is not a thing at all but, rather, the life of the whole within which we live as members of a whole. Roles may be assigned but their assignment is tantamount to their overturning. The first will be last and the last first, not as an exhortation, but as a depiction.

The political virtually requires the effacement of self as the condition for the emergence of what is common. Setting oneself aside is what yields the public space that comes into view as a possibility only when it has occurred. When we ask whence that capacity derives we are faced with the realization that it can only come from itself. It is a pattern we have already noted in taking account of the innermost capacity of the person but, before we shift too quickly to its personalist dimensions, it is worthwhile to dwell on its purely political manifestations. Resorting to the notion of persons begs the question of how the political transposition occurs. It is not just that persons ground the political, for there is a fundamental sense in which the political grounds them. Why else would the political be so indispensable? It is almost as if they need a space in which their reality as persons might be displayed and that nothing short of the visibility of the public realm will suffice. This has nothing to do with the acquisition of fame, although it is very often mistaken for that impulse, for the good man, Plato reminds us, must be compelled to rule. Why is it that the philosopher-king needs the polis? He does not need the gain or glory it can offer him and already possesses the whole of virtue. The question is only obliquely raised in the *Republic*, which is the philosopher-king's own report of the dialogue concerning his rule. Aristotle approaches the question in his account of specific virtues for he presents us with a portrait of the gentleman who aspires to act on a public scale. His *Politics* strains to present a picture of the polis as the realm where alone the full range of virtue can be exercised. Yet even Aristotle does not confront the paradox toward which his thought drives. That is, that the man of practical wisdom can serve the polis most completely when he is no longer concerned with serving it at all. Virtue that reaches its full stature in the polis has already transcended it. We are no closer to plumbing the character of the political if it has become a permeable medium through which we must pass.

Yet that is not an insignificant advance, for even a permeable medium renders visible what would otherwise rest in invisibility. Politics, we begin to see, is the space within which what is invisible becomes briefly visible. As such it partakes of the same fluctuations as that which passes through it. The political community exists through the self-sacrifice of those who are no longer its members although, in another sense, they are more deeply its members than any of the living. It is through them that its innermost truth is revealed. The political community is the community that transcends itself. Never taking account of its own survival, it survives. Or more accurately, it is through the death of the living that the life of its descendants is assured in history. Individually we may be capable of such unbidden selflessness on occasion, on behalf of family members, friends, or even strangers in need. But we have not elevated that thankless generosity into a principle that can be counted upon. That is what the political community has done. It has made self-giving a rule, with all of the drawbacks that such regimentation implies. In many respects the governing authority would rather shift the burden to any sector other than itself and those most favored by it. But none of that would even be possible if there were not the reserve of mutuality on which it can draw. The misuse of power is possible only because power has been authorized. Not every regime has rooted itself in consent but there would be no possibility of coercion if everything had to be coerced. Consent, the surrender of self that yields the common, is constitutive of every regime. Even the most ruthless governments, perhaps they most of all, know the fragility of their power, for it comes from a level utterly inaccessible to their instruments. How can they compel what cannot be compelled? When it is compelled the value of consent has already been lost. This is why, as all the classic literature insists, revolutions occur through dissensions within the ruling class, for they are the class on whose support one must count and whom, for that reason, one cannot coerce. In the limiting instance the power of the powerless is the only genuine font of power.

It is the invisible that is the source of the visible. That is what makes the political so difficult to apprehend for, by the time it is apprehended, it no longer identifies the source whence it derives. Forebearers function, not only as an authorization for its foundation, but also as a marker for a past that remains inaccessible. Always there is an ancientness that lies outside of memory, not because there is no actually remembered transmission, but because that is the only way of denoting the emergence of the present out of what it is not. What makes the political community the preeminent demonstration of this is that it does not simply live off its past, as if that were a fund deposited in the bank. The past is past and can no longer impact the present. Preceding generations no longer vote, pay taxes, or fight wars. They are present only in what they have left behind materially and in memory. But in a more profound sense they are present because they have never left. We meet them in the community that stretches out between us and in which we too will only have a departed membership. It turns out, however, that that is the only membership that counts, for all who have given themselves have placed others first and themselves last. Disappearing behind their contributions they cannot disappear. Tradition, that which is handed on, is not the dead hand of the past but the living hand that comes from the past.[17] We are inclined to think that the state cannot die, and shout, "long live the king," while we as individuals pass on and even the king dies. The state may not be immortal but it does live through history with a durability that outlasts its members. Yet we lack a precise sense of what it is that lives when all of its parts are continually sloughed off to be replaced by new ones. Does this mean that the state is comparable to a living organism? Or perhaps that it is closer to the species that prevails over, and by means of, the demise of individuals? Despite the frequency with which such analogies have been invoked we nevertheless sense something unsatisfactory about them. The state is not an unconscious process whose members can scarcely possess an interest contrary to its own. Instead, we think of the state as, at its most fundamental level, the fruit of their conscious choice and therefore duty bound to consider their interests. Yet there is something surpassing about the political community by which it can require its members to utterly subordinate themselves to the whole. What kind of a community can command a free self-sacrifice?

Evidently it bears only remote resemblance to the voluntary associations we enter into in order to advance our interests. It is this divergence that has been the bane of contract explanations of the origins of the polity. Whatever benefits the political community delivers they are unrelated to our readiness to support it. The terms of our membership require a commitment in the face of a complete absence of any returns. The possibility of benefits for anyone arises only because we have entered a community that is prior to all such possibility.[18] Neither gains nor losses can affect its fundamental nature, which is that it endures through all gains and losses. In that sense it is immortal, although not in the sense of possessing a permanent lease on existence. Its immortality is prior rather than subsequent. No doubt it is a strange status if the transcendence of mortality is the condition of its existence. Yet that is its truth. The members of the political community are already dead, even the future ones, because they have pledged their existence in defense of the whole. They may still be walking around, because the pledges have not yet been redeemed, but that does not alter their basic condition. It is not just philosophy that is the practice of dying; the same imperative applies to citizenship as well. Being already dead they discover, however, that they are deathless. Individual demise, even the disappearance of the whole state, cannot touch an immortality that has already been gained. It is not just that the political community holds its dead in memory, thereby conveying an immortality on them, but that it does this because it is itself constituted by immortality. What is valued is the value that constitutes the community of memory. There is nothing incidental about the assignment of a Memorial Day; it is the very reason for the existence of the nation, not just in fact, but more importantly in itself.

Correlatively, heroes do not die so that they will be remembered; they are remembered because they die. Herein is the source of the formidable strength of the political community, for what is dead cannot be killed. For the same reason its members are immune from coercion into its service, having placed themselves beyond its ultimate sanction. That which is not, that which has placed itself aside, is the durability of what is. Those for whom everything is over have gained all.

That is the secret of the political community that cannot be explained in terms of any of its concomitants. It can be understood only in its own terms as the unique irreplaceable instance of the community that exists between human beings. We might say that the political community is the concretization of that universal community, the point at which the eschatological intersects with time. Like the conferees in Rawls's "original position" we meet outside of place and time, although not as a thought experiment, but as a veritable reality. It is the political that makes it abundantly clear that the eschatological, that which draws us outside of all conditionality, is the most real. The formidable strength of political communities derives from that which is beyond strength. Nothing can assail it for it has overcome all obstacles in its very formation. Composed of those who are ready to give all in its defense, it cannot be defeated by any inner rupture. Dissension cannot occur when every member has already put every other member ahead of himself or herself. Mutual giving and receiving is the ground of its perfect mutuality. For those who have given up all there is no danger that can overwhelm them or, most importantly, dislodge the community they have established between them. Normally we do not think of the polity as a state of perfect union, although it is often so enjoined, because we think it is impossible to be united with so many others whom we scarcely know. Certainly it is not the union of intimacy in family or friendship. Yet in its anonymity it surpasses those more localized allegiances, for it is rooted in a willingness to die for those whom we have not met. Selflessness cannot be improved upon when it is defined by a generosity that transcends all natural limits. The perfection of the political community is not limited to its self-sufficiency but extends most importantly to the finality of its principle. Of course, there still are particular bonds of ethnicity, language, religion, and history, but the political community is already their enlargement in a direction that heads toward universality.[19] This is why it is difficult, although not impossible, to rebuff the stranger and the immigrant. The universal brotherhood of the polity cannot so easily ignore its own foundation.

Echoes of the Christian love of neighbor are not coincidental for the political community is its embodiment. What is the state but the coming together of those whose primary qualification is need, the singular mark that defines who my neighbor is? The brotherhood of all men may be a frequently invoked ideal but it has no concrete reality except within the quasi-universal community constituted by the state. Occasionally we may interact with people elsewhere in the world, we may even engage in humanitarian projects for the relief of their distress, but we cannot live with them unless we are politically united. Mere geographical contemporaneity, a fellowship of mutual good will, does not constitute a community. Amorphous forms of cooperation represent no more than the momentary reality they are. For action to take place, especially when conditions are exigent, there must be a political organization in place that can redeem the irrevocable pledges of its foundation. It is through the political community that we can dedicate ourselves with that last full measure of devotion. We are not just helpful strangers who might choose to minister to one another or not as the situation disposes us. Rather, we have entered an indissoluble union from which we are resolved not to walk away. It may seem plausible to picture ourselves as joined by means of a contract of mutual support but, as we have seen, this only begs the question of what could possibly induce us to uphold it when the contract requires everything of us. The question, we realize, has been misdirected. We do not uphold the contract, for the contract upholds us. The contract is not just the condition of the possibility of our joining together, it is the condition of the possibility of contracting as such.

It is because we are already pledged to one another that we can do so by the formality of contract. Instead of trying to explain the contract in terms of other things, a bargain by which we seek a profit above our contributions, we must look on it as the irreducible horizon of our living. We can only bargain against a background of what cannot be bargained for. Mutual respect and fidelity do not issue from an agreement but instead enable us to enter into agreements. To speak of this as a matter of virtue that we must presuppose and promote is merely to push the issue further away from us, for it is the possibility of virtue that is the irreducibility within which we live. We can become virtuous only because virtue is the setting within which we act. It is not even the case that we find virtue since, strictly speaking, we find ourselves within virtue, virtue that has been there all along as the possibility of our awakening to it. Virtue can be acquired only because we have already been given it. The Greeks were surely right in seeing the polis as the community within which that possibility can be optimally fulfilled, for it is the arena in which the full range and reach of virtue can be realized. But they did not become clear on the primordiality implied. That is, that while the polis may be the community within which virtue is possible, the more decisive aspect is that it is virtue that makes the polis possible. The polity lives in virtue. As a consequence of this misplacement of emphasis, Western political thought has struggled for millennia with the precariousness of its ordering principle. Historical reality, in contrast, has been far more reliable, for we have generally witnessed political continuity that has only occasionally been marred by its downfall. Individuals do not generate the polity. They have been generated by it.

The Person as the Possibility of Politics

We live by living beyond ourselves. The polity is the abundant revelation of this because it so palpably derives from a mutuality of sacrifice extended over time. Everyone has their interests and incentives but, if this were all, there would be no possibility of building something more than our individual selves. Apart from the theories about its genesis, the political community is a fact explicable only by virtue of the powerful priority of others for us. Unlike the economy of reciprocal exchange, whose logic lies completely on the surface, the polity seems to thrive on a logic of nonreciprocity that almost beggars explanation. Why should we reach out to strangers who may never reach out to us? Why expend ourselves in a lifetime of service from which only others will benefit? The notion that we must be paid is so thoroughly embedded in our rationality that it virtually defines it, except that we are surrounded by reminders of its continual overturning. Others have given of themselves, even given themselves, that we might be, and we in turn are drawn by the others whose arrival can only be made possible by our self-giving. We do not give that we might receive for, in the widest dimension, we receive that we might give. The bounded rationality of the market is only made possible by the unbounded rationality of the community that sustains it.[20] Things can be bought and sold only because not everything can be bought and sold, not least of all the buyers and sellers themselves. Their reciprocity is grounded in a mutual openness that exceeds all reciprocity. We cannot even thank our greatest benefactors who have long disappeared from the scene, rendering repayment of the debt impossible. The relationship has been winnowed to the purity of the gift for they are present to us in no other way.

The polity is the community of the gift. When neither giver nor recipient can meet they are joined together only in the gift. Recompense is forever moot when giving excludes the possibility of acknowledgment. Even the satisfaction that might be derived from contemplating the good provided to a future generation hardly constitutes sufficient motive, for it is precisely when one is long gone that the deed will bear the fruition in which such self-congratulation might be warranted. One does not even know that the consequences will be realized, nor fully what they are, nor even if the giver will be known. Besides, such attenuations are too flimsy a thread on which to build an enterprise that seems to possess no substantial basis other than giving itself. When we ask about the nature of the community thereby generated we may take some small pleasure in contemplating our continuation within it. But on closer examination, in asking what it means to be an American or an Australian, we discover that it has very little specificity beyond the same fellowship of self-giving. Our successors must take as their purpose the giving that continues itself. All other bonds that might unite us pale in significance compared to that transcendent generosity of purpose. Ultimately we are hardly even citizens of particular states but cofounders of a spiritual community that exists nowhere but within the universality of its impulse. That is to say, it exists as an eschatological community, as the Church does in its refusal to acknowledge its present institutionalization as its truth.[21] At its surface the political community may be the realm where power, and its corruptions, are ostentatiously displayed, but that would quickly evaporate were it not for the invisible community of those whose self-transcendence silently underwrites it. In giving, the tangible may be released into the world but its character remains the spirit out of which it emanates. That is the real community, the community of giving, of which government is only a shadow. Representation is heavily weighted toward the one who functions as the representative, but its truth is the multitude whose recognition brings it about.

In every decisive respect the political community is a community of persons from whom alone it continually emerges as their most decisive possibility. The president of the United States, for example, is powerless without his recognition as president by those who are not around him.

The person is the possibility of politics. It is persons who can constitute the community of the gift because that is quintessentially the community they form. As persons they are no longer present in the gift, in what they do, and yet they are present in the only way that counts. They are present as persons, that is, in the mode of those who are present through their absence. No natural analogue even approximates this, or it does so only by analogy with a community of persons. Space and time prove no barrier to them for they are only physical impediments that are overleapt in the first stretching forth of gesture. Separation, their enclosure within the fortress of singular consciousnesses, is even less of an obstacle, for it is through the eye of the other that they first glimpse themselves. Isolation with its accompaniments of suspicion and mistrust, in Hobbes's depiction of the state of nature, requires an even greater effort of imagination than visualizing their coalescence around a sovereign. Aristotle's observation that man is a political animal only intimates the most superficial connection, for it fails to penetrate to what makes it possible to be a member of a polis. That is, that he is born into a polis that he already carries within him. Even before he speaks he already contains the word of love that speaks to every other human being. It is not his speech that enables him to communicate with the other; it is his communication with others that enables him to speak. No one needs to be told what language is.[22] It is the possibility of being understood by others and of understanding them. Mutuality is the condition in which we find ourselves, not as a given of nature, but as the possibility of giving that always exceeds nature. The gift can always be identified but its source eludes us. Only persons can know what giving is because only they can give and in the process give what cannot be given and yet must be given, themselves. That is what a community of persons is and what a political community cannot avoid being. It is a community of those who know that they are not present in any of its manifestations because they are so completely present within them.[23]

Persons are never present and, for this reason, are the only ones who can always be present. The self-transcendence that makes a community possible is both an achievement of persons and the definition of persons. A common good constituted by the subordination of individual interests to the whole, the harmonic convergence that characterizes any cooperative functioning system, is more than an afterthought to them. They already contain it in their continuous departure from who they are. Self-transcendence is possible for persons because persons are self-transcendence. But this also means that even when they create the interlocking cooperative patterns within which they live, persons are not simply that. Nothing could be further from who they are than what they create. Paradox is the great law of their existence. The supreme challenge of political communities, therefore, is to learn how to take this into account. Having invested so much in the operations necessary to sustain them, they must find ways of acknowledging that they are not what they appear to be. Unlike any of the marvels of nature or the intricate machines of our own construction, the cooperative arrangements within which human beings themselves live constitute a singular exception. Where all of the others are conceived as systems intended to secure the good of the whole beyond the parts, a society of persons with its framing political structure is a radical reversal of priorities. Here alone in all the universe the part exceeds the whole.[24] This is not merely a matter of aspiration but a matter of fact. The great historical communities organized for action, that is, politically, draw on the endless generosity of the persons who create them, but those persons are nowhere contained within the work of their creation, which must be looked upon, therefore, as pale adumbrations of the higher community in which they are united. Persons cannot be sacrificed for the common good, not only because it is not right, but also because it is impossible. They have already expended themselves on its behalf and, even if they wanted to give more than they can give, they cannot do so. They remain a community of persons, a community of those who know one another as uncontainable in any of their enactments. The only fitting community of persons is the community that mutually embraces one another as persons.

This of course does not mean that persons cannot be killed. They are so dispatched all too frequently, but it does mean that in some sense they cannot be eliminated. How can what is never simply there be eradicated through the removal of the there? Besides, one who has already given himself or herself on behalf of another cannot really die. They have died once and cannot do so again. To be a person is somehow to have reached the imperishability of those who go through death into life. This is what self-transcendence is. It is to die to self and in dying to live beyond life. At the individual level this is dimly glimpsed in the great heroic actions of those who break through to its truth. For the rest of us it may merely remain at the level of aspiration. But for the political community it acquires an affirmation that compels us to recognize its reality, for the political community is the elevation of transcendence into its principle. Where self-transcendence has so evidently become the foundation on which the community is based, fidelity to its own principle requires that it incorporate the acknowledgment of persons as its very essence. It is a community of those who cannot die because they have already died to themselves. Sharing a common space and time is only a beginning for they remain united even when they are no longer so defined. Badges of identity are a pale substitute for the inner embrace that has occurred. Persons are united through sacrifice, which is the only means by which they can hold one another as persons. We may be inclined to think that this is simply a matter of remembering our dead and contemplating our descendants, but that is to characterize it in an excessively subjective way.

Lincoln's formulation in the Gettysburg Address is striking when he insists that it is not up to us to bestow honor on the fallen, who have already sufficiently attained it. We are the ones who must draw from them the dedication to the cause for which they gave "the last full measure of devotion." There is nothing purely inward about the community to which they attested, as if it might now depend on the vagaries of our readiness to keep it in mind through memorialization. On the contrary, as Lincoln insists, nothing we can do can "add or detract" from what has been accomplished. Compared to their final sacrifice we can only offer incremental contributions to an edifice that is fully present. Ours is the unreality, theirs is the reality. This is why the polity is most fully actualized through the dead rather than the living. No accumulation of remembrances and tributes can match what has already been realized. It is indeed fitting that the polity should retain its martyrs in precious memory but it should not make the mistake of thinking that they acquire this status through its recognition of them. In a world where prizes and awards are ubiquitous we are inclined to forget that their bestowal, properly speaking, adds very little to the recipients. They are only of value because the recipients bestow far more on the bestowers. The situation is even more one sided when it comes to acknowledgment of those to whom we owe everything. Lincoln's address is justly celebrated because, apart from the power and economy of language, it arises from a profound understanding of that relationship. There would be no polity to heap grateful remembrance on the dead, were it not for their selflessness. Not only did they secure its existence but, even more significantly, they constitute what must be secured. The community of remembrance is released by those whose deeds are worth remembering. It is not memory that is the basis of the community but the inextinguishable nobility that summons recollection. We may be engaged in remembering, Lincoln understood, but the possibility is furnished by those whose lives have been memorable.

They are the supreme disclosure of the political. We see that there is no community other than the one effected in the outpouring that precedes every community. Each person contains the whole by which she or he is contained. It is for this reason that they must be embraced as the whole. There is a peculiar anticipation of this line of thought in Aristotle's wrestling with the place of the man of preeminent virtue within the polis. Clearly the prospect of such an individual did not fit well with his scheme of a community of equals who rule and are ruled in turn, thereby acquiring the full range of virtues. In a sense this rare specimen already exceeds the polis since he has no need of its schooling. He has surpassed the polis. Again it is a mark of Aristotle's greatness that he does not simply dismiss such an inconvenient case or minimize its impact on his thought. Instead, he acknowledges that justice requires that such an individual should be made king, not simply because he surpasses his contemporaries, but because he surpasses the polis itself.[25] The community that exists for the sake of virtue, for the good life, cannot overlook the individual in whom its nature has been fully realized. Such a man is the polis as a whole. The source of the difficulties with which Aristotle struggled is his conviction that the polis has such a nature as can be realized. This is also why its history is not of particular relevance to him. What he did not consider is that the polis cannot be realized because it has already been realized in the perfect community glimpsed at its foundation. At best the polis can only aim at what it has already been. This is why its existence is unfolded over historical time for it can never capture the eschatological flash from which it begins. What remained to be discovered is what this discovery means and how we might talk about a community that exists before it has existed. But most of all, we need to find a way of affirming the meaning of a community in which the individual is greater than the whole.

It is here that political practice has anticipated our theoretical need in the most striking fashion. The language of rights is inchoate acknowledgment of the transcendence of the person, for it is a language of inexhaustibility. A right that can be used up when its limits are reached scarcely counts as a right. It cannot be alienated, even by its possessors. To accept the logic of rights is to enter into a perspective that defies all logic, or at least the logic of limits by which all our other perspectives are framed. Here alone, it seems to say, we touch upon the limitless. No matter what persons have done or what condition they are in, they never reach a point where they have ceased to require respect for their rights. Even crime does not wholly abolish the rights of criminals. In some respects it brings their rights more acutely into play since they are the more seriously jeopardized. The same applies to those whose hold on existence is so tenuous as to be almost imperceptible. Death does not abrogate the accord that the rights of the deceased may impose upon us. We cannot simply dispose of their remains or sully their reputations as if they have ceased to count.[26] And certainly no social good, no matter how large or enduring, even the good of humanity as a whole, can justify setting aside the rights of its most insignificant member. We are properly appalled at a society that could countenance such indifference, for we judge that any collective benefit cannot be worth so exorbitant a price. One person is larger than the whole. This is what the prescription of rights, a moral imperative that cannot refuse its extension to every single person, uncompromisingly entails. It is a moral force that has gained such uncontested authority across our world, despite the evident uncertainty of its basis, that its very success is as much in need of explanation. The discrepancy between the depth of conviction of rights and the paucity of justifications adduced has now reached such a point that, we might well ask, if rights are not the basis for our understanding of dignity rather than the other way around.[27]

Rights as an Epiphany of the Person

The suggestion that rights may serve as an epiphany of the person should not strike us as so surprising. Nothing is more elusive than the person who never appears in all that he or she says or does. It is only in passing, obliquely, that we catch a glimpse of the inexpressible mystery that each of us is. We meet as persons when we have only initiated a gesture. It is therefore no blot on our acuity that we lack a developed account of the dignity of the human person, for the person as such remains inaccessible to us. How can we account for what can only be glimpsed? The dignity of the person is as elusive as the person. The only reason we have any possibility of catching the reality of the person is that we live within it. It is the same with the notion of dignity that derives from the status of persons. We do not possess an idea of dignity but rather live within it and therefore know it only by living it out. This is a pattern long observed within liberal political thought, in which it is the defense of rights that deepens our adherence to them.[28] Once achieved, they seem to evaporate and we wonder what the source of their conviction was. In the larger sense it is the elaboration of a concept of human rights that heightens awareness of the person whose inextinguishable dignity lies behind them. Kant, as we noted, is the beginning of this pivotal identification of human dignity, while before him dignity attached to the specific social status an individual occupied.[29] Now a heightened sensitivity to the indignity a person may suffer is the fruit of a determination to defend rights that arise from just such an intimation of inviolable dignity. Even Locke's defense of liberty is driven by revulsion at the assault on the dignity of free rational beings.[30] There is nothing more fundamental than the primordial intuition of what is appropriate to persons as such.

It is also an intuition that can be retained only to the extent that it is acted upon in constituting a common world. The modern invocation of human rights is not just a singular political achievement, constituting the authoritative moral framework for global discourse. It is also a prime philosophical event in our self-understanding. In recognizing the validity of rights we say what we cannot say. That is, that all individuals are always limitlessly more than they can ever say or do, that no matter how we define or measure them they are more than can be defined or measured. Each person is an inexhaustible "more than." Of course, this is something we already know in the most elementary encounter with other persons, for it is the condition of possibility for such encounters. But now we have a means of rendering this tangibly manifest in a way that precludes easily forgetting it. Rights are a badge of transcendence in a world pervaded by immanence. They neither need nor require a rationale to support them since any justification adduced would lack their transparency. At best it would provide a reason that itself stood in need of a further reason, and so on. The attempt to make present what cannot be made present would undermine it. This is why arguments that seek to justify the dignity of the person, with their inevitable coalescence around the definition of the person, strike us as not only futile but even blasphemous. Can we define the person with whom we converse? How can we converse if we have ceased to regard him or her as a person? The abbreviated injunction of respect contained in rights avoids such convolutions. Its secret is that it evades all theoretical animadversions and propels us directly into the reality of life. Rights are a language that works infinitely better in practice than in theory.[31] This is because, as the language of the person, rights apprehend the transcendence of the person in the only way it can be accessed. The rights of persons are inseparable from the flash of transcendence that the person is.[32]

The language of rights is superior to any account of it because it embraces the possibility of theory. We can hardly enter into theoretical reflection and debate if we are not already constituted as a community of persons, that is, as a community mutually recognizing the inviolability of our rights. Acknowledgment of rights is the condition of entry, not just in a constitutional sense but, more fundamentally, in a constitutive one. This is also why we cannot demand that our interlocutors produce evidence of their personhood. It is presupposed, not simply logically, but also ontologically. To speak with a person is to speak with one who is not present, for in everything that he or she has said the person has always already evanesced. Requests for a definition of the person are precisely what cannot be asked of any person. We might be able to say what the person has been but even that defeats itself since in what is past he or she has never been fully present either. At most we might say where the person has been, but only if we are prepared to tolerate the ambiguity of their being at all. Rights reflect just this intangibility of the rights holders. We require them neither to meet criteria nor to make contributions, only that they *are* in the most minimal sense of those who present themselves in their bare humanity. Rights are no respecters of differences between claimants. To have a right is to have nothing else on which one's right is based other than the right itself. We might say that the right defines humanity rather than humanity the right. If it were the latter then the right could not be the beginning of the conversation, for there would have to be a conversation about the humanity of the proposed recipient of rights that would be prior to a conversation with him or her. The reason we cannot get back to an account of humanity is that we are ourselves human and therefore cannot step outside of it. Rights are the possibility of our being human. As soon as we begin to inquire into the humanity of the other we have ceased to engage the other on human terms, as equals in our humanity, and have opened up the prospect of behaving inhumanly toward him or her. This is what we must not do. We avoid it by resolutely affirming the humanity of the other through the unconditional assignation of rights. We begin with the rights of the other and cannot make them a topic of conversation.

All of this marvelous preemption is accomplished through the language of rights. But what really sustains the momentum is that rights do not remain tied simply to the acknowledgment of common humanity. They carry us forward to a deeper disclosure of what that humanity is. That is, that the instance of humanity before us exceeds even the whole species. In respecting the humanity of the other we discover that even that boundary is not wide enough to contain the other. Humanity names a species but how can it include what cannot be named for it is more than any name assigned to it? Now we begin to see the deeper source of the difficulty of definitions. If even humanity itself is not large enough to encompass what the other is, for he or she is unencompassable, then no imputed grounds can be sufficient for the limitless respect that is owed. Here the language of rights reaches its crowning achievement, for it has managed to articulate what can scarcely be articulated in any other way. It has overturned the logic of species that seems to be its foundation. If membership in the species of humanity is the basis for inclusion within a regime of rights, then we would expect that that boundary would also define the limits of rights. Yet that is a boundary we regularly expand, not just in insisting that rights be extended to the unborn but, less controversially, in the reverence we accord to the remains and reputation of the dead. The latter fall unqualifiedly outside of the human species. But we do not need to contemplate such limiting cases in order to perceive what is at stake. That is abundantly clear once we consider how thoroughly the conception of rights overturns the logic of species as such, for in no other instance does a species commit itself to the prioritization of the individual over itself. On the contrary, a species is what lives at the expense of its members who must die so that the species can continue through new members. A species never ages in this sense. We on the other hand cannot countenance even the most elementary restrictions that would be required to ensure the level of species flourishing we demand of cattle. Rights of the individual supersede the interests of the whole. The species, humanity, means nothing if a single individual is sacrificed for it. We do not belong to a species, for each member is a unique irreplaceable species in himself or herself.

The language of rights brings into view what it means to be a person. Each one is unique, irreplaceable, incommensurable, outweighing in value everything else in the universe, including the species insofar as it merely is. Nothing tells us this since anything that is would have to partake of the finitude and exhaustibility of what is. Rights and dignity, by contrast, are directly apprehended. They are glimpsed simultaneously with the glimpse of the person by which we know one another more deeply than we can say. It is simply that the language of rights is a public affirmation of what we can scarcely affirm inwardly. We take for granted that each one is an unspeakably precious unique person. But what does that mean and whence do we derive it? The possibility of cloning suggests that we are on the verge of transposing this notion, at least insofar as genetic uniqueness is concerned. Yet even clones would not lose their uniqueness as persons. What revolts us about cloning human beings is that it seems so blatant a devaluation of the singularity of persons.[33] At root, however, it is impossible to clone a person for the person has always already stepped outside what it is to be a clone. If one cannot be a member of a species, then one emphatically cannot be a clone of another. Whatever their characteristics, persons are not what they are. We dimly intuit this all the time about the persons we know, but it is only the language of rights that elevates it into a principle by which it might be stated. Even there, however, it cannot be stated conclusively but only by the indirection of limitlessness implied in the very notion of rights. Inexhaustibility and inalienability are inseparable from the meaning of rights since a right whose limit could be reached is not the kind of unconditional warrant it claims to be. Rights are uniquely attached to persons whose crowning glory is self-transcendence. No limit can be placed upon rights because none can be placed upon persons.

Rights are thus the external recognition of persons. The paradox is that through a finite assignation we acknowledge the infinite. Persons are just what cannot be represented externally. At every point they have departed from what is imputed to contain them. The language of rights is a language that calls attention to its own defective signification; it effects the self-departure that is characteristic of persons it is intended to secure. What is defined through the limits of language turns out to have an unlimited import. In that sense the language of rights partakes of the paradox that constitutes the existence of persons, for they too exist in the mode of externality by not existing within it. The inwardness from which they have emerged could scarcely be or be discerned without the outwardness by which they glimpse their own transcendence. It is because the external is not a mere incidental dimension, a concession to the intangibility of the person, but its essential expression, that the framework of rights plays such a crucial role. The epiphany of the person cannot occur without the medium of expression that it illuminates. Rights are in this sense not an afterthought, an accidental reflection in externality of what is essentially internal. They are the essential means by which what cannot be grasped is grasped, precisely because rights pronounce the ungraspability of the person. The stability of regimes founded on the indefatigability of the person arises from the perfect coincidence of form and content in her or his constitution. Transcendence is finally represented in the only way that it can be, as transcendent. Legal constructs that cannot contain the transcendent contain it in the only way that it can be contained, as transcending it. That is what the language of rights announces in unequivocal terms. The person overflows the state. But this now means that the state is not what it appears to be.

At its core the state is nothing, the person is everything. Like the soldiers that return to retrieve a fallen comrade, the state attests to the primacy of the individual as superseding the collective. The part takes precedence over the whole, even when the part might well be sacrificed for the sake of the whole. Indeed, it is because the soldier has already determined to make such an offering that we prevent it by coming to the rescue before it can be accomplished. We cannot do otherwise, for we cannot take the full measure of devotion for granted without doing everything to render it unnecessary. To expend anything less in return would be to betray the bond from which the mutual pledges of support have arisen. A community of persons cannot be other than one that makes the welfare of each person its overriding concern. It is scarcely even a community to the extent that it is consumed by care for its neediest member. The singular has overtaken the multiple, for it has no interest as a community that overrides the urgency of the most vulnerable. To speak of this as a manifestation of bonds of empathy between us seems to provide a naturalistic explanation but it is, in fact, to displace the inexplicability one step further away. How is it that we are susceptible to the tug of empathy? Feeling one another's pain is more than a matter of feeling. It is a veritable placing of ourselves in the other. We can have such feelings only because we are not bound up within our own feelings, but already feel beyond ourselves in ways that are at the root of what it means to be in communion with others. It is only persons who possess such openness because they are open to the other before they even know themselves. The foregrounding of the other expressed in imprescriptible rights is not derived from the nature of persons; it is their very nature. Rights, by which the other takes precedence over me and over all others in the moment, are merely the external expression of what has already occurred in the mutuality of persons to one another. This is the secret of the appeal of the language of rights that has superseded all other political formulations. In the application of rights there flashes the recognition that this is how persons are in relation to one another. Each is an inexhaustible mystery to us, to themselves, and to all whom they meet.

The discourse of rights embodies an idea of community that is prior to its individual members but only in such a way that it has made them prior to itself. The whole lives for the part. That is the affirmation of rights. Its rationale is that the part is the whole, not as an aspiration, but as the self-effacement of the person open to the whole. There is no limit to the love that the tiniest child might extend to all and therefore he or she must be greeted as if he or she were all. As the possibility of embracing all others, the baby must in turn be embraced by all others as if it were all to them. It is not that the polity is identical with the family but there is a coincidence in this one crucial aspect. The child is all to the parents; each member is all to the political community. For each of us there are of course others or other others and politics is the arena in which it is just what is owed to third persons that is of decisive significance. It is an order of justice, not of love, or at least not primarily of love. The family is crucially the latter. But even the mandate of justice must converge with the mandate of love when it acknowledges the inexhaustibility of the individual person. The other who must be accorded his or her rights must be treated as if all the rights of existence were lodged in this particular instant. To be rights they must be unconditional, as love is. In this sense the rights of one are not really solitary, for they implicate the rights of all. To preclude or exclude in advance what is owed is to condition unconditionality. One can do it but not without overturning the possibility of rights whose very meaning is that the rights of all are bound up with the rights of one. This is not simply a matter of consistency but of inner dynamics. Rights that are merely conditional are not rights at all. They can scarcely be rendered coherent if we fail to see that in their invocation, at the point at which a human being is most exposed, this particular other has become all to us. It is in need that the part becomes the whole.

You are the unique irreplaceable one, we seem to say, without whom we cannot go on. Even when we do go on, we go on as if we are not going on but remain where we were. The loss of an individual member of the family leaves a hole that cannot be filled by any other or by all others. In the family, where we know the person most intimately, this irreplaceability is evident, but that does not mitigate its public acknowledgment.[34] The polity simply finds the more transparent language of rights for what the family holds within the impenetrability of its grief. To the extent that a person means all to us we must find a means of giving voice to what cannot be so easily voiced. How can we say all to a person? How can we convey that this person means all to us, just what we cannot say? Tears are a burning signifier of love, while rights are their more serene counterpart. But they equally say what cannot be said because it can only be pointed. The difference is that the political pointing rises to a transparency that enables us to keep in mind what can only remain subterranean within the feeling of the family. It is in the political that we can discern what is at stake, for it is there that the unique irreplaceability of the person is elevated into a principle. The person may be nurtured in the family but only becomes visible in the political valuation. We know that the person is unique, irreplaceable, incommensurable, because he or she stands outside of all that is, can indeed behold it by virtue of that standing, but we cannot go beyond the intuition of the other as meaning all to us, until we have acquired a language that enables a public acknowledgment of non-exchangeability. It is true, as Aristotle observes, that we can never become intimates with very many people, but even he struggled to find a way of explaining how we are, nevertheless, friends with all members of the human race. It is in political "friendship" that we grasp the grounds of possibility for friendship in the more specific sense. We can become friends because we are already friends in the eschatological sense.

The child is not loved in the family because it possesses a right, but its assignment of unfathomable rights begins to bring into view the meaning of that love. Unconditionality may be cited in passing but its impact can only be seen when we place him or her in relation to all others. That is what a regime of rights does. Derrida speculated about the contradiction entailed by the Christian injunction of universal love when to love one is necessarily to exclude all others. Yet he need not have troubled himself about the paradox since it is routinely navigated, not only in Christianity, but also in the application of rights.[35] For Christians, the neighbor is the one to be loved as if he or she was all that mattered in the world because, in a sense that is so, for the neighbor is the one most in need of love at that particular moment.[36] The language of rights accomplishes the same in its own mysterious dynamic. Rights are never general or abstract. They are wholly exposed in the instance where they are most needed, that is, in those who are most in need of their protection. If rights do not mean something in the case of greatest exigency, then they are rendered nugatory in all others. One stands for all. If we are ready to displace all so that one may not be unjustly displaced, then we have made our treatment of one the measure of our treatment of all. It is because every other is an all that they can rely on the same confidence in their own treatment as the one who has been so singularly valued. But the question arises only when necessity has propelled it to the fore. We cannot treat everyone as if they alone were all that mattered in the world, yet we can so regard them when their hour of need has cast them upon us. Public policy does deal with persons in the aggregate but it can never afford to forget that in the aggregate they cease to be persons. The great achievement of the language of rights is that it has made that transition, if not completely navigable, at least one that can be negotiated.

Individuals in need have ceased to be part of the aggregate and have stepped forward in all of their unique, unfathomable, personhood. As persons they exceed the whole. In particular, their treatment is the barometer of the moral worth of the whole, for what is the purpose of sustaining a community that would cast off its most vulnerable members? How can any collective purpose or destiny, no matter how laudatory, be purchased at the price of the most defenseless member? The language of rights may have originated in nature, the concept of natural rights, but in such reflections we see how far above nature its trajectory soars. We cannot countenance the necessity of perishing that nature imposes on every species. Persons cannot be permitted to die. Even when our efforts can only sustain time for a while longer without net collective benefit, we are still required to do all that we can to preserve them. It is almost as if the amount of time thereby gained for them is irrelevant in comparison to the timelessness of the gesture of never abandoning them. A rational expenditure of health care resources is virtually impossible in a setting where every patient exceeds any rational imposition of limits. The patient may refuse additional treatment in solidarity with those who may need the resources, but we cannot presume to limit the utility of one who may stand ready to exceed all bounds of utility in his or her own self-sacrifice. From a social perspective there may be no compelling need to preserve all or even as many as possible. The consequences of people living forever would even be disastrous since there would be no possibility of renewal through new birth.[37] But from an individual perspective the imperative of preservation is incontrovertible. The challenge is to find a means of coordinating the two perspectives since we cannot simply live wholly within one or the other. How is it that we can view the regular demise of individuals as largely irrelevant while the loss of just one is incalculable?

The answer lies in the perspective of rights by which the infinity of the person comes into view. The other as a person becomes visible, not through her or his death, which is the fate of all organic life, but through the way that we regard it. This is why it is not even what happens to the person that is of the highest relevance to the polity but how we end up treating him or her. We know the death of the other is inevitable just as it is for all of us. What we cannot tolerate, however, is failure to do all that we can to stave off that inevitability, for it is only in this way that we can affirm his or her transcendent worth. Defeat may be unavoidable, indeed, from a collective perspective may even be welcome, but it is transmuted into victory from the highest, personal, point of view. Having done all we can for the other we have reached the eternal dimension that, by definition, cannot suffer any demise or diminution. We live within the deathlessness that is the only appropriate horizon of persons. This is the highest service we can render to the person in need before us, the affirmation that he or she is far more than the need by which he or she is presently constrained. In the same way, it is also the highest return they can make to us, for they have made us caregivers who discover that we are always more than the care we have given.

In giving care we give ourselves and in receiving it we receive other selves. The community in which we are joined, a community that is realized only when it is organized for collective action as a polity, turns out to be almost nonexistent. The persons who transcend it already live outside of it. That is what the meeting of persons affirms. The solid externality of politics guards a ghostly solidarity beyond it. That is the highest transparence of the state and the reason why it cannot afford to countenance even the slightest deviation from the maximum that is owed to the person. Its smallest and frailest members represent therefore an incalculable treasure, for it is through them that the political community can demonstrate the depth of veneration from which it springs. Politics is most complete when it has become politics of the person.

Introduction

1. This is very similar to Rawls's conception of the bond of reciprocity that ultimately defines a liberal political order, but while he focuses on the justness of that relationship I wish to turn attention to the condition of its possibility. Moral agreement is possible only between persons who have somehow found themselves in a political community with one another. It is an old problem of social contract theory but for that reason one that is all the more intractable. The fact that Rawls presupposes what he proposes is not a fatal defect in his thought, or in liberal political theory more generally, but it is a feature that cries out for attention. To suggest as much is not to invoke a "perfectionist" requirement over a "proceduralist" one. It is merely to point to the reciprocity that enables the conversation about reciprocity to take place. The mutuality of persons is prior to all talk of perfections or procedures. Persons are the horizon that cannot be comprehended. John Rawls, *Political Liberalism* (New York: Columbia University Press, 2005).

2. That tension is present in the origin of the term "person" as the *prōsopon*, or the mask worn by actors who thereby establish their identity before an audience. Already in the beginning the term draws our attention to what the person is not, namely the mask, the visible exterior, rather than the interiority for which such visibility is necessary. We are not sufficiently alerted to the person whose mask simultaneously closes and discloses what is within. The person is not simply an identity. This is why it is possible for a person to fashion his or her identity. For an illustration, see the fascinating account of the young Barack Obama's conscious

exploration of alternative identities in David Maraniss, *Barack Obama* (New York: Simon & Schuster, 2012).

3. For a good overview of the many strands of personalism, see the essay "Personalism," by Thomas D. Williams and Jan Olof Bengtsson, in *The Stanford Encyclopedia of Philosophy* (spring 2014 ed.), ed. Edward N. Zalta, http://plato .stanford.edu/archives/spr2014/entries/personalism/. The term "personalism" first emerges with Friedrich Schleiermacher in his book *Über die Religion* (1799). In America it appears with Walt Whitman in his essay "Personalism" published in *The Galaxy*, May 1868. See Jan Olof Bengtsson, *The Worldview of Personalism: Origins and Early Development* (Oxford: Oxford University Press, 2006), and Thomas D. Williams, *Who Is My Neighbor?: Personalism and the Foundations of Human Rights* (Washington, DC: Catholic University of America Press, 2005).

4. Surely it is not just prudishness that prompts Kant to regard lewdness as a greater evil than killing oneself. What offends him is the affront to human dignity that abandonment to lust implies. It is this underlying conception of dignity that he struggles to articulate in *The Metaphysics of Morals* while conceding that "it is not so easy to produce a rational proof that unnatural, and even merely unpurposive, use of one's sexual attribute is inadmissible as being a violation of duty to oneself (and indeed, as far as its unnatural use is concerned, a violation in the highest degree)." Immanuel Kant, *The Metaphysics of Morals*, trans. Mary Gregor (Cambridge: Cambridge University Press, 1991), 425. All citations to Kant are to the Prussian Academy edition now included as marginal page numbers.

5. This shortcoming is not from any want of trying. Indeed, it may be the result of such a focus on the goal of human dignity that the path toward it is overlooked. Even in that preemptive format, however, the emphasis on the centrality of the person has had an invaluable effect. I do not in any sense want to diminish what we can learn from reading Jacques Maritain, Emmanuel Mounier, Gabriel Marcel, Karol Wojtyla, and Robert Spaemann, to name but a few representatives of a movement that goes from German Idealism into existentialism and phenomenology and includes an American personalist school, as well as sociological personalism. A useful overview is provided by Christian Smith, *What Is a Person? Rethinking Humanity, Social Life, and the Moral Good from the Person Up* (Chicago: University of Chicago Press, 2010). In a fine study Holger Zaborowski, *Robert Spaemann's Philosophy of the Human Person* (Oxford: Oxford University Press, 2010), has brought out the extent to which Spaemann has been working toward a more metaphysically unified conception of the person as *Selbstsein*, self-existence, even while operating out of "a conservative pluralism of theories" (248). The aim of the present work is to advance the emergence of a person-centered philosophy rather than a philosophy of the person, which has tended to define and limit the project of the personalists.

6. Kant, *Metaphysics of Morals*, 429.

7. This is not to suggest that there have not been impressive attempts to ground human dignity in terms of itself. George Kateb, *Human Dignity* (Cambridge, MA: Harvard University Press, 2011), and Leon Kass, *Life, Liberty, and the Defense of Dignity: The Challenge for Bioethics* (San Francisco: Encounter, 2002).

8. The coherence of the unfolding of modern philosophy, despite its apparent incoherence, is narrated in David Walsh, *The Modern Philosophical Revolution: The Luminosity of Existence* (Cambridge: Cambridge University Press, 2008). The personalist implications of this development are only touched upon in that volume because they do not come clearly into focus within the mainline of modern philosophical thought. It is the contention of the present study that the modern philosophical revolution culminates in the realization that the person furnishes the horizon of philosophy.

9. Martin Heidegger, "Letter on Humanism (1946)," in *Pathmarks*, ed. William McNeill (Cambridge: Cambridge University Press, 1976), 271.

10. The title of the present work might well have been *Person Without Being*, following from Jean-Luc Marion's groundbreaking *God Without Being*, trans. Thomas A. Carlson (Chicago: University of Chicago Press, 1991). Marion has mined the great potential of phenomenology for an expansive recovery of the whole theological tradition. As a consequence he has also made an inestimable contribution to the enlarged account of the person, although it is not fully recognized as such because of his attachment to the language of the phenomenon. I would argue that his work on the gift overturns the priority of the phenomenon, just as it does the priority of being. The challenge is to find an adequate metaphysical horizon when "metaphysics" has been left behind. This is why the primacy of the person is so indispensable, for the person lives within the gift of self even, and especially, when the gift of the self comes from God. Thus, I affiliate myself strongly with the remark with which Marion closes the 1991 preface to the work. "To give pure giving to be thought—that, in retrospect it seems to me, is what is at stake in *God Without Being*. It is also the task of my future work and, I expect, of the work of many others" (xlv).

11. This is essentially the burden of an influential summary by Joseph Ratzinger, "Retrieving the Tradition: Concerning the Notion of Person in Theology," *Communio* 17 (fall 1990): 438–54, German original 1973. Karol Wojtyla acknowledges something similar: "In that sense one may, and even must, speak about some kind of revolution which has occurred in the ethics of modern times. The substantive subordination of practicality to normativity had to bring with it, not so much (as in the case of Kant) the rejection of the entire teleological structure which had hitherto been dominant, but its demotion." Karl Wojtyla, *Man in the Field of Responsibility*, trans. Kenneth W. Kemp and Zuzanna Maślanka Kieroń (South Bend, IN: St. Augustine's Press, 2011), 54.

12. See Charles Taylor, *A Secular Age* (Cambridge, MA: Harvard University Press, 2007).

13. For Richard Dawkins God must be a far more substantial presence if he is to be present. Richard Dawkins, *The God Delusion* (Boston: Houghton Mifflin, 2008). How can we be deluded about a God who, even as Plato formulated it, is "beyond being" or is transcendent (*Republic* 508)?

14. Eric Voegelin, *Collected Works*, vol. 17, *The Ecumenic Age*, ed. Michael Franz (Columbia: University of Missouri Press, 2000); "Reason: The Classic Experience," in *Collected Works*, vol. 12, *Published Essays: 1966–1985*, ed. Ellis Sandoz (Baton Rouge: Louisiana State University Press, 1990), 265–91, and "Quod Deus Dicitur" in the same collection, 376–94.

15. Norris Clarke demonstrates the extent to which St. Thomas uses self-communication as a central conception even though he never makes it thematic in a question or article. W. Norris Clarke, *Person and Being* (Marquette, WI: Marquette University Press, 1993).

16. See David Chalmers, *The Conscious Mind* (Oxford: Oxford University Press, 1999).

17. This is what is overlooked in the endless controversy over the self as an independent core and as the product of a social-historical formation. The dispute makes sense only within the recognition that the person is neither. Beyond identity is the person himself or herself, whether that identity is defined by a metaphysical core or a social-historical nexus. See John Christman's lucid exposition, *The Politics of Persons: Individual Autonomy and Socio-historical Selves* (Cambridge: Cambridge University Press, 2009), which is itself written from a perspective outside of the alternatives it contemplates. The readers too are invited to consider perspectives that stand apart from them. The person is the condition of possibility for the discussion of the person.

18. Emmanuel Levinas, *Otherwise Than Being or Beyond Essence*, trans. Alphonso Lingis (Pittsburgh, PA: Duquesne University Press, 1987).

19. Parmenides, fragment B3.

20. It is instructive to read Heidegger's extensive meditation on the famous Parmenidean fragment as aiming at the horizon of the person to which he remains excruciatingly close. Martin Heidegger, *Introduction to Metaphysics*, trans. Ralph Mannheim (New Haven, CT: Yale University Press, 1959).

21. "Once we try to picture the life of a society in which no one had the slightest desire to act on these duties, we see that it would express an indifference if not disdain for human beings that would make a sense of our own worth impossible." John Rawls, *A Theory of Justice* (Cambridge, MA: Belknap, 1971), 339.

22. This difficulty was compounded when the terminology was translated into Latin as "una essentia tres substantiae" and the Greek distinction between

ousia and *hypostasis* was almost entirely lost. St. Augustine seems to sense the problem as he notes that, although the Greek word *prosōpa* may be translated as *personae*, everyone prefers to use the technical term *hypostases* so as not to deviate from the formulation. In other words, "person" consistently drops out when we wish to be clear about substances or things. For the issue among the Cappadocian fathers as well as Augustine, see Jaroslav Pelikan, *Christianity and Classical Culture* (New Haven, CT: Yale University Press, 1993), ch. 15. Some evidence of the discomfort in the Greek formulation may be gleaned from the suggestion that the Son is not *homoousios*, the same being, with the Father, but *homoiousios*, of a similar being. This is covered in Jaroslav Pelikan, *The Christian Tradition*, vol. 1, *The Emergence of the Catholic Tradition* (Chicago: University of Chicago Press, 1971), 209.

23. G. W. F. Hegel, *Encyclopedia of Philosophical Sciences*, pt. III, *Philosophy of Mind*, trans. A. V. Miller (Oxford: Oxford University Press, 1971). While the title *Philosophie des Geistes* can be translated as "philosophy of mind or spirit," it might also be rendered "philosophy of the person." The latter is what the vexed terms *Geist* and *esprit* have sought to name but, because they evade the reality of the personal, they inevitably slip into the ambiguity of a vaporous or cosmic spirit. Hegel's thought has suffered as much as any from this misunderstanding.

Chapter One. A Personalist Account of Persons

1. A parallel critique of the limits of social theory has been mounted by the reassertion of theology as the framing horizon of discourse. See John Milbank, *Theology and Social Theory: Beyond Secular Reason* (Oxford: Blackwell, 1990). What Milbank and others who claim theology's preeminence insufficiently articulate is the personal character of the relationship to God on which it depends. It is a personalist theology that is insufficiently attentive to its own possibility.

2. "Tantamne profunditatem creditis esse in homine, quae lateat ipsum hominem in quo est?" St. Augustine, *Enarrationes in Psalmos*, XLI, par. 13, in *Corpus Christianorum*, ed. D. Dekkers and J. Fraipont (Turnholt: Brepols, 1956), XXXVIII:470. This is from St. Augustine's commentary on the lines "Deep calls to deep at the roar of thy waterfalls" (Psalm 42:7, Revised Standard Version).

3. Rainer Maria Rilke, *Letters to a Young Poet*, trans. Stephen Mitchell (New York: Random House, 1984), Letter Seven.

4. Although he is not generally listed as a personalist, Wilhelm Dilthey is probably the most significant theorist of the inner perspective within the human sciences. See Rudolf Makkreel, *Dilthey: Philosopher of the Human Studies* (Princeton, NJ: Princeton University Press, 1992).

5. It seems that confusion engulfs us whenever the question of who we are and where we have come from is posed. "We badly need a clear understanding of what we mean by 'human,' otherwise the question of human origins remains confused." This is the core observation of Brendan Purcell's great synthetic reflection *From Big Bang to Big Mystery: Human Origins in the Light of Creation and Evolution* (Hyde Park, NY: New City, 2012), 35.

6. Blaise Pascal, *Pensées*, S233.

7. This theme is more extensively elaborated in Paul Ricoeur, *Oneself as Another*, trans. Kathleen Blamey (Chicago: University of Chicago Press, 1992), and is central to his whole notion of narrative as the mode of disclosure.

8. Some sense of the issues between them may be gleaned from Emmanuel Levinas's essay "Martin Buber and the Theory of Knowledge," in *The Levinas Reader*, ed. Sean Hand (Oxford: Blackwell, 1989), 59–74.

9. Max Scheler, *Formalism in Ethics and Non-Formal Ethics of Values: A New Attempt toward the Foundation of an Ethical Personalism*, trans. Manfred S. Frings and Roger L. Funk (Evanston, IL: Northwestern University Press, 1973); *On the Eternal in Man* (New Brunswick, NJ: Transaction, 2010); *The Nature of Sympathy*, trans. Peter Heath (New Brunswick, NJ: Transaction, 2009).

10. Henri Bergson, *Creative Evolution*, trans. Arthur Mitchell (London: Macmillan, 1960).

11. Karl Jaspers, *Psychologie der Weltanschauungen* (Berlin: Springer, 1960); Martin Heidegger, *Being and Time*, trans. John Macquarrie and Edward Robinson (New York: Harper, 1972).

12. Emmanuel Mounier, *Personalism*, trans. Philip Mairet (Notre Dame, IN: University of Notre Dame Press, 1952); *A Personalist Manifesto*, trans. monks of St. John's Abbey (New York: Longmans, 1952); Gabriel Marcel, *The Existential Background of Human Dignity* (Cambridge, MA: Harvard University Press, 1963); Jacques Maritain, *The Person and the Common Good*, trans. John J. Fitzgerald (Notre Dame, IN: University of Notre Dame Press, 1985).

13. Karol Wojtyla, *The Acting Person*, trans. Andrzej Potocki (Dordrecht: Reidel, 1979; Polish original 1969); *Person and Community: Selected Essays*, trans. Theresa Sandok (New York: Peter Lang, 1993).

14. No more poignant example of the incomplete state of personalist philosophy today can be conceded than the inability of even its most noted exponent, John Paul II, to effect a deeper intellectual influence. Among religious circles he is more widely admired for his positions and expositions than for the character of his arguments. Cheered for the firmness of his insistence on moral truth, he was nevertheless unable to convey its foundation in what it means to be an acting person. John Crosby is one of the very few who even recognizes the extent to which Wojtyla represents an original voice within a philosophy anchored in the person.

Yet even Crosby's laudable efforts to extend and elaborate the personalist perspective have not been enough to connect it with the philosophical mainstream in which it is properly located. See John F. Crosby, *The Selfhood of the Person* (Washington, DC: Catholic University of America Press, 1996); *Personalist Papers* (Washington, DC: Catholic University of America Press, 2003). See also Kenneth Schmitz, *At The Center of the Human Drama: The Philosophical Anthropology of Karol Wojtyla/Pope John Paul II* (Washington, DC: Catholic University of America Press, 1993), especially the final chapter for the reservations that even a sympathetic reader harbored toward the project. It has proved difficult to allay the fears of the loss of an enduring suppositum of the subject when the focus turns toward the interiority of action.

15. "The two sources which are relevant for the traditional anthropology—the Greek definition and the clue which theology has provided—indicate that over and above the attempt to determine the essence of 'man' as an entity, the question of his being remained forgotten, and that this being is rather conceived as something obvious or 'self-evident' in the sense of *being-present-at-hand* of other created things." Heidegger, *Being and Time*, sec. 10.

16. Even Edith Stein was still held by the convention of a psychological analysis when her philosophical project had been to think through what it is that makes a psychological analysis possible, that is, to think about what is not simply psychological. Edith Stein, *Finite and Eternal Being: An Attempt at an Ascent to the Meaning of Being*, trans. Kurt Reinhart (Washington, DC: Institute of Carmelite Studies, 2002).

17. Peter Singer, *Practical Ethics* (Cambridge: Cambridge University Press, 1993), 186. Jürgen Habermas has given voice to the shock of the reign of biotechnology without finding a way to ground the protestation. See Jürgen Habermas, *The Future of Human Nature* (Cambridge: Polity, 2003).

18. St. Thomas Aquinas, *Summa Theologiae* I, Q. 30, a. 4. Nevertheless, Thomas clearly grasps the incommensurability in the notion of person that is overlooked in the widely quoted definition of Boethius that "a person is an individual substance of a rational nature." See his cautious departure from Boethius in Q. 29, a. 1, where he attempts a definition of person. "Therefore also the singulars of the rational nature have also a special name even among other substances, and this name is person."

19. It is a position that is dangerously close to the vanity of the world so brilliantly analyzed by Jean-Luc Marion. "The one who loves sees the world only through the absence of what he loves, and this absence, for him boundless, flows back on the entire world; if a single person is lacking, all will fall back into vanity." Jean Luc-Marion, *God Without Being*, trans. Thomas A. Carlson (Chicago: University of Chicago Press, 1991), 136.

20. Søren Kierkegaard, *Stages on Life's Way*, ed. and trans. Howard V. Hong and Edna H. Hong (Princeton, NJ: Princeton University Press, 1988), 479.

21. "If those glad tidings of your Bible were written in your faces you would not need to insist so obstinately on the authority of that book: your works, your actions ought continually to render the Bible superfluous, through you a new Bible ought to be continually in course of creation." Friedrich Nietzsche, *Human, All too Human*, trans. R. J. Hollingdale (Cambridge: Cambridge University Press, 1988), par. 98.

22. The situation is well analyzed in Patrick Lee and Robert George, *Body-Self Dualism in Contemporary Ethics and Politics* (Cambridge: Cambridge University Press, 2009), although the argument for the wholeness of a human being turns on a comprehensive view of the person that is not fully explicated. It is personalist without acknowledging it because it continually appeals to what it is like to be a person, that is, that we cannot disregard our bodies. Only a person would know this.

23. Mark Cherry, *Kidney for Sale by Owner: Human Organs, Transplantation, and the Market* (Washington, DC: Georgetown University Press, 2005).

24. The critique of this dualism by which the self is a ghost estranged from the body has been forcefully advanced by the "incarnational personalism" of John Paul II. It is at the core of his massive reorientation of the sexual expression of love between man and woman. Yet even this enormously impressive elaboration of a "theology of the body" has not quite been able to shed the implication that everything turns on how subjects regard the meaning of their actions. It attempts to suggest that persons are not simply free to pick and choose between the interpretations placed upon their expressions of love but, without a sufficiently radical account of the person as what can never be expressed truly, the full emphasis on incarnation is not reached. Incarnate persons are still looked upon from outside as if they were never fully incarnate. It is the difference between seeing the body as a means of expression and acknowledging that it is because it cannot adequately express the person that the full dynamic of the body is so precious. In giving ourselves to one another we give more than we can give: the bearing of children that neither possesses singly. John Paul II, *Man and Woman He Created Them: A Theology of the Body*, trans. and intro. Michael Waldstein (Boston: Pauline Books, 2006).

25. Some sense of the impact of this realization can be gleaned from a remark of Robert Spaemann that seems to capture the provocation for his book on the person. "Suddenly the term 'person' has come to play a key role in *demolishing* the idea that human beings, *qua* human beings, have some kind of rights before other human beings." Robert Spaemann, *Persons: The Difference between 'Someone' and 'Something,'* trans. Oliver O'Donovan (Oxford: Oxford University Press, 2006), 2.

26. Francis Beckwith, *Defending Life: A Moral and Legal Case Against Abortion Choice* (Cambridge: Cambridge University Press, 2007).

27. Derek Parfit, *Reasons and Persons* (Oxford: Oxford University Press, 1985).

28. Michael Tooley, *Abortion and Infanticide* (Oxford: Oxford University Press, 1983); Peter Singer, *Practical Ethics* (Cambridge: Cambridge University Press, 1993); and Parfit, *Reasons and Persons*.

29. The reduction of the person to the phenomenon of consciousness does indeed carry this astonishing implication that we are free to kill non-conscious persons. It has been countered with the assertion that the person is more than consciousness for it is consciousness that is a manifestation of the self-identical whole that is the person. The question is, however, how do we have access to that which by definition does not appear but merely makes appearance possible? One could respond that the very thought of manifestation is already a grasp of what is not manifested precisely because it is what manifests. Consciousness thus contains more than that of which it is conscious. But that is to concede that consciousness is always that of a person, that to be conscious is to know that one is a person who cannot be contained within consciousness. Indeed, even the notions of self-consciousness and self-concept do not properly speaking contain the self that always remains outside of them. The question of access to what is beyond consciousness is, in other words, answerable from within consciousness as its own inescapable dynamic. It does not require invocation of a soul as a depth concealed from its possessor. Above all, we know about the soul, as Robert Spaemann suggests, within the moral life. There the self that is beyond the self, as that which cannot die, is unmistakably perceived as the very core of what is at stake in the moral life of a person. To acknowledge moral obligation is to recognize the immortality of the person for whom the mere passage of time is irrelevant. Spaemann, *Persons*, ch. 13, "Souls."

30. It is notable that Robert George and Christopher Tollefsen in their fine discussion of the science and the philosophy relating to the human embryo begin with the story of Noah, one particular embryo that was saved from a flooded hospital in New Orleans during Hurricane Katrina. The embryo is in each instance a solitary one whom we know only by having named him or her. We might say that it is only because we carry the name of the other within us, even before the name has been given, that we can know the other as other. What it means to be an embryo is derived from the notion of the other. This is why George and Tollefsen, despite their desire to explain the uniqueness of the embryo through science, nevertheless felt compelled to begin their account with Noah, the one. Robert George and Christopher Tollefsen, *Embryo: A Defense of Human Life* (New York: Doubleday, 2008).

31. Judith Jarvis Thomson, "A Defense of Abortion," *Philosophy and Public Affairs* 1 (1971).

32. Emmanuel Levinas, *Totalité et Infini / Totality and Infinity*, trans. Alphonso Lingis (Pittsburgh, PA: Duquesne University Press, 1987), 254 / 277.

33. Søren Kierkegaard, *Fear and Trembling / Repetition*, ed. and trans. Howard V. Hong and Edna H. Hong (Princeton, NJ: Princeton University Press, 1983), 55.

Chapter Two. Persons as beyond Good and Evil

1. This is in contrast to Alasdair MacIntyre's widely influential diagnosis that we have failed to provide a rational justification for morality, thereby precipitating a moral collapse. MacIntyre too does not provide such a justification. Instead, he insists that it cannot be separated from the practice of a moral tradition, yet without fully recognizing the implication of this insistence. That is, that morality already provides the universe for moral discourse, including its philosophic justification. Alasdair MacIntyre, *After Virtue* (Notre Dame, IN: University of Notre Dame Press, 1984).

2. St. Augustine, *The Political Writings*, trans. Dino Bigongiari (Chicago: Regnery, 1962), 177.

3. R. A. Markus, *Saeculum: History and Society in the Theology of St. Augustine* (Cambridge: Cambridge University Press, 1970).

4. See Eric Voegelin on "the balance of consciousness" he so much admired in Plato. Eric Voegelin, *Collected Works*, vol. 17, *The Ecumenic Age*, ed. Michael Franz (Columbia: University of Missouri Press, 2000).

5. Jürgen Habermas and Joseph Ratzinger, *Dialectics of Secularization*, trans. Brian McNeil (San Francisco: Ignatius, 2006).

6. See Richard Dawkins, *The God Delusion* (London: Black Swan, 2007), and the extended discussion of the controversy in Brendan Purcell, "Dawkins' Fear of Reason," in *Human Destinies: Philosophical Essays in Memory of Gerald Hanratty*, ed. Fran O'Rourke (Notre Dame, IN: University of Notre Dame Press, 2013).

7. See Plato, *Statesman*, where the definition of ruling is eventually reduced to taking care of featherless bipeds (276e).

8. Marcel Mauss, *The Gift: Forms and Functions of Exchange in Archaic Societies*, trans. Ian Cunnison (London: Routledge, 1969).

9. See ch. 33, "Predestination," in Peter Brown, *Augustine of Hippo* (Berkeley: University of California Press, 1967).

10. John Finnis has made clear the extent to which natural law is rooted in practical reasonableness. "In other words, for Aquinas, the way to discover what is morally right (virtue) and wrong (vice) is to ask, not what is in accordance with human nature, but what is reasonable. And this quest will eventually bring one back to the *underived* first principles of practical reasonableness, principles which

make no reference at all to human nature, but only to human good. From end to end of his ethical discourses, the primary categories for Aquinas are the 'good' and the 'reasonable'; the 'natural' is, from the point of view of his ethics, a speculative appendage added by way of metaphysical reflection, *not* a counter with which to advance either to or from the practical *prima principio per se nota.*" John Finnis, *Natural Law and Natural Rights* (Oxford: Clarendon, 1980), 36.

11. "Act as if the maxim of your action was to become through your will *a universal law of nature*" is Kant's second formulation of the categorical imperative in Immanuel Kant, *Groundwork of the Metaphysics of Morals*, trans. H. J. Paton (London: Hutchinson, 1969), 421.

12. Immanuel Kant, conclusion, *Critique of Practical Reason.* Eric Voegelin, in an early essay (1931), captures well the centrality of obligation as the unsurpassable horizon of Kant's thought, a centrality that extends even to the *Critique of Pure Reason.* Eric Voegelin, "Ought in Kant's System," trans. M. J. Hanak and Jodi Cockerill, ed. Thomas Heilke and John von Heyking, in *Collected Works*, vol. 8, *Published Essays 1928–1933* (Columbia: University of Missouri Press, 2003), 180–227.

13. We can, Kant observes, "as yet have no insight into the principle that we ought to detach ourselves from such interest—that is, that we ought to regard ourselves as free in our actions yet to hold ourselves bound by certain laws in order to find solely in our own person a worth which can compensate us for the loss of everything that makes our state valuable. We do not see how this is possible nor consequently *how the moral law can be binding.*" Kant, *Groundwork of the Metaphysics of Morals*, 100.

14. "Virtue so shines as an ideal that it seems, by human standards, to eclipse *holiness* itself, which is never tempted to break the law." Immanuel Kant, *Metaphysics of Morals*, trans. Mary Gregor (Cambridge: Cambridge University Press, 1996), 396–97. A similar formulation is provided by Meister Eckhart: "For just men, the pursuit of justice is so imperative that if God were not just, they would not give a fig for God; and they stand fast by justice, and they have gone out of themselves so completely that they have no regard for the pains of hell or the joys of heaven or for any other thing." Meister Eckhart, *Meister Eckhart: The Essential Sermons, Commentaries, Treatises, and Defense*, trans. Edmund Colledge and Bernard McGinn (New York: Paulist, 1981), sermon 6: Justi vivent in aeternum (Ws 5:16), 186.

15. Immanuel Kant, Third Antinomy, *Critique of Pure Reason*, A 444–55 / B 472–83.

16. Immanuel Kant, *Critique of Practical Reason*, trans. Mary Gregor (Cambridge: Cambridge University Press, 1997), 97.

17. Karl Ameriks has tried to salvage Kantian autonomy from what he sees as its later distortions. Karl Ameriks, *Kant and the Fate of Autonomy* (Cambridge: Cambridge University Press, 2000).

18. "Nietzsche's concept of nihilism is nihilistic." Martin Heidegger, *Nietzsche* IV: *Nihilism*, trans. David F. Krell (New York: Harper, 1982), 22.

19. Friedrich Nietzsche, *The Gay Science*, trans. Josefine Nauckhoff (Cambridge: Cambridge University Press, 2001), par. 344.

20. The necessity of penetrating to the existential core was the principal point of the analysis in David Walsh, *After Ideology* (San Francisco: HarperSanFrancisco, 1990), 30–37.

21. This is Grotius's famous "etsiamsi daremus": "even if we should concede what cannot be conceded without the utmost wickedness, that there is no God, or that the affairs of men are of no concern to him." Hugo Grotius, *De Jure Belli ac Pacis*, Prolegomena, par. 11. Quoted in Finnis, *Natural Law and Natural Right*, 43, and the accompanying endnote on classical and scholastic precedents.

22. Samuel Moyn, *The Last Utopia: Human Rights in History* (Cambridge, MA: Harvard University Press, 2010).

23. See the shift in Rawls's thought from *A Theory of Justice* to the "overlapping consensus" of *Political Liberalism* discussed in David Walsh, *The Growth of the Liberal Soul* (Columbia: University of Missouri Press, 1997), 32–38.

24. Quoted in Friedrich Nietzsche, *The Birth of Tragedy Out of the Spirit of Music*, par. 15.

25. G.W.F. Hegel, *Phenomenology of Spirit*, trans. A.V. Miller (Oxford: Oxford University Press, 1977), 406–7.

26. It would seem that the revival of political theology over the past two decades is a direct response to the impossibility of deriving a moral order from autonomy. Only an authoritative source beyond the human realm can sufficiently affirm the imperative of justice. A fine example of this approach is Oliver O'Donovan, *The Desire of the Nations: Rediscovering the Roots of Political Theology* (Cambridge: Cambridge University Press, 1999). But once O'Donovan turns his attention to the application of political theology he follows the enactment of judgment within a practice. "Law is the presupposition of every political act of judgment, because it is a presupposition of every human act that is conscious of itself. It is the reality that determines how we conduct ourselves, the original bridge between the 'is' and the 'ought,' the order within the world that is given to us. We find the law already there in place, we discern it, and we comprehend it." Oliver O'Donovan, *The Ways of Judgment* (Grand Rapids, MI: Eerdmans, 2008), 189.

27. "The fact that man is aware that he can do this just because he ought to discloses within him an ample store of divine capabilities and inspires him, so to speak, with a holy awe at the greatness and sublimity of his true vocation." Im-

manuel Kant, "On the Common Saying, 'This May be True in Theory, but it does not Apply in Practice,'" in *Political Writings*, trans. H. B. Nisbet (Cambridge: Cambridge University Press, 1970), 71.

28. Kant, *Critique of Practical Reason*, 97.

29. "Therefore nothing but the *idea of the law* in itself, *which admittedly is present only in a rational being*—so far as it, and not an expected result, is the ground determining the will—can constitute that pre-eminent good which we call moral, a good which is already present in the person acting on this idea and has not to be awaited merely as a result." Kant, *Groundwork of the Metaphysics of Morals*, 401.

30. This is the issue that Ricoeur skillfully explores in his critique of Derek Parfit, who sought to argue that personal identity can be elided into a mere replication of the self. Ricoeur objects that there remains the unassimilated self as always over and above identity as mere sameness. Paul Ricoeur, *Oneself as Another*, trans. Kathleen Blamey (Chicago: University of Chicago Press, 1992), 129–39.

31. It is called by Kant simply a "fact of reason" in the *Critique of Practical Reason* (5:31). For an extensive discussion, see John Rawls, *Lectures on the History of Moral Philosophy*, ed. Barbara Herman (Cambridge: Cambridge University Press, 2000), 253–72.

32. This seems true of the most profound contemporary reflections along the lines of the between, the "metaxological" ethics of William Desmond, *Ethics and the Between* (Albany: State University of New York Press, 2001), which still speaks of an agapeic outpouring of love as an "impossible ideal." It could not be an impossible ideal if it were not first and more profoundly possible, as the possibility of the person.

33. A striking expression of the perplexity is encountered in Adam Smith's review of the academic curriculum in *The Wealth of Nations* (1776) in which he finds philosophy divided into Metaphysics or Pneumaticks and Physicks, corresponding to the division of reality into spiritual and corporeal entities. "When these two sciences had thus been set in opposition to one another, the comparison between them naturally gave birth to a third, to what was called Ontology, or the science which treated of the qualities and attributes which were common to both the subjects of the other two sciences. But if subtleties and sophisms composed the greater part of the Metaphysicks or Pneumaticks of the schools, they composed the whole of this cobweb science of Ontology, which was likewise sometimes called Metaphysicks." Adam Smith, *An Inquiry into the Nature and Causes of the Wealth of Nations* (Indianapolis, IN: Liberty Fund, 1981), V,i,f,29.

34. Søren Kierkegaard, *Fear and Trembling and Repetition*, ed. and trans. Howard V. Hong and Edna H. Hong (Princeton, NJ: Princeton University Press, 1983), 55.

Chapter Three. Reality Transcends Itself in Persons

1. "But then with me, the horrid doubt always arises whether the convictions of man's mind which has developed from the mind of the lower animals, are of any value or at all trustworthy. Would any one trust in the convictions of a monkey's mind, if there are any convictions in such a mind?" Charles Darwin, letter to W. Graham July 3, 1881, in *The Life and Letters of Charles Darwin*, ed. Francis Darwin (New York: Basic, 1959), 285.

2. See, for example, the ambitious project of Sebastian Seung, *Connectome: How the Brain's Wiring Makes Us Who We Are* (London: Allen Lane, 2012).

3. Max Scheler, *The Human Place in the Cosmos*, trans. Karin Frings (Evanston, IL: Northwestern University Press, 2008). For an empirical confirmation, see the account of a neurosurgeon's discovery that thought continued even when his neocortex was shut down by bacterial meningitis during a coma that lasted seven days. Eben Alexander, *Proof of Heaven: A Neurosurgeon's Journey into the Afterlife* (New York: Simon & Schuster, 2012).

4. This is the perspective of continuity between subjectivity and objectivity that is overlooked by Thomas Nagel in his treatment of "a single problem: how to combine the perspective of a particular person inside the world with an objective view of that same world, the person and his viewpoint included." Thomas Nagel, *The View from Nowhere* (Oxford: Oxford University Press, 1986), 3. The analysis is a brilliant refutation of reductionism in its various guises but it fails to recognize its own source. That is, that the author already occupies a position beyond either subjectivity or objectivity. This is what makes it possible for him to discourse about them. Only toward the end does he begin to concede his own eschatological status, in contemplating the possibility of his death as not only an event in the world but also the end of his world. "This is not just a realization about the future. The submerged illusion it destroys is implicit in the subjective view of the present. In a way it's as if I were dead already, or had never really existed" (228).

5. Michael Polanyi, *Personal Knowledge: Towards a Post-Critical Philosophy* (Chicago: University of Chicago Press, 1962); *The Tacit Dimension* (Chicago: University of Chicago Press, 2009). Polanyi's influential account of the pre-given and inarticulate background of scientific investigation ends where the present reflection begins. It is one thing to point to the personal dimension of knowledge, it is another to think through what it means to be a person who bears such a possibility of knowledge within. A similar restriction to the psychological marks the equally impressive work of Bernard Lonergan, *Insight: A Study of Human Understanding* (London: Longman, 1958). Lonergan even draws out the implied understanding of metaphysics but he does nothing to illumine the metaphysics of understanding.

6. Peter Berger and Thomas Luckmann, *The Social Construction of Reality* (New York: Anchor, 1967); Thomas Kuhn, *The Structure of Scientific Revolutions* (Chicago: University of Chicago Press, 1970).

7. The conventional definition of evidence as what is publicly available or repeatable, "what all similarly situated observers would discover," already contains within it the mutuality of persons in their access to the truth. Again, Heraclitus had the controlling formulation in referring to this as the "common" world, as opposed to the private musings of each individual mind.

8. The search for extraterrestrial life, SETI (Search for Extraterrestrial Intelligence), as the project has come to be known is now fifty years old. Beginning with a solitary radio telescope it has now enlarged to become a cooperative enterprise of observatories on five continents, most recently in Project Dorothy (in keeping with the originally named Project Ozma, from *The Wizard of Oz*). The investigation is boosted by the discovery of exoplanets, planets that orbit suns outside of our solar system and could contain life in the same way as Earth. Marc Kaufman, "A Global Extraterrestrial Pursuit," *Washington Post*, November 7, 2010, A4.

9. An interesting case is provided by Derek Parfit's demolition of personal identity as philosophically untenable. It turns out, however, that the real grounds for his perspective are that it is only by forgetting ourselves that we can see the world truly. "My claim [is] that we could describe our lives in an *impersonal* way." Derek Parfit, *Reasons and Persons* (Oxford: Oxford University Press, 1985), 217. His insistence that "Personal identity is not what matters" (255) is exactly what characterizes the identity of persons. Ricoeur objects (*Oneself as Another*, trans. Kathleen Blamey [Chicago: University of Chicago Press, 1992], 138) that this does not necessarily require the elimination of the self, but in a certain sense it is self-elimination that marks the identity of persons. He is surely correct that there is a Buddhist quality to Parfit's inspiration, yet he fails to exploit the full implication of that insight. That is, persons continually transcend their selves; the self is in the mode of self-transcendence. Conventional treatments of identity and self fall short because they operate with the assumption that persons are somehow present.

10. Albert Einstein, "Physics and Reality," *Franklin Institute Journal* (March 1936). Quoted in *The Oxford Dictionary of Quotations*, 5th ed., ed. Elizabeth Knowles (Oxford: Oxford University Press, 1999), 290.

11. "The truth is precisely the opposite of what is asserted here: science today has absolutely *no* belief in itself, let alone an ideal above it—and where it still inspires passion, love, ardor, and *suffering* at all, it is not the opposite of the ascetic ideal but rather *the latest and noblest form of it*. Does that sound strange to you?" Friedrich Nietzsche, *On the Genealogy of Morals*, trans. Walter Kaufmann (New York: Vintage, 1969), sec. 23.

12. One of many recent examples is the celebrated victory of the IBM computer, Watson, over the reigning champions on the quiz show *Jeopardy!* The title of John Searle's op-ed sums up the issue. "Watson Doesn't Know It Won on 'Jeopardy!'" *Wall Street Journal*, February 23, 2011.

13. Most often of course the issue of what intelligence is has simply been avoided, as in the famous "Turing Test," announced by Alan Turing in 1950: a machine is intelligent if it exhibits behavior that cannot be distinguished from intelligent behavior. See the informative summary in Graham Oppy and David Dowe, "The Turing Test," in *The Stanford Encyclopedia of Philosophy* (fall 2008 ed.), ed. Edward N. Zalta, http://plato.stanford.edu/archives/fall2008/entries/turing-test/. The one criterion overlooked in most of the discussion is that machines are incapable of raising the question of their status as machines.

14. Neither subjective nor objective, since they are the grounds of both, they are "metaphysical," a term that ironically points to our own lack of a term to name what is more real than ourselves. It was of course Aristotle's first editors that initiated the coinage of "meta ta physica" but it was St. Thomas's commentary on it that fixed its usage as a philosophical science based on natural reason. See Eric Voegelin, *Collected Works*, vol. 6, *Anamnesis*, trans. M. J. Hanak and Gerhart Niemeyer, ed. David Walsh (Columbia: University of Missouri Press, 2003), 391.

15. John Paul II refers to this as the "threshold of wonder" in the late poem *Roman Triptych*, trans. Jerzy Peterkiewicz (Washington, DC: United States Catholic Conference of Bishops, 2003), 8.

> The threshold which the world crosses in him
> Is the threshold of wonder.
> (Once this very wonder was given a name: "Adam.")
> He was alone in his wonderment,
> Among creatures incapable of wonder
> —for them it was enough to exist and go their way.

It is evident from these late poems that Wojtyla carried on his philosophic exploration as pope but in the mode of poetic meditations. See John McNerney, "Triptych Reflections: The Philosophy of John Paul II," in *The Heritage of John Paul II*, ed. Ciarán Ó Coigligh (Dublin: Veritas, 2011), 61–93.

16. Isaac Newton, *Opticks*, bk. 3, pt. 1, q. 30.

17. Heraclitus, "Nature loves to hide" (fragment B 123).

18. Immanuel Kant, *Critique of the Power of Judgment*, trans. Paul Guyer and Eric Matthews (Cambridge: Cambridge University Press, 2000).

19. Robert Sokolowski has coined the phrase "agent of truth" as a synonym for "human person." Robert Sokolowski, *Phenomenology of the Human Person* (Cambridge: Cambridge University Press, 2008).

20. Thomas Nagel approaches this thought in his powerful rebuttal of reductionist naturalism when he insists on the cognitive shift humans introduce into biological evolution. "Each of our lives is a part of the lengthy process of the universe gradually waking up and becoming aware of itself." Thomas Nagel, *Mind and Cosmos: Why the Materialist Neo-Darwinian Conception of Nature Is Almost Certainly False* (Oxford: Oxford University Press, 2012), 85. Nagel intuits what this implies in the term "panpsychism," although it can only be adequately named within the notion of the person.

21. See Brendan Purcell, *From Big Bang to Big Mystery* (Hyde Park, NY: New City, 2012), 120–21, on the problems in the "intelligent design" argument that smuggles in an intelligence at the point where the sciences do not require it.

22. See Lonergan, *Insight*, 452–54, on the notion of emergent probability. Nagel also understands the alternatives as reductionist or emergent although he lacks the nuance of Lonergan's account. Nagel, *Mind and Cosmos*, 54–56. See also Purcell, *Big Bang to Big Mystery*, 137–38, on how this notion overcomes the famous problem of "gaps" in the fossil record that so bedeviled both Darwin and his creationist critics.

23. G. W. F. Hegel, *Phenomenology of Spirit*, ch. 5, "The Certainty and Truth of Reason."

24. Kant, *Critique of the Power of Judgment*, 253.

25. Nietzsche understood this, but he hardly improved on Aristotle's formulation that the polis exists, not for the sake of life, but for the good life. This is why the life subordinate to its mere continuation, through the arts that ministered to its material needs, was thoroughly despised. Aristotle, *Politics*, bk. VI. Nagel has his own more restricted formulation. "As I have said, the judgment that our senses are reliable because their reliability contributes to fitness is legitimate, but the judgment that reason is reliable because its reliability contributes to fitness is incoherent." Nagel, *Mind and Cosmos*, 125.

26. The necessity for the introduction of the term "human revolution" into paleoanthropology is almost sufficient evidence of the preponderant tendency to assimilate human beings to their evolutionary antecedents. See Purcell, *Big Bang to Big Mystery*, ch. 5, "On the Threshold of the Human Mystery: Was There a 'Human Revolution'?"

27. Richard Dawkins, *The Selfish Gene* (Oxford: Oxford University Press, 1989), exhibits not the slightest distorting self-interest in its exposition. He has overcome the "selfish" gene. The deeper problem is surely that only a self can be selfish.

28. The Large Hadron Collider (LHC) near Geneva was opened in September 2008 with the pooled resources of the European countries. Its recent announcement of the discovery of the Higgs boson particle goes a long way toward

comprehending how mass is acquired in the universe. Of course, it is only persons who, lacking mass entirely, could evince such a curiosity.

29. See the amusing report by some of B. F. Skinner's students who repeated the master's animal-conditioning experiments in *The Behavior of Organisms*. It turned out that when the setting was altered, the animals reverted to their untrained state and refused to cooperate, thereby meriting the new title of "The Misbehavior of Organisms." The incident is recounted in David Ehrenfeld, *The Arrogance of Humanism* (Oxford: Oxford University Press, 1978), 79–81.

30. Friedrich Nietzsche, *The "Birth of Tragedy" and Other Writings*, trans. Ronald Speirs (Cambridge: Cambridge University Press, 1999), sec. 15.

31. "This sublime metaphysical illusion [of the attainability of truth] is an instinct which belongs inseparably to science, and leads it to its limits time after time, at which point it must transform itself into *art; which is actually, given this mechanism, what it has been aiming at all along*." Nietzsche, *"Birth of Tragedy,"* sec. 15.

Chapter 4. God as the Seal of the Personal

1. This is the personalist horizon within which Marion writes *God Without Being*, trans. Thomas A. Carlson (Chicago: University of Chicago Press, 1991) without fully acknowledging it, although he continually approaches it in his excavation of giving and the gift. In this sense his criticism of St. Thomas for privileging the perspective of being, "the primacy of human conception" (81), may itself be a case of the same incomplete recognition by Thomas of the presupposition of his thought. Marion arrives at the more striking formulation: "Only love does not have to be. And God loves without being" (138). But would it be fair to say that this prioritization of love is absent from Thomas's thought? As with all thinking that confesses its inability to ground its own beginning, even that confession cannot be fully said. Persons alone can grasp it without its needing to be said.

2. St. Thomas Aquinas, *Summa Contra Gentiles*, bk. 3, chs. 37–51.

3. Martin Heidegger, *Identity and Difference*, trans. Joan Stambaugh (New York: Harper, 1969).

4. Parmenides, fragment 3: *to gar auto noein estin te kai einai.*

5. Martin Heidegger, *Introduction to Metaphysics*. St. Augustine's *Confessions* is the first text that fully concedes this realization in a way we have yet to appreciate, for he is not just confessing his sins to God but recognizing that his thinking takes place in relation to God. The work is written within the awareness of God's knowledge. "If a man confesses to you, he does not reveal his inmost thoughts to you as though you did not know them" (bk. V, ch. 1).

6. It is remarkable how many of Heidegger's formulations about being find their meaning only under the conception that being is personal. "The truth of being is the be-ing of truth." Martin Heidegger, *Contributions to Philosophy (From Enowning)*, trans. Parvis Emad and Kenneth Maly (Bloomington: Indiana University Press, 1999), sec. 44. Where is the be-ing of truth but within the person? Even the formulation depends on making the person the summit of being, and it can be grasped only by persons who are open to truth. The central notion of *Ereignis*, as event, appropriation, or "enowning," is only a possibility for persons. This, it seems, must be admitted despite Heidegger's protestations that "the *great turning around* is necessary, which is beyond all 'revaluation of all values,' that turning around in which beings are not grounded in terms of human being, but rather human being is grounded in terms of be-ing" (sec. 91). How could he know about the event of be-ing if he were not a person whose being is the event of be-ing?

7. A demonstration of this is provided in part three of Derek Parfit's *Reasons and Persons* where he asks the question of his identity if a replica of his brain were to be transmitted to another planet and survive there. Would it be the same as he himself is? In every way it is indistinguishable, we may say, except in asking the question of its identity. The self that raises the question of his identity, of mere sameness as constituting it, has stepped outside the limits of sameness. In raising the question Parfit is the unique unrepeatable one.

8. "Not we, not you or I, know about God. For reason, insofar as it affirms God, can affirm *nothing* else, and in this act it annihilates itself as a particularity, as something that is *outside* God." G. W. F. Schelling, "Schelling's Aphorisms of 1805," trans. Fritz Marti, *Idealistic Studies*, no. 42 (1984).

9. "I cannot respond to the call, the request, the obligation, or even the love of another without sacrificing the other other, the other others." Jacques Derrida, *The Gift of Death*, trans. David Wills (Chicago: University of Chicago Press, 1995), 68. Derrida points out, in line with Kierkegaard and Levinas, that this aporia can only be addressed in the turn toward God, who fills up all that is lacking in our love for all others.

10. Martin Heidegger, *Being and Time*, sec. 24.

11. "He who only wants to be the giver does not give enough. Christianity teaches that the ultimate gift of God is that he makes himself into a receiver with regard to us. He who gives someone to understand that he is ready to be everything for him, but that he is not interested in being loved himself, humiliates the other. The *amor benevolentiae* is love only if it is also *amor concupiscentiae*. And the same is true *vice versa*." Robert Spaemann, *Love and the Dignity of Human Life* (Grand Rapids, MI: Eerdmans, 2012), 21.

12. See the conclusion of "Nietzsche Contra Wagner" in Friedrich Nietzsche, *The Anti-Christ and Other Writings*, trans. Judith Norman (Cambridge: Cambridge University Press, 2005).

13. The young John Rawls provided as eloquent a formulation of this idea as anyone, thereby reminding us of the deeply personalist roots of the account of liberal political society he later elaborated. "Ultimately all personal relations are so connected for the reason that we all exist before God, and by being related to Him we are all related to each other although we may never have met one another. That personal relations form such a nexus leads to the conclusion that religion and ethics cannot be separated." John Rawls, *A Brief Inquiry into the Meaning of Sin and Faith, with "On My Religion,"* ed. Thomas Nagel (Cambridge, MA: Harvard University Press, 2009), 116.

14. "God Himself is reconciled to nature by virtue of a spontaneous love, that is, He is not dependent *on nature* and yet He does not want to exist without her. For love does not exist where two beings are in need of each other but where each could exist independently, such as in the case with God who is already *in and of Himself—suapte natura*—the being God; here then, each one could be for itself without considering it an act of privation to be for itself, even though it will not want to, and morally cannot, exist for itself with the other. Of such a kind, then, is also God's true relation to nature, that is, not a *unilateral* relation. Nature, too, is drawn to God by love and therefore strives with infinite zeal to bear divine fruit." F. W. F. Schelling, "Stuttgart Seminars," in *Idealism and the Endgame of Theory: Three Essays of F. W. F. Schelling*, trans. Thomas Pfau (Albany: State University of New York Press, 1966), 221.

15. Jean-Luc Marion, *Being Given: Toward a Phenomenology of Givenness*, trans. Jeffrey L. Kosky (Stanford, CA: Stanford University Press, 2002).

16. "Whoever seeks to save his life will lose it, and whoever loses his life will save it" (Luke 17:33).

17. "Just as by unconditionally not requiring the slightest reciprocal love, the one who truly loves has taken an unassailable position; he can no more be deceived out of his love than a man can be tricked out of the money he tenders as a gift and gives to someone." Søren Kierkegaard, *Works of Love*, trans. Howard V. Hong and Edna H. Hong (Princeton, NJ: Princeton University Press, 1995), 242.

18. St. Thomas reaches this formulation in his questions on the Trinity. "But since relation, considered as really existing in God, is the divine essence itself, and the essence is the same as person, as appears from what was said above, relation must necessarily be the same as person." St. Thomas Aquinas, *Summa Theologiae* I, Q. 40, a. 1.

19. "The father does not simply cause the son. *To be* one's son means to be I in one's son, to be substantially in him, yet without being maintained there in

identity." Emmanuel Levinas, *Totality and Infinity*, trans. Alphonso Lingis (Pittsburgh, PA: Duquesne University Press, 1987), 255–56.

20. St. Thomas, who gave us the analogia entis, knew that it is not enough to respond with the explanation that we are created, for it is not just the idea of analogy that is at issue but our capacity to grasp it as an analogy that does and does not succeed. Analogy does not explain but rather deepens the mystery of analogical thinking. This is not unrelated to the metaphysics of the person that Norris Clarke concedes was not elaborated by St. Thomas yet remains available within his thought. W. Norris Clarke, *Person and Being* (Marquette, WI: Marquette University Press, 1993).

21. Friedrich Heinrich Jacobi, *The Main Philosophical Writings and the Novel Allwill*, trans. George Di Giovanni (Montreal: McGill-Queen's University Press, 2009).

22. This is a problem that Aristotle notes as he concedes "it is a very great puzzle to answer another question concerning reason. At what moment, and in what manner, do those creatures which have this principle of reason acquire their share in it, and where does it come from?" Aristotle, *On the Generation of Animals* 736b5, quoted in Brendan Purcell, *From Big Bang to Big Mystery* (Hyde Park, NY: New City, 2012), 314. The purely biological explanation could not suffice.

23. The seminal treatment by St. Augustine insists that "in this question concerning the Trinity and the knowledge of God, nothing else is to be particularly considered, except what is true love, or rather what is love." St. Augustine, *The Trinity*, trans. Stephen McKenna (Washington, DC: Catholic University of America Press, 1963), bk. VIII, ch. 7. See also Hans Urs von Balthasar, *Theodramatik* (1983) and *Love Alone is Credible*, trans. D. C. Schindler (San Francisco: Ignatius, 2004). In an even more existential vein Piero Coda has written: "God is One and Triune, because his existence is constitutively tripersonal; and on the other hand, the mystery of the divine Person is included specifically in the mystery of the intrinsic trinitarity of divine existence." Piero Coda, *Il negativo e la trinità: Ipotesi su Hegel* (Rome: Città Nuova, 1987), 372; see also *Evento Pasquale: Trinità e Storia* (Rome: Città Nuova, 1984); *Il logos e il nulla: Trinità, religioni, mistica* (Rome: Città Nuova, 2003). I am indebted to a very fine exposition of Coda's work in Brendan Purcell, "Towards a Trinitarian Humanism: Piero Coda's Development of a Heuristic of Radical Fraternity as a Lived Theology of History," *Sophia: Ricerche su i fondamenti e la correlazione dei saperi* (Rome) 4, no. 2 (2012): 247–71.

24. This has been eloquently expressed within the Eastern tradition, especially as most recently expounded by John Zizoulis, *Being as Communion: Studies in Personhood and the Church* (Crestwood, NY: St. Vladimir's Seminary Press, 1985). "The expression 'God is love' (1 John 4:16) signifies that God 'subsists' as Trinity, that is, as person and not as substance. Love is not an emanation or 'property' of

the substance of God . . . but is *constitutive* of His substance, i.e. it is that which makes God what He is, the one God . . . Love as God's mode of existence 'hypostasizes' God, *constitutes* His being" (97). This is discussed in Eugene Webb, *Worldview and Mind: Religious Thought and Psychological Development* (Columbia: University of Missouri Press, 2009), ch. 8, "Religion and Personhood."

25. "When one proclaims 'God' the altogether 'highest value,' this is a degradation of God's essence. Here as elsewhere thinking in values is the greatest blasphemy imaginable against being . . . Only from the truth of being can the essence of the holy be thought. Only from the essence of the holy is the essence of divinity to be thought. Only in the light of the essence of divinity can it be thought or said what the word 'God' is to signify." Martin Heidegger, "Letter on Humanism," in *Pathmarks*, trans. William McNeill (Cambridge: Cambridge University Press, 1998), 265, 267.

26. Søren Kierkegaard, *Philosophical Fragments, or a Fragment of Philosophy*, ed. and trans. Edna H. Hong and Howard V. Hong (Princeton, NJ: Princeton University Press, 1985), 30.

27. This is the upshot of Charles Taylor's vast reflection on *The Secular Age* (Cambridge, MA: Belknap, 2007).

28. This is the complaint of the Grand Inquisitor in Dostoevsky's unmatched presentation of Christ as the one who authenticates human freedom in *The Brothers Karamazov*.

29. St. Thomas Aquinas, *Summa Theologiae* I, Q. 14, a. 10, reply obj. 4.

30. Søren Kierkegaard, *Eighteen Upbuilding Discourses*, ed. and trans. Howard V. Hong and Edna H. Hong (Princeton, NJ: Princeton University Press, 1990), 69–78.

31. Joseph Ratzinger, "Retrieving the Tradition: Concerning the Notion of Person in Theology," *Communio* 17 (fall 1990): 438–54, German original 1973. See above, introduction, n. 17.

32. "The free man is, if he is really free, freedom itself, yet only insofar as he is free." Quoted in the fine article on Eckhart by Burkhard Mojsisch and Orrin F. Summerell, "Meister Eckhart," in *The Stanford Encyclopedia of Philosophy* (summer 2011 ed.), http://plato.stanford.edu/. The core understanding of the person as self-creating gets its first dramatic expression in Eckhart's formulation "I am the cause of myself." What this means, he understood, could only be glimpsed as the process by which God is. "Therefore I pray to God that he may make me free of 'God' for my real being is above God if we take 'God' to be the beginning of created things. For in the same being of God where God is above being and above distinction, there I myself was, there I willed myself and committed myself to create this man." Meister Eckhart, *Meister Eckhart: The Essential Sermons, Commentaries, Treatises, and Defense*, trans. and intro. Edmund Colledge and Bernard McGinn (New York: Paulist, 1981), sermon 52.

33. Heidegger, "On the Essence of Truth" and "Plato's Doctrine of Truth," in *Pathmarks*, 136–82.

34. Emmanuel Levinas, *Otherwise Than Being or Beyond Essence*, trans. Alphonso Lingis (The Hague: Nijhof, 1981). A more personalist formulation is given by Chiara Lubich: "In the light of the Trinity, being reveals itself, if we can say this, as guarding deep within itself the non-being that is gift of self: not the non-being that negates being, rather the non-being that reveals being as love: *being that is the three divine Persons*." Chiara Lubich, *Essential Writings*, ed. Michael Vandeleene (Hyde Park, NY: New City, 2007), 212.

Chapter Five. Art as the Radiance of Persons in Reality

1. One can trace the shift in meaning of the term "art" from a means to an end in itself as confirmed by the nineteenth-century embrace of the slogan "art for art's sake." See Walter Pater, *The Renaissance: Studies in Art and Poetry* (New York: Oxford University Press, 1998). For the contrasting view that art has its genesis in the sacred, see Titus Burckhardt, *Sacred Art in East and West* (Louisville, KY: Fons Vitae, 2002). R. G. Collingwood provides a good overview in *The Principles of Art* (London: Oxford University Press, 1956).

2. The standard histories of art begin, for example, with the art of Paleolithic cave painting even though these paintings are often displayed in extraordinarily inaccessible locations. See H. W. Janson, *History of Art*, 2nd ed. (Englewood Cliffs, NJ: Prentice Hall, 1977).

3. As with art it is only retrospectively that aesthetics as a field is reconstructed. A standard anthology is *Philosophies of Art and Beauty: Selected Readings in Aesthetics from Plato to Heidegger*, ed. Albert Hofstadter and Richard Kuhns (Chicago: University of Chicago Press, 1976).

4. The mere fact that we are able to make aesthetic judgments that claim universal validity was what struck Kant as most decisive. "How is a judgment possible which, merely from **one's own** feeling of pleasure in an object, independent of its concept, judges the pleasure, as attached to the representation of the object **in every other subject**, *a priori*, i.e. without having to wait for the assent of others?" Immanuel Kant, *Critique of the Power of Judgment*, trans. Paul Guyer and Eric Matthews (Cambridge: Cambridge University Press, 2000), 288 (emphasis in original). See also his *Observations on the Feeling of the Beautiful and the Sublime and Other Writings*, trans. Patrick Frierson and Paul Guyer (Cambridge: Cambridge University Press, 2011).

5. G. W. F. Hegel, *Philosophy of Mind*, trans. A. V. Miller (Oxford: Oxford University Press, 1971); *Aesthetics: Lectures on Fine Art*, 2 vols., trans. T. M. Knox (Oxford: Clarendon, 1975).

6. F. W. J. Schelling, *Philosophy of Art*, trans. Douglas W. Stott (Minneapolis: University of Minnesota Press, 1989); *System of Transcendental Idealism*, trans. Peter Heath (Charlottesville: University of Virginia Press, 1978).

7. Fyodor Dostoevsky, *The Idiot*, trans. Constance Garnett (New York: Bantam, 1981), 370.

8. A recent visit to Skellig Michael, the astonishing monastic village that sits atop a rock in the Atlantic just ten miles off the coast of County Kerry, Ireland, provided an interesting example. The Irish government, through its Office of Public Works (OPW), had just completed twenty-five years of restoration work and sought to celebrate the occasion. Yet it did not seem appropriate that this great public effort to preserve a spiritually significant site should be marked by a religious event. Instead, the OPW invited eleven poets to spend time on Skellig Michael in order to pen their responses to the unique spirituality of the place. The result was indeed an impressive anthology, *Voices at the World's Edge: Irish Poets on Skellig Michael*, ed. Paddy Bushe (Dublin: Daedalus, 2010). The choice of poetry as the voice of public meaning was so unremarkable that neither political nor ecclesiastic circles seemed to demur.

9. For a very different view that sees art as succumbing to the same disintegration that has marked the modern world, see Hans Sedlymayr, *Art in Crisis: The Lost Center* (New Brunswick, NJ: Transaction, 2006). His thesis, first published in 1948, seems less plausible today in light of the extraordinary resistance to disorder led by such artists as Dostoevsky, Eliot, Camus, Solzhenitsyn, Havel, Milosz, Wojtyla, and many others. The authoritative truth of art is eloquently presented in Glenn Hughes, *A More Beautiful Question: The Spiritual in Poetry and Art* (Columbia: University of Missouri Press, 2011).

10. This thought seems to have been first expressed by Percy Bysshe Shelley as the conclusion of his *Defense of Poetry* (1821): "Poets are the hierophants of an unapprehended inspiration; the mirrors of the gigantic shadows which futurity casts upon the present; the words which express what they understand not; the trumpets which sing to battle, and feel not what they inspire; the influence which is moved not, but moves. Poets are the unacknowledged legislators of the world." *The Oxford Dictionary of Quotations*, 5th ed., ed. Elizabeth Knowles (Oxford: Oxford University Press, 1999), 714–15.

11. All of this reflection is well developed in the central discussion of art in Hans-Georg Gadamer, *Truth and Method*, 2nd rev. ed., trans. Joel Weinsheimer and Donald G. Marshall (New York: Continuum, 1989), especially ch. 2, "The Ontology of the Work of Art and its Hermeneutic Significance."

12. Aleksandr Solzhenitsyn, "Nobel Lecture," in *The Solzhenitsyn Reader*, ed. Edward Ericson and Daniel Mahoney (Wilmington, DE: Intercollegiate Studies Institute, 2006), 512–26.

13. Solzhenitsyn evocatively develops this in "Live Not By Lies," in *Solzhenitsyn Reader*, 556–60.

14. Friedrich Nietzsche, "On the Uses and Disadvantages of History for Life," in *Untimely Meditations*, trans. R. J. Hollingdale (Cambridge: Cambridge University Press, 1997), 57–123.

15. Friedrich Nietzsche, *"The Birth of Tragedy" and Other Writings*, trans. Ronald Speirs (Cambridge: Cambridge University Press, 1999), sec. 5.

16. Even when particular artistic visions have been eclipsed, faith in art not only endures but often becomes the main theme of art. The operas of Paul Hindemith epitomize this preoccupation with art itself. Often they revolve around the fascination with particular artists, as in *Mathis der Maler*, which concerns the life of the Renaissance painter Mathias Grünewald.

17. It is notable that Thomas Nagel in his suggestion of teleological naturalism as the bridge between mind and matter does not include art as one of its most illuminative points of connection. Thomas Nagel, *Mind and Cosmos* (Oxford: Oxford University Press, 2012).

18. The manifesto of German Idealism, the anonymous "Oldest Systematic Programme," opens with the observation that "in the future the whole of metaphysics will collapse into morals," but then concludes with the evocation of beauty as the culminating idea. "I am now convinced the highest act of reason is an aesthetic act since it comprises all ideas, and that *truth* and *goodness* are fraternally united only in beauty. The philosopher must possess as much aesthetic power as the poet." *The Early Political Writings of the German Romantics*, ed. and trans. Frederick Beiser (Cambridge: Cambridge University Press, 1996), 3–5.

19. J. G. Fichte formulates this view perhaps most succinctly. "I *am* immortal, imperishable, eternal as soon as I decide to obey the law of reason; I must not first *become* so. The supersensible world is no future world; it is present." J. G. Fichte, *The Vocation of Man*, trans. Peter Preuss (Indianapolis, IN: Hackett, 1987), 99.

20. Andrew Bowie, *Aesthetics and Subjectivity: From Kant to Nietzsche* (Manchester: Manchester University Press, 2000).

21. Paul Ricouer, *The Rule of Metaphor*, trans. Robert Czerny (Toronto: University of Toronto Press, 1981), makes this point in a more conventional way.

22. This was the big moment in the life of Hellen Keller when she discovered the mystery of language, "that 'w-a-t-e-r' meant that wonderful cool something that was flowing over my hand." Helen Keller, *The Story of My Life* (New York: Airmont, 1965), 21.

23. See the creations of Wagner, Lewis, and Tolkien, and the popularity of movies that transport us to such magical realms near and far.

24. A remarkable example of this concession is contained in the work of the neuroscientist Giulio Tononi, who in trying to communicate the science of the

brain that underpins consciousness discovered that it could best be done by means of an imaginative journey undertaken by Galileo. Giulio Tononi, *Phi: A Voyage from the Brain to the Soul* (New York: Pantheon, 2012).

25. In his 1936 essay, "The Origin of the Work of Art," Heidegger reflected on Van Gogh's famous painting of a crumpled old pair of shoes as an elevation of their being over their utility. Before they can be used, the shoes simply are. "In the work of art the truth of their being has set itself to work . . . the opening up of beings in their being, the happening of truth." When he returned to this essay Heidegger added the more precise formulation that the disclosure of truth in art cannot itself be grasped. "Art is then conceived as disclosive appropriation (*Ereignis*)." Martin Heidegger, *Off the Beaten Path*, trans. Julian Young and Kenneth Hayes (Cambridge: Cambridge University Press, 2002), 16–18, 55.

26. Even in Edgar Allen Poe's famous formulation the condition of the possibility of poetry seems overlooked. "We have taken it into our heads that to write a poem simply for the poem's sake, and to acknowledge such to have been our design, would be to confess ourselves radically wanting in the true poetic dignity and force: — but the simple fact is that would we but permit ourselves to look into our own souls we should immediately there discover that under the sun there neither exists nor can exist any work more thoroughly dignified, more supremely noble, than this very poem, this poem per se, this poem which is a poem and nothing more, this poem written solely for the poem's sake." Edgar Allen Poe, "The Poetic Principle," *Home Journal*, August 31, 1850, 1.

27. Marie König, *Am Anfang der Kultur: Die Zeichensprache des frühen Menschen* (Berlin: Mann, 1972); *Unsere Vergangenheit ist älter* (Frankfurt: Krüger, 1980).

28. The One who created "saw"—He saw that it "was good."

"He saw," yet the Book continued to await the fruition of his "vision."
You, O man, you who also see, come—
I am calling you, all "who see," down the ages.
I am calling you, Michelangelo!
In the Vatican a chapel awaits the fruition of your vision!
The vision was awaiting an image.
From the time that the Word became flesh, the vision continued to wait.

John Paul II, *Roman Triptych*, trans. Jerzy Peterkiewicz (Washington, DC: United States Catholic Conference of Bishops, 2003), 14–15.

29. Voegelin's adoption of metaxy from the *Symposium* scarcely improves on this because the metaxy is separated from the person through whom it is accessed, and by which alone it can be known. Eric Voegelin, "Reason: The Classic Experience," in *Collected Works*, vol. 12, *Published Essays, 1966–1985*, ed. Ellis Sandoz (Columbia: University of Missouri Press, 1990), 279. A similar lacuna affects the

thought of William Desmond, who has developed a powerfully "metaxological" metaphysics. The difficulty is that the person cannot be located in the between without admitting that the notion of the between arises from the person as such. Are persons in the between or are they the source of it? Besides, the very pronouncement of the between seems to have stepped outside of it. The only way of handling such challenges is surely to admit that the person not only thinks but also is the horizon of thought. See William Desmond, *Being and the Between* (Albany: State University of New York Press, 1995), and the other volumes in his trilogy, *Ethics and the Between* (Albany: State University of New York Press, 2001) and *God and the Between* (Malden, MA: Blackwell, 2008).

30. The great Protestant mystic Jacob Boehme grappled with this problem of the unfolding of God from the *Ungrund* without ever finding the adequate means of distinguishing between the human and the divine processes of self-expression. David Walsh, *The Mysticism of Innerworldly Fulfillment: A Study of Jacob Boehme* (Gainesville: University Presses of Florida, 1983).

31. That does not of course mean that metaphor exhausts our penetration of the world in which we find ourselves, as Jacques Derrida reminds us in *Margins of Philosophy*, trans. Alan Bass (Chicago: University of Chicago Press, 1982).

32. Brendan Purcell, *From Big Bang to Big Mystery: Human Origins in the Light of Creation and Evolution* (Hyde Park, NY: New City, 2012), ch. 8.

33. Martin Heidegger, *The Fundamental Concepts of Metaphysics: World, Finitude, Solitude*, trans. William McNeill and Nicholas Walker (Bloomington: Indiana University Press, 1995).

34. Or in the fragment (B 92) of Heraclitus: "The Lord at Delphi neither speaks nor conceals; he rather gives a sign."

35. Mircea Eliade, *The Sacred and the Profane*, trans. Willard R. Trask (New York: Harcourt, Brace, 1959); *Dreams and Mysteries: The Encounter Between Contemporary Faiths and Archaic Reality*, trans. P. Mairet (New York: Harper & Row, 1961).

36. It is in this sense that Derrida's notorious "différance," the differing and deferring of every saying from what is said, is never a fatal objection. Metaphor exemplifies difference. See his *Writing and Difference*, trans. Alan Bass (London: Routledge, 1978), which nevertheless fails to grasp the condition of possibility for its own analysis. That is, that it is only a person that can glimpse the inexhaustibility of metaphor because he lives within it.

37. Voegelin drew attention to this in his late analysis of cosmological order. "This play, in which the several areas of reality supply one another with analogies of being, is possible only because gods and men, celestial phenomena and society are conceived as intracosmic things, i.e. as consubstantial partners in the community of being, so that they all can represent the cosmos that is present in them

all . . . For the primary experience of reality is the experience of a 'cosmos' only because the non-existent ground of existent things becomes, through the universe and the gods, part of a reality that is neither existent nor non-existent." Eric Voegelin, *Collected Works*, vol. 17, *The Ecumenic Age*, ed. Michael Franz (Columbia: University of Missouri Press, 2000), 127.

38. Immanuel Kant, "Idea for a Universal History With a Cosmopolitan Purpose," in *Political Writings*, ed. Hans Reiss (Cambridge: Cambridge University Press, 1991), Third Proposition.

39. Some sense of this continuity drives the intriguing presentation of the brain by Tononi, *Phi*, in which art and metaphor are pressed into service as the means of presenting the scientific understanding of the human brain. The neurophysiology of the brain assumes the form of Galileo's dream for phi (the brain) can only make sense as psi (mind). Tononi remains a convinced materialist in his science of the brain yet the whole book concedes that art provides the more surpassing mode of understanding.

Chapter Six. History as the Memory of Persons

1. Søren Kierkegaard, *Concluding Unscientific Postscript to Philosophic Fragments*, ed. and trans. Howard V. and Edna H. Hong (Princeton, NJ: Princeton University Press, 1992).

2. Paul Ricoeur has provided an eloquent meditation on the dynamics of memory, history, and forgetting that form the background of historiography and its role in living our lives together. It is a subtle and sensitive reflection that yet remains within the phenomenology of historical memory without asking about the condition of its possibility. That which surpasses the phenomenon eludes him although it continually hovers as the absent presence that is the person. "Every act of memory (*faire mémoire*) is thus summed up in recognition." Paul Ricoeur, *Memory, History, Forgetting*, trans. Kathleen Blamey and David Pellauer (Chicago: University of Chicago Press, 2004), 495. Phenomenology points obliquely to the metaphysical horizon within which it unfolds. That is, to the person who is and who is not contained in the phenomenon and therefore provides the possibility of a phenomenological analysis.

3. G. W. F. Hegel, *Phenomenology of Spirit*, trans. A. V. Miller (Oxford: Oxford University Press, 1977).

4. Eric Voegelin, "Homer and Mycenae," in *Collected Works*, vol. 15, *The World of the Polis*, ed. Athanasios Moulakis (Columbia: University of Missouri Press, 2000), ch. 3.

5. Eric Voegelin, *Collected Works*, vol. 17, *The Ecumenic Age*, ed. Michael Franz (Columbia: University of Missouri Press, 2000).

6. See Voegelin, *The Ecumenic Age*, introduction.

7. Voegelin grappled with a formulation of this in his memorable phrase "flow of presence" although he hesitated to allow it to overturn itself, for it really means the non-flow of what is non-present. Eric Voegelin, "Eternal Being in Time," in *Collected Works*, vol. 6, *Anamnesis*, trans. M. J. Hanak and Gerhart Niemeyer, ed. David Walsh (Columbia: University of Missouri Press, 2002).

8. The modern preoccupation with apocalypse moves toward its location within the person without fully recognizing that directional logic within itself. See David Walsh, *The Modern Philosophical Revolution* (New York: Cambridge University Press, 2008), especially the chapters on Hegel, Heidegger, and Derrida.

9. The echo of the famous opening line of Voegelin's *Order and History* is not coincidental. "The order of history emerges from the history of order." The difference is that here we are attempting to present a formulation that takes account of itself. Voegelin's sentence seems to suggest a vantage point outside of it, rather than one that includes the condition for its own possibility.

10. William Desmond has devoted considerable attention to the articulation of a "metaxological metaphysics," a metaphysics of the between in which persons live. This has given rise to some strikingly parallel observations to those above. "It might seem that posthumous mind is an impossibility, for we exist in the between. Yet posthumous mind tries to think the beyond in the midst of the between, to become awake to what is at issue in the being of the between." William Desmond, *Being and the Between* (Albany: State University of New York Press, 1995), 193. The only question is how this insight itself is possible. The horizon of the person seems ineluctable.

11. Søren Kierkegaard, "How Can an Eternal Happiness Be Built on Historical Knowledge?" in *Concluding Unscientific Postscript*, II, ch. 4.

12. Cicero, *The Nature of the Gods*, bk. II.

13. Jacob Neusner, "Who Needs 'The Historical Jesus?' An Essay-Review," *Bulletin for Biblical Research* 4 (1994): 113–26.

14. Charles Taylor comes very close to this recognition in his conception of "immanent transcendence" but he cannot see how it would function because he neglects the horizon of the person. Instead, he regards it as the inconclusive aspiration of a secular age. "But there is a new paradox: there seems to be a renewed affirmation of transcendence, of something beyond flourishing, in the sense of pointing to life beyond life. But at the same time, this is denied, because this point has absolutely no anchorage in the nature of reality." Charles Taylor, *A Secular Age* (Cambridge, MA: Belknap, 2007), 726. To be a person is to live within that paradox by which it ceases to be a paradox. It is simply how a person is.

15. "The order of society in history is theoretically irrelevant to Aristotle because he is convinced that perfect order can be realized within history; the order of

history itself becomes of absorbing interest only when perfection is recognized as a symbol of eschatological fulfillment beyond history." Eric Voegelin, *Collected Works*, vol. 16, *Plato and Aristotle*, ed. Dante Germino (Columbia: University of Missouri Press, 2000), 390.

16. Eric Voegelin, *Collected Works*, vol. 14, *Israel and Revelation*, ed. Maurice P. Hogan (Columbia: University of Missouri Press, 2001).

17. Voegelin brilliantly raised the issue of historical equilibrium, especially in the last two volumes of *Order and History*. Yet he stopped short of the realization that the advent of Christ is more than the culminating elevation of the tension between a process of transfiguration and transfiguration itself. He is its resolution. Such an insight only becomes apparent within the personalist horizon that Voegelin approached without definitively reaching. See David Walsh, *The Third Millennium* (Georgetown: Georgetown University Press, 1999), ch. 5, "Christ as the Heart of Civilization."

18. St. Augustine, *City of God*, bk. XX.

19. Alexandre Kojève, *Introduction to the Reading of Hegel*, ed. Allan Bloom and trans. James H. Nichols (New York: Basic 1969), and Barry Cooper, *The End of History* (Toronto: University of Toronto Press, 1984).

20. "What remains disconcerting about all this is firstly, that the earlier generations seem to perform their laborious tasks only for the sake of the later ones, so as to prepare for them a further stage from which they can raise still higher structures intended by nature; and secondly, that only the later generations will in fact have the good fortune to inhabit the building on which a whole series of their forefathers (admittedly, without any conscious intention) had worked without themselves being able to share in the happiness they were preparing. But no matter how puzzling this may be, it will appear as necessary as it is puzzling if we simply assume that one animal species was intended to have reason, and that, as a class of rational beings who are mortal as individuals but immortal as a species, it was still meant to develop its capacities completely." Immanuel Kant, "Idea for a Universal History with a Cosmopolitan Purpose," in *Political Writings*, ed. Hans Reiss (Cambridge: Cambridge University Press, 1991), Third Proposition. Kant's discomfort is in marked contrast to the response of St. Thomas Aquinas, who raises the question as to whether Christ is the head of all men and answers resoundingly in the affirmative. None are merely superfluous. "Therefore we can say that in general throughout the history of the world, Christ is the head of all men but in different degrees." St. Thomas Aquinas, *Summa Theologiae*, III, Q. 8, a. 3.

21. This is essentially the question posed by Jacob Burckhardt, *Reflections on History* (Indianapolis, IN: Liberty Fund, 1979).

22. It is noteworthy that the secondary literature on Kant rarely turns its attention to the discomfort Kant acknowledges in contemplating the sacrifice of the indi-

vidual on the altar of historical progress. See the most recent sample in *Kant and Modern Philosophy*, ed. Paul Guyer (Cambridge: Cambridge University Press, 2006).

23. Samuel Moyn, *The Last Utopia: Human Rights in History* (Cambridge, MA: Belknap, 2010).

24. Aleksandr Solzhenitsyn, *The Gulag Archipelago*, vol. 2, trans. Thomas Whitney (New York: Harper, 1975), 611–12.

25. Victor Frankl, *Man's Search for Meaning*, trans. Ilse Lasch (New York: Washington Square, 1963), 124.

26. Aleksandr Solzhenitsyn, *The First Circle*, trans. Thomas Whitney (New York: Bantam, 1968), 96.

27. This is an issue not fully confronted by Leo Strauss in his famous juxtaposition of natural right and history. He is left merely asserting the incompatibility of philosophy based on natural right with the historicism that opposes it. "By denying the significance, if not the existence, of universal norms, the historical school destroyed the only solid basis of all efforts to transcend the actual." Leo Strauss, *Natural Right and History* (Chicago: University of Chicago Press, 1953), 15. The problem is that natural right is an historically emergent discovery and the historicist objection is itself a claim to have transcended history. History as the horizon of the nonhistorical must be conceded if such difficulties are to be avoided.

28. Martin Heidegger, "On the Essence and Concept of φύσις in Aristotle's *Physics* B, I" (1939), in *Pathmarks*, ed. William McNeill (Cambridge: Cambridge University Press, 1998), 183–230.

Chapter Seven. *Politics of the Person*

1. In Plato, *Timaeus* (22b) the Egyptian priest says to Solon: "O Solon, Solon, you Hellenes are always children; there is no such thing as an old Hellene." See Eric Voegelin, *Collected Works*, vol. 17, *The Ecumenic Age*, ed. Michael Franz (Columbia: University of Missouri Press, 2000), ch. 1, "Historiogenesis."

2. Homer, *Iliad*, bk. IX. See the discussion in Eric Voegelin, *Collected Works*, vol. 15, *The World of the Polis*, ed. Athanasios Moulakis (Columbia: University of Missouri Press, 2000), ch. 3, "Homer and Mycenae."

3. James Edward Peters, *Arlington National Cemetery: Shrine to America's Heroes* (Bethesda, MD: Woodbine, 2000).

4. The anthropological principle is announced in Plato, *Republic* 368. Socrates claimed in the *Gorgias* that he was the only true statesman in Athens since he alone knew its true good. Even one who follows a less public path can nevertheless carry the city within, as Matryona does in Aleksandr Solzhenitsyn's short story "Matryona's Home," in *The Solzhenitsyn Reader*, ed. Edward Ericson and Daniel Mahoney (Wilmington, DE: Intercollegiate Studies Institute, 2006), 24–56.

5. Michael Oakeshott, *On Human Conduct* (Oxford: Clarendon, 1990).

6. Jacques Maritain, *The Person and the Common Good*, trans. John J. Fitzgerald (Notre Dame, IN: University of Notre Dame Press, 1966).

7. Hannah Arendt, *The Human Condition* (Chicago: University of Chicago Press, 1958). It is noteworthy that the term *idiōtēs* designated one who remained in the private realm, concerned only with the self rather than the public good of the city. The burden of being forced to conceal oneself without the opportunity to appear in the visibility of the common world is movingly narrated by Socrates in Plato, *Republic* 495–96.

8. This Heideggerian formulation demonstrates the closeness between his account of being and the elevation of the political as the realm of action in Hannah Arendt. "The pre-political essence of the πόλις, that essence that first makes possible everything political in the originary and in the derivative sense, lies in its being the open site of that fitting destining [*Schickung*] from out of which all human relations toward beings—and that always means in the first instance the relations of beings as such to humans—are determined. The essence of the πόλις always comes to light in accordance with the way in which beings as such in general enter the realm of the unconcealed in keeping with the expanse of those limits within which this occurs, and in keeping with the way in which the essence of human beings is determined in unison with the manifestness of beings as a whole." Martin Heidegger, *Hölderlin's Hymn "The Ister,"* trans. William McNeill and Julia Davis (Bloomington: Indiana University Press, 1996), 82–83.

9. The modern view of liberty as noninterference is different, in elevating the exercise of private liberty as the humanly meaningful realm. Yet it does not obviate the primacy of political liberty as the framework that makes private liberty possible. Indeed, the validation of the private realm is itself a publicly political act. Benjamin Constant has a classic reflection on the mutual interrelation of the two forms of liberty. Benjamin Constant, "The Liberty of the Ancients Compared with the Moderns (1819)," in *Political Writings*, ed. Biancamaria Fontana (Cambridge: Cambridge University Press, 1988), 309–28.

10. The whole of the *Republic* can be read as this great contest between truth and appearance concerning the question of justice, but its culmination is surely the portrait of the tyrant who is the most abjectly isolated individual in the whole city. Plato, *Republic* 562–79.

11. This is the issue that is confronted in the trial and death of Socrates, especially as presented in the *Apology, Crito,* and *Phaedo.* But it is not simply a classical confrontation, as Vaclav Havel made clear. See his "The Power of the Powerless," in *Open Letters: Selected Writings, 1965–1990*, ed. Paul Wilson (New York: Vintage, 1992), 125–214.

12. Yves Simon made this argument plain in *A General Theory of Authority* (Notre Dame, IN: University of Notre Dame Press, 1991).

13. Even Hobbes who makes the sovereign the author of truth cannot dispense with the consent that must take place in the covenant by which we exit the state of nature, the pre-political state. "It is not therefore the Victory, that giveth the right of Dominion over the Vanquished, but his own Covenant." Thomas Hobbes, *Leviathan*, ch. 20.

14. "It is not our aims that primarily reveal our nature but rather the principles that we would acknowledge to govern the background conditions under which these aims are to be formed and the manner in which they are to be pursued. For the self is prior to the ends which are affirmed by it; even a dominant end must be chosen from among numerous possibilities. There is no way to get beyond deliberative rationality. We should therefore reverse the direction between the right and the good proposed by teleological doctrines and view the right as prior." John Rawls, *A Theory of Justice* (Cambridge, MA: Harvard University Press, 1971), 560.

15. *The Roots of Liberty: Magna Carta, Ancient Constitution, and the Anglo-American Tradition of the Rule of Law*, ed. Ellis Sandoz (Columbia: University of Missouri Press 1993); for the way "the kingdom issues from the people," see John Fortescue, *In Praise of the Laws of England* (1471), ch. XIII, in *On the Laws and Governance of England*, ed. Shelley Lockwood (Cambridge: Cambridge University Press, 1997).

16. "Then if we suppose that people of this sort ought to be subject to the highest type of man, we intend that the subject should be governed, not, as Thrasymachus thought, to his own detriment, but on the same principle as his superior, who is himself governed by the divine element within him. It is better for everyone, we believe, to be subject to a power of godlike wisdom residing within himself, or, failing that, imposed from without, in order that all of us, being under one guidance, may be so far as possible equal and united." Plato, *Republic* 590.

17. This is to vary Jaroslav Pelikan's memorable formulation: "Tradition is the living faith of the dead, traditionalism is the dead faith of the living." Jaroslav Pelikan, *The Vindication of Tradition: The 1983 Jefferson Lecture in the Humanities* (New Haven, CT: Yale University Press, 1986), 65.

18. Michael Oakeshott understood some of this, although he did not necessarily press his reflections as far as they might have taken him. "Thus, *respublica* cannot be authoritative on account of its providing shelter from some of the uncertainties of a human life . . . this cannot be a reason (let alone the reason) for recognizing the authority of *respublica*: civil association can provide these blessings only on account of this recognition." Oakeshott, *On Human Conduct*, 152.

19. Bergson glimpsed something of this but downplayed the extent to which closed and open moralities form a continuum. Henri Bergson, *The Two Sources of Morality and Religion,* trans. R. Ashley Audra and Cloudesley Brereton (New York: Doubleday, 1932).

20. The great contemporary economic challenge is not only to affirm "that traditional principles of social ethics like transparency, honesty and responsibility cannot be ignored or attenuated, but also that in *commercial relationships* the *principle of gratuitousness* and the logic of gift as an expression of fraternity can and must *find their place within normal economic activity.*" Benedict XVI, *Caritas in veritate* (2009), par. 36.

21. The City of God, Augustine insists, is not the same as the Church, which is merely on its way toward it. But to visualize that eschatological city he still employed the conception of a city, thereby demonstrating the primacy of the political in our thought. See St. Augustine, *The City of God.*

22. The difficulty of explaining language is well illustrated by the famous story of Helen Keller, who at the age of nine made the momentous discovery that words stand for things, which she reports as a great liberation of her mind. Helen Keller, *The Story of My Life* (New York: Airmont, 1965), 21.

23. An extended meditation on giving, although without suggesting the political implications, is available in Jean-Luc Marion, *Being Given: Toward a Phenomenology of Givenness,* trans. Jeffrey L. Kosky (Stanford, CA: Stanford University Press, 2002).

24. Aquinas acknowledges this most clearly in noting that "the rationality of a part is contrary to the rationality of a person." St. Thomas Aquinas, III *Sentences,* d. 5, q. 3, a. 2. See also his observation that "man is not ordered to the body politic according to all that he is and has." St. Thomas Aquinas, *Summa Theologiae* I-II, Q. 21, a. 4, ad 3.

25. "A whole is never intended by nature to be inferior to a part; and a man so greatly superior to others stands to them in the relation of a whole to its parts. The only course which remains is that he should receive obedience, and should have sovereign power without any limit of tenure—not turn by turn with others." Aristotle, *Politics* 1288a.

26. Michael Rosen makes our duty to reverence the remains, even of a dead fetus, the crucial indicator of human dignity. What he seems unable to acknowledge is what this indicates, namely the flash of transcendence the person is. Michael Rosen, *Dignity: Its Meaning and History* (Cambridge, MA: Harvard University Press, 2012), ch. 3, "Duty to Humanity."

27. Compelling confirmation of that precedence is provided by Brian Tierney's investigation into the genesis of the idea of natural rights, which arose within

canonist and juridical disputes long before any theoretical foundation had been elaborated. Brian Tierney, *The Idea of Natural Rights* (Atlanta, GA: Scholars, 1997).

28. Contrary to Nietzsche's observation that liberal institutions "cease to be liberal as soon as they are attained," it is precisely this awareness that awakens liberal reassertion. Friedrich Nietzsche, *The Twilight of the Idols*, sec. 38.

29. Peter Berger, "On the Obsolescence of the Concept of Honour," in *Liberalism and Its Critics*, ed. Michael Sandel (New York: New York University Press, 1984), 149–58.

30. See the motto to the *Two Treatises of Government*, which consists of a passage from Livy that concludes: "They are not to be placated unless we yield to them our blood to drink and our entrails to tear out." John Locke, *Two Treatises of Government*, ed. Peter Laslett (New York: New American Library, 1965), 170.

31. The prioritization of practice over theory, as well as the characterization of political principles as abbreviations, has long been associated with the thought of Michael Oakeshott, especially in *Rationalism and Politics*, rev. ed. (Indianapolis, IN: Liberty Fund, 1991). It is doubtful, however, that Oakeshott would have applied his notion to the language of rights although, I would argue, that a more thorough application of the primacy of practice would have required it. His closest approach is in the notion of a "civil association," which he distinguishes sharply from an "enterprise association" in *On Human Conduct*. The essential thrust is covered in David Walsh, *The Growth of the Liberal Soul* (Columbia: University of Missouri Press, 1997).

32. This conviction seems to be the guiding thread of George Kateb's interesting attempt to ground human dignity on a purely secular basis. He invokes Emerson's characterization of every person as an "infinitude" but goes on to explain what this means in his own reflection. It is that without being immortal we can nevertheless have immortal longings. "We need to stay true to what we know—the immensity beyond immensity of space and time and the universe's purposeless waste—because that knowledge is an incomparably superior encouragement to wonder." In light of that true immortality we disdain the false immortality of mere endless life. George Kateb, *Human Dignity* (Cambridge, MA: Belknap, 2011), 125, 215. As with so many "secular" accounts, Kateb's explains everything except the source of his own perspective. Only infinity can apprehend the finite.

33. This is the core of the objection presented by Jürgen Habermas, *The Future of Human Nature* (Cambridge: Polity, 2003). A very different but convergent approach is developed in Leon Kass, *Life, Liberty, and the Defense of Dignity: The Challenge for Bioethics* (San Francisco: Encounter, 2002). See also *Human Cloning and Human Dignity: The Report of the President's Council on Bioethics* (New York: Public Affairs, 2002).

34. Hegel uses *Antigone* as the test case for the clash of rights between the family and the state, which cannot be resolved precisely because they draw on the same spiritual substance. G. W. F. Hegel, *Phenomenology of Spirit*, trans. A. V. Miller (Oxford: Oxford University Press, 1977), 276. He handles the same issue quite differently in *The Philosophy of Right*, where the family is the intuitive unity of what is also unfolded as civil society and the state. All are forms of ethical life in which the individual sustains and is sustained by the whole.

35. Curiously Derrida acknowledges the Christian resolution of the paradox but does not seem to notice the parallel outcome in the language of rights. This is discussed in relation to Kierkegaard's reflections on Abraham's sacrifice of Isaac. Jacques Derrida, *The Gift of Death*, trans. David Wills (Chicago: University of Chicago Press, 1995), 96.

36. St. Thomas asks whether we are bound to succor all who are in need and responds that the answer turns on the particularity of the person before us. St. Thomas Aquinas, *Summa Theologiae* II-II, Q. 71, a. 1.

37. Arendt connects the uniqueness of each individual with the fact that the birth of each of us is a new beginning. Natality is the condition for the possibility of the unexpected in human action. Arendt, *The Human Condition*, 178.

INDEX

DAVID WALSH

is professor of politics at the Catholic University of America.

He is the author and editor of a number of books, including

The Modern Philosophical Revolution: The Luminosity of Existence.